49.95

D0148332

Serving the Urban Poor

SERVING THE URBAN POOR

DAVID FANSHEL,
STEPHEN J. FINCH,
and JOHN F. GRUNDY

PRAEGER

Westport, Connecticut
London

Library of Congress Cataloging-in-Publication Data

Fanshel, David.
　　Serving the urban poor / David Fanshel, Stephen J. Finch, and John
　F. Grundy.
　　　　p.　cm.
　　Includes bibliographical references and index.
　　ISBN 0-275-94075-6 (alk. paper)
　　　1. Lower East Side Family Union—History.　2. Child welfare—New
　York (N.Y.)—Case studies.　3. Family social work—New York (N.Y.)—
　Case studies.　I. Finch, Stephen J.　II. Grundy, John F.
　III. Title.
　HV743.N49L694　1992
　362.82′8′097471—dc20　　　　91-44572

British Library Cataloguing in Publication Data is available.

Library of Congress Catalog Card Number: 91-44572
ISBN: 0-275-94075-6

First published in 1992

Praeger Publishers, 88 Post Road West, Westport, CT 06881
An imprint of Greenwood Publishing Group, Inc.

Printed in the United States of America

The paper used in this book complies with the
Permanent Paper Standard issued by the National
Information Standards Organization (Z39.48-1984).

10 9 8 7 6 5 4 3 2 1

Contents

Acknowledgments

We wish to express our appreciation for the support received from Alfred B. Herbert, Jr., the executive director of the Lower East Side Family Union. He facilitated our work and encouraged full cooperation of the staff. He also made available a complete set of forms about all subjects in the study from the agency's management information system. The information we extracted from the forms proved very valuable in the work that we describe in this book.

The social work associates and the team leaders were full participants in the research and often appeared to find participation in the research interviews challenging and interesting. They were helpful in explaining the research to the clients and were usually successful in enlisting client participation in research interviews. The high response rate (81%) achieved in the client interview phase of the study owes much to their efforts.

Dean Mitchell Ginsberg of the Columbia University School of Social Work encouraged the initiation of the project and similar strong support was received from his successor, Dean George Brager. Subsequently, Dean Ronald Feldman helped to create conditions under which the project could come to successful closure.

The work has involved close collaboration with Dr. Jaime Alvelo in the design of the research, construction of instruments and codebooks, and the collection of data. He was a full partner in this effort.

Paul A. Marsters made a significant contribution to our research. Chapters 12 and 13 reflect the work he put into the analysis of the agency's management information system data. At the time of his contribution, he was a member of the Statistical Laboratory in the Department of Applied Mathematics and Statistics at the State University of New York at Stony Brook.

Dr. Amelia Chu performed many tasks as a graduate student serving as a viii Acknowledgments

research assistant on the project. Her work included translating the client interviewing schedule into Chinese, interviewing the Chinese clients, and carrying
out coding and computer operations. She carried out the major assignments
involved in codifying the case closing information and in codifying the family
system information for the study.

Margaret Polinsky made valuable contributions in the early phases of the
research working as a research assistant in instrument construction and data
gathering tasks.

The research reported here was funded by a grant to the Lower East Side
Family Union from the William T. Grant Foundation and the Robert Sterling
Clark Foundation. The Columbia University School of Social Work received a
contract from the agency to carry out the research reported here.

Obviously, much is owed to the clients who consented to be interviewed about
their service experiences. Their candor in interviews and the thoughtfulness of
their responses were impressive. We learned a great deal from them about problems of survival under conditions of urban blight. We hope our appreciation for
the clients comes through in the way we have described them.

Part **I**

Introduction to the Study

Chapter 1

Introduction: The Agency, Its Environment, and Design Issues

The Lower East Side Family Union (LESFU) was established in 1972 as "a social service brokerage for at risk families whose low educational level and ethnic heterogeneity made it difficult to link with social service agencies in time to prevent a family breakdown" (Rapoport 1987). It serves the Lower East Side of Manhattan and has as its purpose the provision of preventive services to families whose children are at risk of placement in foster care. The program has received national recognition for its innovative approach to problems of the urban poor and has previously been discussed in detail by Weissman (1978), Beck (1979), Young (1985), and Rapoport (1987).

We studied all 160 client families who applied for service from LESFU over the 11-month period from April 1982 through March 1983. A family was designated as a subject when a member of the family signed an official Application for Services form of the New York State Department of Social Services (DSS-2560). A client's signing the form was a requirement before any agency offering child welfare preventive services involving state funding of local programs could provide assistance.

THE LOWER EAST SIDE ENVIRONMENT

The Lower East Side was, and remains, an area containing large pockets of extreme poverty. The area includes Alphabet City (a blighted neighborhood that was a notorious center for the wholesale drug trade during the study period), the infamous Bowery section, Chinatown, Little Italy, and the original Jewish settlement areas of Hester Street and Orchard Street. The area was the object of intense real estate speculation.

There have been dramatic changes in the area. For example, in 1880, there were 700 Chinese living on the Lower East Side. Over the years, Chinese immigration accumulated and accelerated when in 1965 the federal government opened up Chinese immigration to the United States. By 1982, Chinatown had grown into a dynamic community of 80,000 people.[1] Many of the families were recent immigrants to the United States. They supplied the male work force for the large restaurant industry in the area and the female work force for the garment industry. Most worked in small business sites, many of which failed to meet minimal Labor Department health standards.

The range of problems LESFU's clientele faced was far wider than those usually encountered by family service agencies. Most notably, police, prosecutors, and city officials were combating the rampant heroin and cocaine trade firmly entrenched on the Lower East Side during this period. Many of the transactions were carried on seemingly without effort, often in daylight, on street corners and inside buildings (*New York Times,* July 5, 1983). The despair and devastation of neighborhoods were so overwhelming that residents no longer regarded the sight of addicts "shooting up" in public as unusual. A police commander described the area as "the retail drug capital of the world."

Our encounters with the physical environment surrounding the agency at the assigned research office with Team I at East 6th Street (between Avenue B and Avenue C) confirmed the worst of these reports. The area resembled the destruction in Europe during World War II. In the destroyed and half-destroyed buildings that surrounded Team I's quarters, we constantly saw drug dealers zigzagging everywhere as they plied their trade in a manner that was striking for its brazenness. Once, we returned to the Team I offices to find the apartment house across the street the site of a drug raid, complete with heavily armed police officers in bulletproof vests and suspects sprawled on the streets. Our memories contained images that were a mixture of Fellini-like grotesqueries and the animated fast-changing action scenes of a police movie. We often wondered what social workers could be expected to accomplish with families in this particular context. What kind of powerful interventions would be required to overcome the noxious forces in this blighted urban environment?

ORIGINS OF LESFU

Young (1985) described the circumstances surrounding the creation of LESFU, which he saw as having been dominated by the energy, skill, and determination of Bertram Beck, then the executive director of the Henry Street Settlement on the Lower East Side. Beck chaired a committee of five directors of settlement houses in the area that became the vehicle for applying to foundations for funding and in helping to found a new agency in the area. In time, the board of trustees was expanded from this core group to one that included representatives from other organizations.

A report of the New York-based Citizen's Committee for Children, *A Dream*

Deferred (1971), documented the need for such an agency from the long and disappointing history of foster care in New York City. At the time of the report, there were such phenomena as overcrowding of children in public shelters; increasing difficulties in placing older, behaviorally difficult minority group children into the City's system of voluntary agencies, and concerns over inappropriate and prolonged care and rising costs associated with children in care. The report concluded that a whole new system was needed that would minimize the need for care by preventing or reducing the crises that led to the placement of children. Foster care was to become a last resort rather than the primary mode of service delivery it appeared to have become.

LESFU began operation in 1972. Weissman (1978) described it as a community-based child welfare agency. It was an attempt to create an agency that would act as a general practitioner integrating social welfare service delivery. It would serve as an entry point for a family to be linked with a range of specialized services and as an intermediary between the public social service systems and private sector systems. It was to operate as a union of professionals and neighborhood residents. Its operating style was to intervene early in a client's problems and to involve the community in its decision making.

The formation of LESFU anticipated the current national policy regarding child welfare services that made "permanency planning" for children the stated goal of service interventions on behalf of beleaguered families. As a policy defined by the Adoption Assistance and Child Welfare Act of 1980 (Public Law 96-272), child welfare services were given the mission of preventing the unnecessary separation of children from their families by identifying family problems, assisting families in resolving their problems, and forestalling the breakup of the family where the prevention of child removal was desirable and possible (Maluccio, Fein, and Olmstead 1986).

THE LESFU STRUCTURE FOR SERVICE DELIVERY

LESFU is one type of child welfare preventive service agency among whose interesting features are its team approach, its use of workers residing in the community, its mix of clients from three very different ethnic groups, its location in an urban area under extreme stress, and its history of having been brought into being by settlement house agencies in its neighborhood. The team concept has evolved over the years. During the study period, LESFU had four teams, with caseload as shown in Table 1.1.

LESFU was not intended to duplicate existing service agencies on the Lower East Side already involved with families and children. Its main objectives were resource development, referral, and case management. It used the residents of the area to deliver social services and homemaker service. An assumption in the structure of the organization was that many functions could be performed as well or better by members of the community who did not have professional training. Beck (1979) gave the following rationale for such a staffing arrangement:

Because the Union is located in the same neighborhoods as the families it serves, and because its direct-service staff is drawn from the neighborhood, it is in a position to know which families are in trouble, or to hear from one family that another needs help. The Union staff enters into a partnership with the parent or parents of these families helping them to find and to organize support services that are wanted and available.   (p. 5)

Beck also felt that workers drawn from the residents of the area would be more effective because of higher expectations and less likelihood of burnout:

It is the belief of the Union that people whose life experience is close to that of the families expect the families to succeed and that these expectations motivate the families to do so. Highly educated, middle-or-upper-class people who have never endured the life of the desperately poor tend to underestimate the strength of poor families and do not provide sufficient challenge to them to build on these strengths. Work with these families is extremely difficult and fatiguing. The use of an approach to management that involves team decision-making creates a framework that lessens the danger of staff burnout that might occur with great frequency in the conventional bureaucratic structure.   (p. 7)

A second assumption (Weissman 1978) was that teams organized along ethnic lines would be more efficient. Team I had a preponderance of Spanish-speaking workers, while Team II was made up largely of Chinese workers. Team III was largely black. Team III was an evolution of the concept of teams in that it was staffed by civil service workers on loan from the Office of Special Services for Children of the Department of Social Services of New York City. While the members of the public-sector team were civil service personnel who could not be hired, fired, or disciplined by the executive director of LESFU, they were, in fact, serving under the administrative leadership of the executive director of LESFU in a relationship similar to that of the other three teams.

Another experiment was to have a team (Team IV) that focused its efforts on a poverty-stricken, devastated block, seeking to organize among the tenants natural systems of support that would prevent family deterioration and that would help families solve some of their most serious problems. Its efforts also included services delivered to individuals in groups, such as teenaged job programs and after-school help for children with homework assignments. This team had the smallest number of clients.

STAGES IN THE MODEL OF SERVICE

The agency had structured its model to help clients mobilize their own coping capacities as well as to make better use of the resources available in the community. The model's core was the concept of a contract that was written individually for each client and that clearly stated the client's needs and what services would be offered.

During the study period, the model was conceptualized as a sequence of seven stages in which the social work associate (SWA) acted as case manager and mediator between the client and the agencies providing services the client required. These stages were:

1. *Intake* or *Pre-work Agreement:* The purpose of intake was for LESFU and the client to come to a shared understanding of the problems that the family faced. As many as three interviews with the client were needed before an understanding of the client's problems was achieved.

2. *The Work Agreement:* The model's structure was to establish the problems that were to be worked on mutually with the client. The work agreement was a clearly written understanding between the client and the SWA concerning the problems they would work on and the tasks each would perform.

3. *The Goal Statement:* The intent was to establish with the client joint expectations on how or how much of the problem would be resolved. For example, the client was entitled to know what the chances were of achieving such goals as obtaining public housing given long waiting lists. The goal statement was a mutual agreement on the longer-term objectives to be achieved. It was broader than the specific problems outlined in the work agreement. For example, if a work agreement had been made to help a mother get her child into a special education classroom, the goal statement might specify promoting the child's intellectual and social development, which may in the future include a work agreement related to enrolling the child in an after-school program or to obtaining tutoring. The model stressed the importance of mutuality and client self-determination in the identification and assignment of priorities to problem areas and goals.

4. *The Convening:* Since a LESFU "high-risk" client usually had more than one problem, there were often a number of service providers involved with the family. *Convening* refers to a meeting or other means of gathering together the client and other agencies and organizations that carried out functions in service provision to the client. The aim was to begin the process of coordinating services. A major LESFU task was to ensure that the efforts of all providers involved in a case were coordinated. Through the process of convening, the client, LESFU, and other providers would come to agreement about what each party would do to strengthen the family.

5. *The Contract:* Through the process of convening, the client, LESFU, and other providers should have come to an agreement about what each party would do to strengthen the family. The contract was a written statement concerning the goals and tasks of each party. The contract was intended to prevent duplication or fragmentation of services, dispel false expectations by all parties, and ensure continuity and accountability of services (Maluccio and Marlow 1974).

6. *Monitoring:* LESFU workers continually reviewed the extent to which LESFU, the client, and the providers were living up to the terms of the contract and whether circumstances had changed sufficiently so that the service contract should be revised.

7. *Follow-up/Termination:* The SWA was responsible for following up with the client and service provider to insure that the correct services were made available and that additional problems had not arisen in the family. For high-risk cases, termination could occur if the client's problems had been resolved or were under control or had been terminated for other reasons. For example, a joint client and LESFU decision that LESFU was not assisting the client would result in closing the case.

Because the essence of the LESFU model was that the client and the SWA have a formal mutually agreed upon agenda, we sought to identify what clients expected in the way of service, what the SWAs said they would attempt to do, what the SWAs and clients agreed to work on, and what the clients were told was expected of them with regard to their participation in the service effort as well as what was expected of family members. Alcabes and Jones (1985) have argued that would-be clients often do not become socialized to the client role. They make the point that an effort to evaluate service in such cases can be pointless because the necessary commitment for ongoing work with the agency simply has not taken place.

In her well-known study of casework practice, *Motivation, Capacity, and Opportunity: Studies in Casework, Theory and Practice* (1964), Ripple stressed the importance of defining the "problem at issue" with respect to client requests for service. Her point was that not everything noxious and unsatisfying that the client has to cope with necessarily winds up as an agenda item for service activity. The client might not be ready to address the issues involved in a change effort and other problems might be more pressing. Consequently, we asked clients to identify the "precipitating events" that propelled them into seeking service, the "main" problems that principally concerned them, the "other" problems for which they were also seeking solutions, and the "conditions" that were onerous to the family (such as housing, income, ill health, neighborhood circumstances, and family relationships) but where service directed toward improvement of these conditions was not sought.

As we scanned the problems reported by the SWAs and the clients themselves, we were impressed with the phenomenological complexity involved in the professional assessment tasks. There were a myriad of problems and conditions that could be addressed. Further, some impairments might be located within clients' attitudes and behaviors, while others had to be attributed to the surrounding distressed environment in which they lived. Part of the problem configuration also would likely include the lack of resources made available by the larger society, such as affordable housing, health services, and drug treatment.

DESIGN ISSUES

We did not perform a simple field experiment in which clients were assigned randomly to experimental and control groups as was done in the study *A Second Chance for Families* (Jones, Neuman, and Shyne 1976) because an experiment was premature in this situation. Neither the "problems to be prevented," nor the "treatments" to be applied, nor the "responses" to be observed were clearly defined prior to the start of the study. Even now that we have completed the study, we feel that we can only begin to formulate hypotheses that describe the processes these families experience. The problem of defining "treatments" and "responses" is even more formidable.

The next most rigorous study design is a matched-pair, case-control study

(Cochran 1983). Indeed, our original plan for the study was to evaluate the outcomes of the LESFU service offered by tracking the client families and comparing their experiences to those of a comparative group of non-LESFU families. After we began our field work and encountered the realities of this population, we realized that we had to modify our design. First, it took a year to accumulate the desired number of LESFU clients—160 cases. Second, we could not satisfactorily define a control population much less provide a solid basis for designating non-LESFU families as appropriate matches for study subjects. Families can come to LESFU because they have been evicted from their housing, because their welfare benefits have been cut off, because a child has been expelled from school, or because of any other disaster to which poor families are vulnerable. How does one define the matching subject? For example, who would be a match for a Chinese family in Chinatown with marital problems? A Chinese family in Queens? One not living in a Chinese community? One working with one of the settlement houses? Third, the expenditures on measuring the LESFU families grew beyond the amounts budgeted. In view of the growing complexity of the research problem, we were increasingly concerned that the budget left to locate and interview a suitable contrast group would not be adequate. Explorations with potential referral sources to secure recruits for the study were not encouraging. For these reasons, we decided to revise the design to a population survey focusing on an exploratory approach gathering data on the service encounters of the 160 clients.

While we were interested in the outcomes of agency interventions, and this study does have evaluative implications, our basic aim was to understand the clients' cognitive and emotional states when they sought help. With what problems were they contending? Were there problems they had a particular investment in solving? Were there problems they had learned to live with? How much value did they place upon what had been done for them? What had they been able to do for themselves? What could and could not be done given the resources available to LESFU? We sought to learn what was in the "black box" of problem-oriented service delivery to poor people.

The absence of studies concerning what is included in the service processes that constitute the heart of preventive services makes the rich descriptive information we have gathered useful and timely in filling an important void in knowledge. Past research on preventive child welfare services has concentrated almost exclusively on studying a narrow range of case outcomes, such as prevention of foster care placement, and has not studied the nature of services rendered and the changes in family functioning associated with service investments. Consequently, we described the detailed nature of the problems presented by the client families, the areas worked on in the service encounters, and the changes in the lives of the families reported in the interviews with the SWAs and with the clients. Our aim was to develop clarity about what the service system is all about and to develop a theoretical understanding about the processes in a preventive service agency.

Rapoport (1987) discussed our LESFU research and quoted Fanshel as having eight questions in the early stages of the research:

1. What are the implications of studying cases that included many chronic and intractable problem families—"tough cases." How does this affect discussing evaluation of results with them?

2. What expectations are realistic for the persistence of any changes that may occur? If public responsibility requires that service systems avoid throwing "money at problems," is this the best use of the funds?

3. How much does the effect of the LESFU service model depend on its specific leadership, its specific history as an innovating unit, its specific skill and experience?

4. What evaluation strategy is reasonable to hold the interest and involvement of a staff that works under difficult, often discouraging conditions? . . . How can an evaluation scheme be developed in which the emphasis is upon proof that the agency is moving in the right direction, rather than that it has found a "magic cure" that "works"?

5. How should the researcher interpret claims of the agency's uniqueness by the media? While the emphasis on innovation highlights special elements in the LESFU model, there is no doubt that much or all of this has been done before, and to ignore this would be failing to learn from prior experience.

6. What is the relevance of ethnic subcultures on family functioning, and how does this affect application of the LESFU model? Are Puerto Rican one-parent families different, for example, from Chinese, black, or white ethnic one-parent families at the same socioeconomic level, and what consequences do the differences have in relation to preventive intervention?

7. How can the vulnerability of those involved in the project be approached, both on the side of the agency being evaluated and the research team?

8. Given all the difficulties, what benefit is it reasonable to expect from the project: service lessons? scientific information? methodological findings? skills training? (Rapoport 1987, pp. 49–50)

BASIC QUESTIONS

There was an evolution in our thinking about the questions that our research could answer and about the ones that we should be asking. Since LESFU's purpose is the prevention of foster care placement, a key question is:

1. What was the placement rate of children in foster care, both absolutely and in comparison to other agencies offering preventive services?

As we analyzed our data, we found that a substantial fraction of the teenagers in the client population were already seriously involved in criminal activity. Our next question was almost rhetorical:

2. Was the definition of LESFU's mission as the prevention of foster care placement unwisely restrictive? Less rhetorically, was there an indication of the possibility of prevention of juvenile criminality and drug involvement?

The principal constraint on our design of this study was the absence of measures of the success of the service effort on behalf of a client family. If a valid and comprehensive measure of success in social work practice in a service program such as LESFU were available, then more rigorous comparative designs could be executed:

3. Does a measure of case success exist that is consistent with both the SWA's and the client's reports? If so, what is it?

The 160 client families who were in this study were not a random sample of the overall population of families needing social services. The data describing them and their experiences were thus limited in their usefulness for providing insights into the mechanisms trapping families in poverty. Nevertheless, a key question is to understand the client background factors causing a family's problems:

4. What insights can be gained about the external economic, social, and medical factors associated with the plight of these families?

The structuring of LESFU was unique. The team concept of using members of a poor community who were not formally trained as SWAs under the supervision of an experienced and fully trained worker has promise for providing social services more economically and of a relatively high quality. Additionally, the direct contributions to the SWAs in income and job satisfaction were no doubt considerable. Additionally, there is the issue of the value of the seven-stage LESFU model. The questions are:

5. To what extent is LESFU effective, and what is the evidence that the effectiveness is related to aspects of the model or the organization of the service delivery? Are parts of the LESFU structure so attractive that they merit special attention? What problems can the SWAs deal with effectively? Does the organization accomplish its mission as a general practitioner by being an effective entry point and source of referrals?

An aspect of the service delivery that has received less attention from researchers is the process that the client family experiences. Some questions in this domain are:

6. What services does a client family especially value? What are effective ways of developing productive working relationships with clients? What are the clients' thoughts and feelings about their treatment?

The next chapter is a description of the methodological organization of the study and some of the statistical issues. The second part of the book, Chapters 3 through 6, discusses the external variables affecting the family. The third part, Chapters 7 through 10, discusses the members of the family. The fourth part, Chapters 11 through 14, discusses the effectiveness of the service process and the conclusions of our research.

NOTE

1. In 1991 about 150,000 Chinese lived in Chinatown and 150,000 in New York City's outer boroughs. See the articles about Chinatown by Gwen Kinked in *The New Yorker*, June 10, 1991, and June 17, 1991.

Table 1.1
Distribution of Cases among LESFU's Teams

	Frequency	Percent
Team I	47	29.4
Team II	48	30.0
Team III	40	25.0
Team IV	25	15.6
Total	160	100.0

Chapter 2

Organization of the Study

The data of this study were time ordered and were collected from two sources, the social work associate (SWA) responsible for a case and the client, so that the opinions of both important actors were captured. These parallel views of what took place in the service encounter were important tools for the validation of the information. The data were particularly valuable because they captured the history of the case as it progressed from opening to closing, on average a period of 11 months.

The study's design is different from Fanshel's and Shinn's longitudinal study of foster children in that the data-gathering activities did not involve repeated inquiries of the same actor in the service situation (Fanshel and Shinn 1978). The design is closer to the authors' more recent study of children in foster care with The Casey Family Program in five western states, where a content analysis of caseworkers' records was followed by direct interviews with the subjects (Fanshel, Finch, and Grundy 1990).

LESFU MANAGEMENT INFORMATION SYSTEM (MIS) (M)

The agency had used a management consultant to develop a management information system (MIS) several years prior to the start of the study. The input document was a one-page form, shown in Figure 2.1, that collected a great deal of relevant information. Every month, the SWAs recorded on each case the problems worked on (using a three-digit code), the total time spent on the case during the month, whether problems were resolved, changes in the status of problems previously identified, the stage of the LESFU model of service the case was at, and information about service providers that were brought into the case. Table 2.1 contains the listing of the problem codes used in the MIS system. There were ten large problem areas with a number of subproblems as shown. To help the reader keep in mind the various sources and processing that the data represent, we will attach a letter to each variable indicating its origin. The letter *M* will denote a variable from the LESFU MIS.

The agency used the MIS as a management tool to create service counts and to deal with the accountability requirements of the New York City Human Resource Administration's Special Services for Children,[1] the public agency providing funds for the agency as well as providing staff for Team III. We considered the research potential of the information in the MIS system. Paul Marsters, then a graduate student at Stoney Brook, defined many of the key variables that we have used here.

A key summary statistic developed by Marsters was the rate of reported resolution. This statistic was equal to the number of a type of problem reported resolved at the end of the case divided by the number of cases in which the SWA reported the problem as present. These rates were problem specific. Following the standard approach for summarizing rates using indirect adjustment (see, for example, Fleiss [1981]), Marsters then calculated for each case the expected number of problems reported resolved based on the mix of problems present in the case and the agencywide rates of reported resolution. For example, a case that had the four reported problems of conflicts between adult family members (code 002 with agencywide rate of reported resolution 30%), adult public assistance problems (205 with rate of reported resolution 64%), child not enrolled in school (704 with rate of reported resolution 61%), and other child health problems (910 with rate of reported resolution 41%) would have 1.96 problems expected to be reported resolved based on the agencywide rates.[2]

The indirectly standardized ratio of the number of problems reported resolved was a summary measure for each case that had obvious content validity about the success of the client's and the SWA's efforts. It was the ratio of the number of problems reported resolved at the end of a case to the number of problems that were expected to be resolved based on the overall experience of the agency. An indirectly standardized ratio equal to one for a case meant that the number of problems reported to be resolved by the SWA was exactly equal to the number expected based on the agency's total experience. A ratio greater than one meant that the SWA reported more problems resolved than would have been expected based on the agency's overall experience. We hypothesized that this ratio was a natural measure of case success. Similarly, an indirectly standardized ratio of less than one suggested that the work in the case was less than successful.

Marsters also analyzed the time data submitted by the SWA. Each month, the SWA reported the total amount of time spent on each case and the problems that the SWA and the client worked on. He used each report as the unit of data, the total time reported spent as the dependent variable in a regression analysis, and the 70 variables indicating whether a problem in the MIS system had been reported as worked on as independent variables. From his regression analysis, we were able to estimate how much time the LESFU SWAs had spent working on each of the problems. In addition, we calculated the expected amount of time that the SWA would spend on each case based on the mix of problems reported in the case and our estimate of the amount of time spent on each problem based on our analysis of the MIS time reports.[3] The ratio of the amount of time that the SWA reported spending on a case to the expected amount of time for a case was a variable that we used in our analyses. Our hypothesis was that there would be a positive association between this variable and measures of case success.

CASE CLOSING (X)

There were many clients who could not go the whole way in working on their problems. Their cases "fizzled out" in that the client was not able to sustain a commitment to work on all the problems brought to the agency. To document this, we extracted information from the SWA's case records about the nature of the closing: whether it reflected the unilateral action of the SWA or the client or whether the closing was jointly agreed upon. Variables from the case closing information will be identified with the letter X.

FAMILY COMPOSITION MODULE (F)

We created a Family Composition Module to capture the various family forms reflected in our client population from the case records of the SWA and the client interviews. The family composition is an exogenous variable in the "black box" of this process, and Chapter 3 contains a summarization of our results. The letter F will denote a variable from the Family Composition Module.

DEBRIEFING I (A)

As shown in Figure 2.2, the first direct contact of our research team with the LESFU staff was an interview with the SWA assigned to the case. We call this interview Debriefing I and will label all variables derived from this interview with the letter A. The interview usually took place within a week of the case opening. It took one-half hour to complete on average and used the standard interviewing schedule shown in Appendix A.

The decision to conduct a debriefing interview with the SWA as a way of measuring early perspectives on the clients was based upon three considerations. First, the SWAs were key informants since they had the most in-person contact with the clients. Second, an interview with them would be superior to a written questionnaire because we could go beyond the standard questions and elicit their special insights. Third, the interview would also serve to motivate the SWAs to cooperate with the project, since the purposes of the research could be explained and an ongoing relationship developed.

The first Debriefing I interview took place on April 28, 1982, and the last took place on July 1, 1983. The interviews were tape recorded to permit checks on the quality of the interviewing and to provide the researchers with narrative accounts containing the SWA's impressions of the client. Interviewing in the field offices gave the research staff an opportunity to observe the environment of each team site, and the many encounters with agency staff members that this required led to insights about the service environment. For example, we became more sensitive to the fact that the physical quarters of the agency were modest at each site. Since space was at a premium, research interviews had to be scheduled carefully so as not to interfere with the use of the offices for client service appointments. When the clients came in with their children, we witnessed their transactions with agency staff and often sensed the warmth in the interplay between the clients and staff.

In the analysis of the data from the interviews, we developed indexes of the SWA's evaluation of the client's motivation to work with LESFU, the client's degree of optimism as to whether the problems of concern in seeking help from the agency could be solved, any evidence of client resistance to ongoing LESFU involvement, areas in the client's situation targeted for work, the degree of responsibility shown by the mother toward her parental duties, the adequacy of the family's living arrangements, and the involvement of other service organizations deemed necessary for resolution of the client's problems.

DEBRIEFING II (B)

About three months after the Debriefing I interview, we had a follow-up interview with the SWA, again using a prepared interviewing schedule, shown in Appendix B. We refer to this interview as Debriefing II and will identify variables collected from this interview with the letter *B*. The first Debriefing II interview took place on August 4, 1982, and the last took place on July 1, 1983. The Time II survey procedure was a telephone interview.

The SWA reported on how active the case currently was, the client's priorities about problems to be solved, any changes that had taken place since the first debriefing interview, the frequency of contact with the client and other family members, the client's present level of motivation, whether the frequency of contact had changed since the opening of the case, any evidence of resistance to seeing the SWA, the failure to keep appointments or the inability to discuss personal problems, the quality of the working relationship with the client, whether the situation of the client had improved, and, finally, the prospects for helping the client resolve major problems facing the family. The SWA identified factors that continued to put the family at risk.

As shown in Figure 2.2, 25 cases closed within the first five months. We obtained 135 Debriefing II interviews. Our analysis of the differences between the 135 cases still open at Debriefing II and the 25 closed cases showed that the closed cases had been identified earlier largely as clients whose service requests and expectations were such that the SWA had not expected long-term contact.[4]

The 25 closed cases represented 16% of the original population. Although it is known that client populations such as those seen at LESFU often come with problems that do not demand extended contact, the reduction was surprisingly small. The length of time cases were open with LESFU is shown in Table 2.2. On average, a case was open 11 months.

It has been well established in prior studies of social agencies delivering services to families and children that a fairly sizable percentage of cases are short term largely because the clients are not motivated to go the long course in attempting to resolve their problems. For example, Briar (1966) reviewed characteristic patterns of service in voluntary family service agencies and found that in the studies cited a high proportion of cases did not continue beyond the initial interview, over 50%, and only about one in five clients continued for five or more interviews. In comparison, the percentage of LESFU clients who continued to the second debriefing was between 76% and 92% with 99% confidence, a percentage far higher than Briar's report.

Since the shrinkage in the study population may conceivably have favored the retention of those clients who were more motivated to overcome their problems, we compared the continuers—the 135 clients covered by the second debriefing interview—to the closed cases—the 25 clients who were included in the first debriefing interview but not in the second—using the major variables derived from the Debriefing I interviews and some of the variables derived from the interviews with the clients. The two groups were not significantly different on most variables, such as the type of problems they brought to the agency, their expectations for specific service interventions, and their demographic characteristics. There were no significant differences between the groups based on ethnicity or family composition.

There were significant differences on some variables. On average, the continuers were under much more stress at case opening than the closed cases ($p <$ .05), had more physical health problems among their children ($p <$ .05), had a higher count of problems cited in the reports submitted to the agency's MIS system ($p <$ .01), and had their cases closed on the basis of service having been completed more frequently ($p <$ .05). Closed cases had more contact with LESFU staff in addition to the SWAs ($p <$ .001). A greater percentage of cases closed early (36%) moved out of the area served by LESFU than was true of continuers (18%, $p <$ .05); and a greater percentage of cases that closed early (20%) had children in foster care at the time of case opening than continuers (7%, $p <$ .05).

CLIENT INTERVIEW (C)

A major research effort was made to survey the clients starting some 15 months after the Debriefing I interviews. The client was usually seen after the case closing. Some cases were still active at the time of the client interview. Appendix C contains the client interview schedule, and variables derived from it will be labeled with the letter *C*.

The client reported on the experience in seeking help from LESFU, the problems demanding resolution in the client's life, the contractual relationship with the SWA on what phenomena in the client's life were to be worked on, and conditions faced by the family that placed it at risk. A significant feature of the interview involved reports by the client about changes that had taken place over the past year and the degree to which the LESFU service effort had contributed to improving conditions and to problem resolution. As the persons most directly affected by the service that the agency was able to offer, the views of the clients were indispensable for developing a fully realized portrait of the agency. Mayer and Timms (1970) and Maluccio (1979) are earlier examples of research seeking the views of clients of agencies serving the poor for the purpose of providing a more sound knowledge base for evaluating social programs.

The "hello and good-bye" politeness factor is the informal term for the problem of obtaining valid responses from clients because they might be inclined to be polite and generous when asked to evaluate the agency even if they in fact did not get much help. Lenski and Leggett (1960) studied the influence of the deference orientation shown by survey respondents of low social status and found that the social norm can significantly reduce the validity of survey findings. They offer the following advice to researchers:

When the interview requires communication between the castes and classes and when the respondent occupies the lower status, then investigators would be well advised to avoid questions which invite the respondent to express mere agreement or disagreement to statements which have a stereotype quality. . . . Such questions seemingly create a pattern of response in a significant minority of respondents which can only confuse the results. (p. 467)

The interview questionnaire was quite comprehensive and consisted of 64 pages containing many questions that required respondents to select from categorical responses presented to them. In keeping with the advice of Lenski and Leggett, we also created many open-ended questions which allowed the respondents to answer in their own words.

We interviewed the clients face-to-face using the questionnaire prepared by us and field tested before undertaking the formal study. The interviewing was conducted by the researchers and additional part-time staff recruited for this purpose. We required that questions be asked as they appeared in the questionnaire while at the same time making an effort to put the respondent at ease, to interpret the intent of questions when confusion arose, and to probe prudently when it was obvious that the respondent had more information to provide about the experience with LESFU. Because of the multiethnic nature of the study population, it was necessary that our interviewing staff be able to meet the language requirements of the respondents. Interviews were conducted in English, Spanish, or Chinese.[5]

The translation of the questionnaire into a Spanish and a Chinese version was carried out in a manner to insure that the meaning of questions would be equivalent across language forms. Some English words might not have the same meaning in other languages. For example, the Chinese clients seemed not to view a child's sojourn with relatives, even for extended periods, as a "separation" experience.[6]

GAINING ACCESS TO THE SUBJECTS

We sought the help of the SWAs to achieve as high a participation rate as possible from the 160 client families. Usually we chose the person who had approached LESFU for service and who was identified by the SWA as the most involved family member. A letter was sent to this person both from the agency and the Columbia University School of Social Work research team explaining the purposes of the study. The letter cited the study's potentially useful contribution to strengthening services for people like themselves. The policy of protecting the confidentiality of what was learned in the interview received clear emphasis. The letters were followed by telephone calls from LESFU staff and the researchers.[7]

We decided to offer a payment of $25.00 to a client for participating in the interview, and this was mentioned in the effort to gain cooperation. We desired to keep the refusal rate as low as possible and were uncertain about our ability to garner cooperation from subjects not accustomed to being asked to participate in research interviewing. Paying an interview fee to subjects in social work research efforts had become more widely accepted as appropriate compensation for their contributions in providing vital information. To ease the client's travel burden, we used the four team sites as locations for the interviews. If care of children was a problem, we offered payment for a baby-sitter to remain with the children while the respondent visited the office. If the respondent brought young children to a team office, LESFU staff cooperated in the care of the children while the parent was interviewed, or a paid baby-sitter was brought in to care for the children. We also offered to interview at the respondent's home, and the majority of clients chose this option.

SURVEY OPERATIONS

Of the 160 cases in the study, 81% ($n = 129$) were interviewed. We achieved such a high rate of participation because of a considerable investment in the task of setting up interviews with the clients. A substantial number of clients responded to the invitation to participate, and this was in large measure due to the active involvement of the SWAs who collaborated in the effort to secure participation in the interview by writing to clients, setting up appointments for the research team, and introducing the research staff to the clients.

When clients did not show up for appointments, interviewers were instructed to make immediate efforts to engage the clients. This usually meant going directly to the client's home to arrange another appointment or gaining the cooperation of the SWA to make such a contact. Repeated efforts to contact the client personally and to dispel mistrust eventually opened some doors. Certain streets could be visited only during the morning hours when drug pushers were still in bed. Contacting a client sometimes required waiting outside a closed building entrance for an extended time until a client showed up or until admission to the building could be gained so that the interviewer could knock on the apartment door. In the absence of a response, the interviewer left a note under the door.

When contact was made, some clients did not agree to an appointment but were willing to be interviewed on the spot. A fair number of clients had moved, and interviews had to be conducted in places like El Barrio (East Harlem), the south Bronx, Harlem, Washington Heights, and Brooklyn. Some interviews were held in emergency shelter hotels and places of opportunity such as a park bench. A few interviews were conducted out of town in places that included Boston and Puerto Rico.

Twelve clients (8%) refused to be interviewed. Initial information of client refusal to participate was conveyed to the LESFU staff. Because of the potential bias introduced by nonparticipation, follow-up contact was made by the research staff to confirm the refusal. Some subjects expressed the view that they did not have the time while others did not wish to discuss personal family problems, and some indicated a lack of interest.

Repeated "no-shows" or failure to keep appointments accounted for 5% of the study population. Another 5% were out of town: two clients had moved to Puerto Rico without leaving a forwarding address, and two clients were in India with their addresses unknown. One client moved to Buffalo, and another to California. Team IV had the largest nonresponse rate (30%), followed by Team II (23%), while Teams I and III showed the same nonresponse rate (13%).

The interviews with the 129 subjects had the following characteristics:

- The first interview took place on August 1, 1983, and the last on January 15, 1984.

- Of those interviewed, 79% were mothers, 9% were fathers, 7% were grandmothers, 2% were children, 1% was another relative, and 2% involved joint interviews.

- The average length of time of the interviews was 2 hours and 10 minutes. The shortest was 1 hour and 15 minutes, while the longest was 3 hours and 57 minutes.

- With respect to language use, 38% of the interviews were conducted entirely in Spanish, 32% entirely in English, 19% entirely in Chinese, 9% mostly in English but partly in Spanish, and 3% mostly in Spanish but partly in English.

- The research interviewers described the conditions for the interview: good, 55%; interruptions, 11%; distractions, 5%; interruptions and lack of privacy, 5%; combinations of these phenomena, 4%; noise interfering, 3%; lack of privacy, 3%; heat and lack of ventilation, 2%; lack of space, 1%; unknown, 8%; and other, 5%.

- The interviewers rated the behavior of the interviewees with respect to being suspicious or guarded: very much, 4%; somewhat, 12%; not at all, 82%; and other, 2%. About 75% were seen as not showing anxiety about the interview, being friendly, showing interest, and giving appropriate responses.

ANALYSIS STRATEGY

The two debriefing interviews and the client interview were the three primary data-gathering occasions of this study. In addition, we were interested in dealing with the interconnections between these three data sets and the information extracted from the LESFU MIS and the case closing data. The variables in the two debriefing interviews and the client interview were too numerous and diffuse to analyze efficiently. We reduced the number of variables by developing indexes that were extracted from the data at hand using a variable reduction strategy developed over many studies including our study of the Casey program (Fanshel, Finch, and Grundy 1990). These indexes are a key feature of our research effort. Simply put, an index is a composite of items reflecting what is perceived as a common domain of information. Aside from the fact that multi-item indexes are usually stronger measures than their individual components, the indexes were a more readily grasped description of the clients. When one does not have a theory exactly specifying the variables to be used in a study and seeks to find coherence among them through exploratory techniques, factor analysis is an effective variable extraction strategy. Appendix D provides a fuller discussion of our computational process. We then used these measures in analyses of variance and multiple regression analyses.

We also used factor analysis to identify the broad sweep of connections among the diverse data elements. The factor analysis we report on used 100 cases. In order to work with complete data sets, we eliminated the 25 cases where there was no Debriefing II data because of early case closing. We also eliminated the 31 cases in which there was no client interview. Together, these two categories accounted for the removal of 51 cases from the factor analysis computations. An additional nine cases were removed because of the lack of completeness of data in the family file. The issues that we sought to address with this analysis were: (1) Is there agreement between the reports of the SWAs and those of the clients about the problems that were the focus of the case? (2) What patterns in the data describe what is going on in the families? (3) What explains the nature of service outcomes in these cases?

We ran a series of factor analyses with the number of factors starting with two and continuing through to 36. We found that certain factors brought together important information in a quite cohesive and easily interpretable manner rather early, say when the number of factors was constrained to six, and then continued to emerge clearly and endure in their cohesiveness even when the number of factors in the solution was 36.[8] Other factors came into the picture rather late, after many factors had been generated, and were more tenuous. We found these factors suggestive but sometimes difficult to interpret. After inspection of all the computer runs up to a 36-factor solution, we chose to display the varimax rotation of the 14-factor solution. We present the rotated factors and discuss them because of the fertility of the associations suggested. In addition, we supplement our presentations with more standard statistical analyses, such as regression analysis and analysis of variance, to confirm the more important details suggested by the factor analysis results.

NOTES

1. Special Services for Children is a unit of the New York City Human Resources Administration that deals with children's social welfare issues including foster care and protective services. Its name was changed to the Child Welfare Administration in 1989.

2. Over the whole agency's experience, the fraction of each of these problems reported resolved were .30, .64, .61, and .41. The value 1.96 is the sum of these four fractions. The definition of the number of problems expected to be resolved in the jth case (called NE_j) is

$$NE_j = R1*I(\text{case } j \text{ has problem 1}) + R2*I(\text{case } j \text{ has problem 2}) + \ldots + R70*I(\text{case } j \text{ has problem 70})$$

where $R1, \ldots, R70$ are the problem specific rates of reported resolution and where $I(\text{case } j \text{ has problem } k)$ is a variable that has the value 1 if problem k were reported for case j and has the value 0 if problem k were not reported for case j.

3. The time expected to be spent on case j, ET_j, is given by the formula

$$ET_j = cb1*N1_j + cb2*N2_j + \ldots + cb70*N70_j$$

where $cb1, cb2, \ldots, cb70$ are the regression coefficients that estimate the amount of time spent each month that a problem is reported worked on based on Marsters' analysis of the MIS time reports and where $N1_j, \ldots, N70_j$ are the number of times the ith problem ($i = 1, \ldots, 70$) was reported worked on in the jth case.

4. While 25 cases were excluded from the Debriefing II survey, information about them was included in the review of closing case information and of the MIS information submitted by the SWAs on a monthly basis.

5. Jaime Alvelo, a senior research associate on the project, carried out 47 interviews, many in Spanish. Amelia Chu, a doctoral candidate at CUSSW and a research assistant on the project carried out 24 interviews; most were conducted in Chinese. Three interviewers of Puerto Rican background in social work graduate training were Mona Liza Ortiz (20 interviews), Guillermo Noriega (18 interviews), and Yolada Morales (seven interviews). David Fanshel carried out 11 interviews in English. Peter Li and Agnes Rivera-Casiana, both doctoral candidates at CUSSW, conducted one interview each as part of the task of testing the language equivalence of the Chinese and Spanish versions of the interviewing questionnaire.

6. Agnes Rivera-Casiana first translated the questionnaire into Spanish, and Jaime Alvelo translated the Spanish version back into English to insure that equivalence was achieved. Amelia Chu created the Chinese version of the questionnaire, and Peter Li translated it back into English.

7. The SWAs quite often hand delivered the letters to the clients.

8. We used the Statistical Package for the Social Sciences (SPSS-X) to carry out the factor analyses reported here.

Figure 2.1
Monthly Case Summary Form to Be Completed by Social Work Associates

CASE SUMMARY

WORKER:

CLIENT:

MONTH: _____ 19 ____

OPENED: __ / __ / __   CLOSED: __ / __ / __

TYPE	____ HIGH RISK	____ NON-HIGH RISK	____ LIMITED SERVICE	____ UNCLASSIFIED

STATUS	____ PRE-WORK AGREEMENT	____ WORK AGREEMENT	____ GOALS	____ CONVENE
	____ CONTRACT	____ MONITOR	____ FOLLOW-UP	____

NUMBER OF ACTIONS TAKEN THIS MONTH: _____   TIME SPENT ON CASE: _____ HOURS _____ MINUTES

PROBLEM AND ISSUE CODING

STATUS: ID = IDENT.   O = OPEN   R = RESOLVED
CHANGE: + = IMPROVE   O = SAME   − = WORSE
ASTERISK (*): CHECK (✓) COLUMN IF ADDRESSED DURING THIS MONTH.

	PROB. CODE	STATUS	CHANGE	(*)		PROB. CODE	STATUS	CHANGE	(*)		PROB. CODE	STATUS	CHANGE	(*)		PROB. CODE	STATUS	CHANGE	(*)
1					5					9					13				
2					6					10					14				
3					7					11					15				
4					8					12					16				

ISSUES	STATUS	CHANGE	(*)	PROBLEM AREAS AFFECTED 1	2	3	4	5	6	ISSUES	STATUS	CHANGE	(*)	PROBLEM AREAS AFFECTED 1	2	3	4	5	6
PROVIDER NOT AVAILABLE										TAKING ACTION									
PAYMENT ELIGIBILITY										NEGOTIATING WITH PROVIDERS									
LANGUAGE										KEEPING APPOINTMENTS									
TRANSPORTATION										FOLLOWING SERVICE PLAN									
CHILD CARE										OTHER:									
RECOGNIZING PROBLEMS										OTHER:									

PROVIDER CODING

STATUS (A-E):
A = INITIAL APPOINTMENT SET
B = ASSESSMENT FOR SERVICES
C = ACCEPTED FOR SERVICES
D = SERVICE ON-GOING
E = SERVICE TERMINATED

ISSUES (0-6):
0 = SERVICE UNAVAILABLE
1 = REFUSES TO SERVE CLIENT
2 = NOT PROVIDING SERVICES
3 = POOR QUALITY SERVICES
4 = RESISTS CONTRACT
5 = RESISTS MONITORING
6 = OTHER

No.	PROVIDERS	STATUS	ISSUES	PROBLEM AREAS AFFECTED 1	2	3	4	5	6
1									
2									
3									
4									
5									
6									

LESFU-2

Table 2.1
LESFU Management Information System Frequencies and Number of Active Periods by Problem Code

	Cases with Problem	Mean Active Periods
0: Family Relations, Adult		
001 Physical Abuse of Child	14	4.0
002 Conflicts between Family Members	79	5.8
003 Neglect of Child's Physical Needs	12	3.7
004 Neglect of Child's Emotional Needs	11	4.1
005 Unwanted Child or Pregnancy	10	2.9
006 Unwilling to Cooperate with Agency	44	6.1
007 Other	38	4.3
1: Social Relations, Adult		
101 Social Isolation	12	3.8
102 Uncontrollable Emotions	12	5.1
103 Inappropriate Behavior	3	4.6
104 Compulsive Gambling	1	2.0
105 Cannot Plan/Structure Time	17	3.5
106 Other	15	4.1
2: Income and Employment, Adult		
201 Poor Money Management	12	5.7
202 Unable to Get or Keep Job	17	3.8
203 Unmotivated to Work or Train	3	5.6
204 Educational or Vocational Skills Poor	18	5.5
205 Public Assistance Problems	89	5.2
206 Other	54	4.5
3: Housing and Environment, Family		
301 Housing in Bad Condition	20	4.9
302 Apartment Too Small	44	6.1
303 Housekeeping Is Poor	·5	1.4
304 Eviction/No Housing Available	37	4.8
305 Utilities Shut-Off	6	2.0
306 No Heat or Hot Water	2	2.0
307 Other	55	4.9
4: Health, Adult		
401 Alcohol Dependency	11	5.9
402 Drug Dependency	10	8.4
403 Mental Illness	10	6.0
404 Mental Retardation	5	5.0
405 Chronic, Long-Term Illness	26	7.9
406 Injury, Short-Term Illness	2	8.0
407 Handicap, Physical Disability	9	8.5
408 Hygiene Inadequate	4	4.2
409 Other	58	4.9

(continued)

Table 2.1

(Continued)

	Cases with Problem	Mean Active Periods
5: Family Relations, Child		
501 Hostility toward Parent	22	5.0
502 Fighting or Temper Tantrums	11	6.5
503 Afraid of Parents	5	5.0
504 Runaway from Home	12	3.8
505 Conflict/Rivalry with Siblings	10	4.2
506 Other	18	4.7
6: Social Relations, Child		
601 Behavior Inappropriate for Age	19	5.4
602 Engages in Criminal Activity	19	4.0
603 Juvenile Offenses/Court Dates	18	3.8
604 Sex-Related Problems	10	3.3
605 Socially Isolated	7	2.8
606 Poor Self-Image	4	2.2
607 Other	17	3.2
7: Educational and Vocational Training, Child		
701 Improper Grade/Class Placement	16	2.9
702 Learning Disability	29	8.3
703 No Skills or Training for a Job	8	4.0
704 Not Enrolled in School	18	3.7
705 Disruptive Behavior at School/Work	25	4.0
706 Truancy from School/Work	39	6.8
707 Trouble with School Work	14	5.3
708 Other	65	5.6
8: Life Skills, Child		
801 Unable to Do Age-Appropriate Tasks	4	2.0
802 Refuses Household Responsibility	6	4.8
803 Unable to Manage Money	1	1.0
804 Does Not Use Time Constructively	17	6.9
805 Other	5	5.0
9: Health, Child		
901 Alcohol Dependency	0	---
902 Drug Dependency	7	4.5
903 Pregnancy Inappropriate	3	3.6
904 Mental Illness	2	12.5
905 Mental Retardation	9	6.7
906 Chronic, Long-Term Illness	13	7.4
907 Injury, Short-Term Illness	10	2.0
908 Handicap, Physical Disability	15	6.6
909 Hygiene Inadequate	2	2.0
910 Other	58	4.6

Figure 2.2
Data-Gathering Activities of the Study

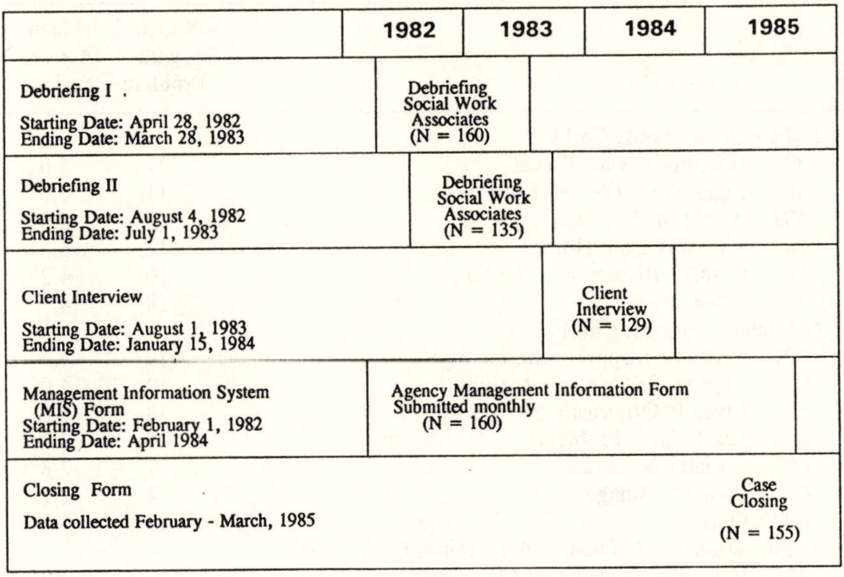

	1982	1983	1984	1985
Debriefing I . Starting Date: April 28, 1982 Ending Date: March 28, 1983	Debriefing Social Work Associates (N = 160)			
Debriefing II Starting Date: August 4, 1982 Ending Date: July 1, 1983		Debriefing Social Work Associates (N = 135)		
Client Interview Starting Date: August 1, 1983 Ending Date: January 15, 1984			Client Interview (N = 129)	
Management Information System (MIS) Form Starting Date: February 1, 1982 Ending Date: April 1984	Agency Management Information Form Submitted monthly (N = 160)			
Closing Form Data collected February - March, 1985				Case Closing (N = 155)

Table 2.2
Number of Months Case Remained Open

Months	Frequency	Percent	Cum Percent
1	1	.6	.6
2	2	1.3	1.9
3	3	1.9	3.8
4	6	3.8	7.5
5	8	5.0	12.5
6	14	8.8	21.3
7	14	8.8	30.0
8	10	6.3	36.3
9	8	5.0	41.3
10	9	5.6	46.9
11	8	5.0	51.9
12	11	6.9	58.8
13	6	3.8	62.5
14	8	5.0	67.5
15	8	5.0	72.5
16	8	5.0	77.5
17	12	7.5	85.0
18	6	3.8	88.8
19	5	3.1	91.9
20	10	6.3	98.1
21	1	.6	98.8
22	1	.6	99.4
23	1	.6	100.0
TOTAL	160	100.0	100.0
Mean	11.456	Std Dev	5.239
Minimum	1.000	Maximum	23.000

Part **II**

Exogenous Variables

Chapter 3

The Client Families

In our analysis, we seek to understand the service experience of clients based on their personal and social characteristics. Variables descriptive of the clients at their entry into work with LESFU that were not caused by their contact with the agency are commonly called exogenous. One group of exogenous variables is the nature of the families of the clients with respect to their ethnicity, their family composition, and the location of their children at the time LESFU began its casework.

We begin our presentation of substantive results with these issues. Insofar as we are able, we will begin each chapter by discussing a case in the population that illustrates the type of issues discussed in the chapter.

The following case is an example of the doubling up of families and illustrates well some of the problems implicit in the phenomenon.

Case Study III

Mrs. III is a separated mother of three in her thirties. She came to LESFU for help in solving the conflicts with her in-laws. Their living habits and critical attitudes toward her had caused harm to her own mental health and to the children as well, placing her on the verge of a mental breakdown. The apartment was not only overcrowded since the in-laws came from China, but also the client and her children were feeling depressed and irritable. The children yearned to move out.

The coming of the in-laws also affected the marital relationship. The mother-in-law complained about the client to her son, and he accused his wife of having wrong attitudes and complained about her lack of feeling for him. The husband recently indicated he wanted to file for divorce.

She consulted a lawyer about her marital situation, and he recommended that she seek community service to resolve the family conflict. She later heard about LESFU from one of her children's teachers. She spoke of her initial negative reactions to her SWA whose manner and attitudes had turned her off. The client then lost interest in the agency and returned to her lawyer. She gave her in-laws a time limit to move out of the apartment. At the same time her husband was pushing for a divorce. The in-laws overstayed the time allowed. Finally, during a family dispute, the in-laws attacked her physically and her husband also joined them. Her screams led to the police being called, and they quieted the situation. Her husband and her in-laws moved out as a result of the fight, and since then they have separated.

Her husband seldom paid the allowance she and the children were supposed to get, and she was facing financial difficulties. She indicated she was too proud to accept public assistance and found it difficult to have to keep telling the welfare staff about her problems. In the interview, she seemed evasive and not comfortable in revealing her feelings. She revealed that her decision not to continue with LESFU was based upon her impression that the SWA was not sympathetic to her plight, and she did not like hearing that her husband could easily find another woman.

ETHNICITY OF CLIENT FAMILIES (F)

LESFU served clients of Hispanic, Chinese, and black ethnic/racial backgrounds and a small group of white clients. As shown in Table 3.1, the Hispanic group was the largest. The group was mainly Puerto Rican, with some persons of Dominican background. Together, 60% of the 160 client families in the study were identified as Hispanic. Chinese families constituted 18% of the families; black families, 14%; and a residual group of white and "others," 8%. The "other" clients included mixed Asian and white marriages and were subsumed under the "white, other" classification.

CENSUS OF CLIENT FAMILIES (F)

Table 3.2 is a census of all family members identified from the various forms the agency was required to keep by Special Services for Children (NYC-HRA) and from the client interview. Our accounting used the mother as the reference point. For the 160 client families, there were 765 individuals enumerated in the forms.

We found that the average age of the 160 mothers was 32 years with a range that was quite wide, from a minimum of 14 to a maximum of 64 years. Most (82%) of the mothers were in the households specified as the residential location of the children. There were fewer identified fathers, 62 (39% of the client families), with 76% of them in the residential households of the children.

The client families contained a host of children. There were 391 children under 18 years among the 160 families with an additional 37 adult children.[1] The families also cared for another 23 children who were nieces, nephews, grandchildren, and stepchildren.

FAMILY STRUCTURE (F)

We categorized each client family into one of four types as shown in Table 3.3. One-fourth (25%) of the client families were husbands and wives sharing households in the conventional manner. These families were usually self-contained with only immediate family members present. The most common arrangement (38%) was a family in which the mother lived alone with her children. Another 20% of the client families were ones in which the mother lived with her children and another adult. In half of these, the maternal grandmother was in the household. In most of these cases, a young mother remained in her parent's home after giving birth. There were a few cases, however, where a grandmother joined her daughter in the daughter's home. The mother was not in the client family household in 18% ($n = 28$) of the families. In five families, the mother had died. There were seven households among these mother-absent households in which the father was residing with his children.

There were significant differences among the ethnic groups with respect to the mix of family types. As shown in Table 3.4, 62% of Chinese families had a mother and father living together, a far higher percentage than the 17% of non-Chinese families that had a father and mother living together ($p < .001$). Almost two-thirds of the black mothers (65%) were living alone without another adult. This was a much higher percentage than the 34% of the other ethnic groups living alone ($p < .001$). While a considerable percentage of Hispanic mothers were also living on their own (39%), the social isolation of the black mothers was particularly striking. They lacked the resources of intact families or other adults. The fraction of families with the mother out of the home was roughly the same (18%) for the four ethnic groups.

GRANDPARENTS BY FAMILY TYPE (F)

Poor families are certainly not alone in the fact that many of them have a parent missing, usually the father, and that children in a given family may have different fathers. Nevertheless, the amount of "doubling up" these families experienced was a particular hallmark of poverty, especially the striking extent of grandparent involvement. On the maternal side, there were 25 grandmothers and eight grandfathers identified. On the paternal side there were nine grandmothers and four grandfathers listed.

Table 3.5 displays the distribution of the 34 grandmothers according to family living arrangements. A grandmother was present in 68% (19 of 28) of the families in which the mother was out of the home. Another ten grandmothers shared residence with the mothers, and another four grandmothers were residing in a household in which both the father and mother were present. The grandmother present was usually the maternal grandmother.

A research assistant, Amelia Chu, reviewed all records of the family at the agency as well as our research materials to make a determination of who was the main caretaker of the children. Table 3.6 presents these results. The mother was the sole caretaker in over one-third of the cases (38%). In 25 cases (16%), there was shared responsibility with a grandmother.

CENSUS OF CHILDREN AND THEIR LOCATION (F)

Table 3.7 is a census of the whereabouts of the children of the mothers and includes those who were out of the home as well as those living in the households. In all, we accounted for 391 children.[2] We have categorized the whereabouts of each in one of four large groups: in the household, in the child's own residence or living with an unrelated adult, in a subsystem of the child care system, or in some other undesired location. In Fanshel, Finch, and Grundy (1990), we argued that emergency shelters, the correctional system, and the medical system should be considered as subcomponents of the child care system. We followed this convention in Table 3.7.

The overwhelming majority (91%) of these children were in their own households. In families in which the mother was out of the home, only 63% of the children resided in the household, while an additional 5% lived with relatives. While only 3% of the children lived in their own residence outside of the household or with an unrelated person, the vast majority of these were from families in which the mother was out of the home.[3] About 18% of children in families whose mother was out of the home were living with an unrelated person or on their own.

There was a pattern for a child whose mother was out of the home to be at greater risk (7% compared to 3% overall, not statistically significant) of being in the child care system. The last category included such undesired outcomes as undomiciled, whereabouts unknown, or runaway. These outcomes were somewhat more likely for a child whose mother was out of the home.

On balance, Table 3.7 shows that a child whose mother is out of the home is at a somewhat greater risk of being in the child care system (the fate of 7% of these children) or at an undesired location (7%) than a child whose mother is in the home. There were no major differences in the distribution of locations for the three types of families in which the mother was present.

Table 3.8 is a cross-tabulation of the location of the child (whether with family or in the child care system or undesirable outcome) by the mother's presence or absence in the home, the grandmother's presence or absence, and the age of the child. For children under two, the mother was much less likely to be out of the home: only 8% of children under two had their mothers out of the home, compared to 15% overall. The grandmother's presence greatly reduced the risk of a child's placement in child care or of an other undesirable outcome when the mother was out of the home. For the 21 children whose mother was out of the home but who had a grandmother present, none were in child care or had an undesirable outcome. For the 35 children whose mother was out of the home and whose grandmother was not present, 23% were in child care or had an undesirable living arrangement. It was surprising that children who had both mother and grandmother in the household were more likely to have been placed in child care or were in an undesirable living arrangement: four of 43 such children (9%) were in child care or in an undesirable living arrangement.

INVOLVEMENT OF FATHERS (F)

The complexity of the client families extended to the involvement of the fathers. Table 3.9 documents that 70% of the families had children from one father and that 21% of the families had children from two fathers.

This complexity extends to the involvement of the most recent father, as shown in Table 3.10. In over half of the families, the most recent father was absent. Although the most recent father was a full-time resident in 32% of the families, the predominant picture was that of children growing up without the presence of their fathers.

INDEX OF FATHER'S ROLE IN FAMILY (A)

Table 3.11 shows the items in the index based on answers to questions in the first debriefing interview that reflected upon the father's role in the life of his family. The internal reliability of the index as measured by Cronbach's alpha was .72. A family that had father and mother together had a father who was more involved ($p < .0001$), and Chinese families had fathers who were more involved ($p < .0001$), reflecting the greater likelihood that a Chinese family had both father and mother.

FATHER'S MOTIVATION AS LESFU CLIENT (B)

Table 3.12 defines the index constructed from the second debriefing interview measuring the motivation of the father in working with LESFU. The internal reliability coefficient as measured by Cronbach's alpha was .91. The index was based on seven items. The ones with the highest item-criterion correlations were the SWA's assessment of the working relationship with the father and the SWA's assessment of whether the father was resistant or late for appointments. Chinese families showed the highest involvement of fathers as measured by this index, and black families the lowest ($p < .001$). As expected, fathers in families in which both husbands and wives were living together had a higher degree of father involvement as measured by this index ($p < .001$).

The correlation of the two indexes of father involvement was .57, a strong correlation indicating that the information about the presence of the fathers in the relationship with LESFU is consistent across the Debriefing I and Debriefing II interviews.

Of the 135 client families covered in the Debriefing II interviews, fathers were in the picture and considered available for service contacts in 31% ($n = 42$) of the Debriefing II population. Of those who were available, 64% showed a willingness to keep appointments with the SWAs. More than a third (36%) revealed problems in keeping appointments, with 24% showing considerable difficulty and 12% showing somewhat of a problem. The SWAs reported that 15 fathers, putative fathers or boyfriends of the mother, ought to have been involved with the efforts at LESFU but were not. Resistance to involvement was frequently cited in these cases.

INDEX OF INVOLVEMENT OF SPOUSE (C)

Table 3.13 defines an eight-item index based on items from the client interview related to the involvement of the spouse, usually the father, in the service relationship with LESFU. The internal reliability of the index as measured by Cronbach's alpha was .80. The items that were grouped together were natural measures of spousal involvement and ranged from the direct statement of the interviewee to the attitude of the spouse about the first approach to LESFU. Confirming the report of the SWA, Chinese families had the highest involvement of the spouse, and black families the lowest ($p < .0001$). As before, when the father and mother were living together, the spouse was more involved as measured by this index ($p < .0001$).

FACTOR ANALYSIS RESULTS (FA)

The factor analysis of the five data sets in this study found a well-defined factor revealing consistent associations of the father indexes. The loadings of this factor are shown in Table 3.14. The variables with the largest loadings were the client interview index of involvement of the client's spouse (loading = .83), the SWA's report that the father was seen by the LESFU staff ($-.81$), the client's report that the spouse had changed for the better (.79), the index of the father's motivation from the second debriefing (.75), and the index of the father's involvement with LESFU from the first debriefing (.68). One large theme was the consistency of report of the three indexes. A more substantive theme was the positive association suggested between the involvement of the spouse and the report of a change for the better in the spouse.

MAJOR FINDINGS

The mother's absence from her home was a fundamental variable associated with placement of her children in foster care or other undesired living arrangements. Although families with both mother and father present had somewhat better outcomes, the analyses of this chapter did not find a major difference in the location of the children when the mother was present. We have documented an extremely complex family structure with many grandparents present and with children having different fathers. When the mother was out of the home, the presence of a grandparent in the home was associated with the children being at lower risk of placement in the child care system or of having an undesirable living arrangement.

There was a notable consistency of the reports characterizing the involvement of the fathers for both debriefing interviews and the client interview. More substantively, the father's extent of association with his family was associated with a change for the better reported by the client. In households in which the mothers were absent, the fathers were more likely to be present and active than in cases in which the mothers were living alone or in which the mothers were living with others.

Chinese families were the most likely to be intact, and black families the most likely to be isolated. Hispanic mothers were less likely to be on their own, with a higher fraction of the mothers residing with other adults, usually family.

NOTES

1. The sum of the entries of child no. 1 through child no. 8 is 386. The discrepancy in the count is due to families with more than eight children and the four unborn children.

2. Whereabouts of the children were determined from examination of DSS Form 2560 and MIS forms used by the agency, from Debriefing I and II interviews, and from interviews with the clients.

3. In one case, three Chinese youngsters were orphaned when both of their parents died of natural causes. They decided to live alone in a household with an aunt looking after them, although she did not live with them.

Table 3.1
Ethnic/Racial Background of Clients

	Frequency	Percent
Total Hispanic:	96	60.0
Puerto Rican	80	50.0
Dominican	12	7.5
Other Hispanic	4	2.5
Chinese	29	18.1
Black	23	14.4
White, other	12	7.5
Total	160	100.0

Table 3.2
Family Composition Information for Study Subjects: Identified Members in Household

	Count	Mean Age	S.D.	Min. Age	Max. Age	% in Household
Mother	160	32.1	9.1	14.0	64.0	82.5
Husband	62	38.9	11.7	18.0	74.0	75.8
Boyfriend	10	24.5	7.8	19.0	30.0	40.0
Mother's mother (MGM)	25	50.5	6.5	41.0	60.0	100.0
Mother's father (MGF)	8	59.5	18.9	37.0	83.0	87.5
Mother-in-law (PGM)	9	51.5	7.2	39.0	60.0	88.9
Father-in-law (PGF)	4	57.0	3.6	53.0	60.0	75.0
Sister	13	23.0	10.7	13.0	45.0	100.0
Brother	11	19.9	9.6	7.0	36.0	100.0
Aunt	5	47.5	16.3	36.0	59.0	80.0
Uncle	2	39.0	39.0	39.0	50.0	100.0
Niece	5	6.8	6.9	1.0	15.0	100.0
Nephew	6	11.2	6.7	1.0	17.0	100.0
Grandson	6	1.7	1.2	1.0	4.0	100.0
Granddaughter	3	2.0	1.7	1.0	4.0	100.0
Sister-in-law	3	17.3	6.8	12.0	25.0	100.0
Brother-in-law	3	13.0	7.1	8.0	18.0	66.7
Stepparent	5	30.5	11.2	18.0	45.0	80.0
Stepchild	3	8.0	9.5	2.0	19.0	100.0
Child No. 1*	156	9.6	5.4	1.0	17.0	89.7
Child No. 2	113	8.0	4.8	1.0	16.0	91.2
Child No. 3	64	6.9	3.9	1.0	14.0	93.8
Child No. 4	34	4.8	3.4	1.0	11.0	88.2
Child No. 5	13	3.5	2.6	1.0	8.0	84.6
Child No. 6	3	5.0	3.5	1.0	7.0	66.7
Child No. 7	2	4.0	1.4	3.0	5.0	100.0
Child No. 8	1	1.0				100.0
Adult Child No. 1	26	19.4	2.2	18.0	26.0	80.8
Adult Child No. 2	8	20.0	2.2	18.0	24.0	87.5
Adult Child No. 3	2	18.0				50.0

*Four cases are expectant mothers awaiting their first children.

Table 3.3
Family Types According to Living Arrangements

	Frequency	Percent
Mother and father living together	40	25.0
Mother alone	60	37.5
Mother and other adult	32	20.0
Mother out of home	28	17.5
Total	160	100.0

Table 3.4
Family Living Arrangements, by Ethnicity

	Mother & Father [40]	Mother Alone [60]	Mother & Other [32]	Mother Out of Home [28]	Total [160]
	(percentaged across)				
Chinese	62.1	10.3	13.8	13.8	29
Hispanic	18.8	38.5	25.0	17.7	96
Black	4.3	65.3	13.0	17.4	23
White, Other	25.0	41.7	8.3	25.0	12
Total	25.0	37.5	20.0	17.5	160

Table 3.5
Location of Grandparents According to Types of Family Arrangements

	Mother & Father No.	Mother & Father %	Mother Alone No.	Mother Alone %	Mother & Other No.	Mother & Other %	Mother Out of Home No.	Mother Out of Home %
	(percentaged across)							
Maternal grandmother In household (N=25)	1	4.0	--	--	8	32.0	16	64.0
Mother-in-law (PGM) In household	3	37.5	--	--	2	25.0	3	37.5
Own household (N=9)							1	100.0

Table 3.6
Main Caretaker in Family Unit

	Frequency	Percent
Mother alone	60	37.5
Mother with Father in home	40	25.0
Mother & Maternal Grandparent	16	10.0
Mother & Paternal Grandparent	9	5.6
Maternal Grandparent	10	6.3
Paternal Grandparent	2	1.3
Other Relatives	4	2.5
Father	4	2.5
Nonrelatives	2	1.3
Other	11	6.9
Total	160	100.0

Table 3.7
Location of Children by Types of Family Living Arrangements*

	Mother & Father		Mother Alone		Mother & Other		Mother Out-of-Home		Total	
	No.	%	No.	%	No.	%	No.	%	No.	%
With Family	106	96.4	150	96.1	60	92.3	41	68.3	357	91.3
Independent Living	2	1.8	0	0.0	0	0.0	11	18.4	13	3.3
Child Care Subsystem	2	1.8	5	3.1	3	4.6	4	6.7	11	2.8
Undesired Location	0	0.0	1	0.6	2	3.1	4	6.6	7	1.8
Total (Row %)	110	28.1	156	39.9	65	16.6	60	15.3	391	100.0

*Data applies only to children 18 years or younger in the family.

Table 3.8
Location of Child by Presence of Mother and Grandmother by Age of Child

| | Mother Home | | | | | | Mother Not Home | | | | | |
| | GM Present | | | GM Absent | | | GM Present | | | GM Absent | | |
Age:	<2	2-13	14-17	<2	2-13	14-17	<2	2-13	14-17	<2	2-13	14-17
With Family	9	25	5	33	184	59	4	16	1	-	21	6
Child Care or Undesirable Location	1	3	-	1	7	-	-	-	-	-	3	5
Total	10	28	5	34	191	59	4	16	1	-	24	11

Table 3.9
Number of Fathers Relative to Mother's Children

	Frequency	Percent
One father only	112	70.0
Two fathers	34	21.3
Three fathers	3	1.9
No. unknown, but more than one	7	4.4
Unknown	3	1.9
Other	1	.6
Total	160	100.0

Table 3.10
Extent of Most Recent Father's Involvement with Family

	Frequency	Percent
Involved, full-time resident	51	31.9
Yes, part-time	4	2.5
Not resident, but is involved	17	10.6
Other	2	1.3
No	83	51.9
Unknown	3	1.9
Total	160	100.0

Table 3.11
Debriefing I: Index of Presence of Father in the Home

Item	Item-Total Correlation
A. How motivated is father to keep the family intact? (low/high)	.68
B. Does most recent father live with the family? (no/yes)	.59
C. What are the sources of income? (no father support/ father support)	.43
D. Is there more than one father? (no/yes)	.35

Cronbach alpha coefficient = .72

Table 3.12
Debriefing II: Index of Father's Motivation as LESFU Client

Item	Item-Total Correlation
A. Quality of working relationship between father and social work associate (good/fairly good/mixed/ poor/very poor)	.86
B. Is father resistant? (very much/somewhat/no)	.84
C. Did father fail to keep appointments? (very much/ somewhat/no)	.77
D. Was father late for appointments? (very much/ somewhat/no)	.76
E. Was father unable to discuss personal problems? (very much/somewhat/no)	.71
F. Father: frequency seen (no contact/once a month or less/ 3 times a month/once a week or more)	.68
G. Father: level of motivation (high/moderate/low)	.61

Cronbach alpha coefficient = .91

Table 3.13
Client Interview: Index of Involvement of Spouse

Item	Item-Total Correlation
A. Identified as married respondent, common law, or shared living arrangement (yes/no)	.75
B. If yes, did he go with R to agency? (regularly/never)	.68
C. Was he seen when SWA made home visits? (yes/no)	.68
D. Does R object to questions about father/mother of child? (no/yes)	.54
E. Is R satisfied with involvement of spouse? (yes/no)	.47
F. Attitude of spouse to first approach to LESFU (favorable/unfavorable)	.42
G. Was father/mother of child seen by SWA or otherwise involved with agency? (yes/no)	.34
H. Amount of contact children had with father/mother (much/none or little)	.35

Cronbach alpha coefficient = .80

Table 3.14
The Role of Fathers in the LESFU Service Effort*

Variable			Loading
Debriefing I			
2. AFATHER	Father's involvement with LESFU		.68
8. AMONEY	Financial problems identified		.28
16. ARISKPLC	Risk of placement of children		.25
Debriefing II			
20. BFATHER	Father's motivation to work with LESFU		.75
33. BCHELTHN	Focus of work on child's health needs	(-)	.31
42. BOB058	Father seen by LESFU staff	(-)	.81
Client Interview			
49. CSPOUSE	Involvement of spouse with LESFU		.83
66. CQE11A02	Spouse reported as changed for better		.79
84. CWRKTHER	Agreement to work on relationship	(-)	.27

*This table is Factor 2 from the factor analysis varimax rotation (14-factor solution).

Chapter 4

Financial Issues

INTRODUCTION

Financial issues loomed large in the problems presented by the clients, and crises related to the lack of income were frequently reported. These concerns reflected the next most important group of exogenous variables, after those describing the client family, and are the subject of this chapter.

Case Study IVA

Mrs. IVA spoke with directness and clarity about the very limited and constricted use she had made of LESFU's services. She needed Medicaid eligibility established to get counseling for her son at a hospital-based mental health clinic. In her discussion of this, she revealed a strong need to hold on to her sense of independence and was reluctant to let anyone help her. She restricted her request to LESFU to the Medicaid question. Even with this issue, she did not bring the necessary papers when the SWA accompanied her to the Medicaid office. As a result, she did not get her application successfully processed in her first attempt. Just before the research interview, Mrs. IVA made better use of the agency when her SWA helped her obtain a one-time payment from public assistance covering three months of overdue rent. Following this, she agreed to join a parent's group at another LESFU team's office.

Mrs. IVA was in her late thirties and the mother of four children who were at home with her. Her husband died 14 years ago in an accident, The two youngest children were fathered by another man who has played no part in the family's life. She was on public assistance for about ten years. For the last five years she has been off public assistance working as a waitress four hours a day. She received Social Security benefits, and she earned wages to supplement her income. Overall, she regarded the family's income as minimal, and she felt that money issues constantly plagued her. She wanted job training for herself but was afraid to go to school at night and leave her children alone at home. Her oldest son appeared to engage in drug-related activities and needed help.

Her change of attitude toward LESFU was rather recent, and she expressed more positive attitudes than she had expressed earlier. She was looking forward to participation in the parent group. Overall, the case reflected limited use of LESFU with an improvement in utilization and evaluation of LESFU just prior to the interview.

Case Study IVB

Mrs. IVB lived in New York City since she left the Dominican Republic eight years ago. She worked in a factory for five years and then had to be hospitalized for a major operation. At this time, she and her husband separated, and she applied for welfare. While she was recuperating in the hospital, the hospital social worker began efforts to get her on welfare and referred her to LESFU with hopes of getting assistance for her in the search for housing. She had lived with her children and husband in a run-down two-room apartment with a bathtub in the kitchen for two years before her operation. She said that within four months of getting in contact with LESFU she had been accepted into a public housing project. She expressed very warm, positive feelings for her SWA and had been dealing with LESFU for several years.

Mrs. IVB had proud feelings about her four children and felt good about the whole parenting experience despite the fact that she was a single parent. She described her children as well behaved, sweet, intelligent, and loving and indicated her child-rearing experience had been easier than most. She also had many friends and a supportive family.

MIS RESULTS (M)

Almost three-quarters (74%) of the client families had one or more adult income and employment problems, and the SWA reported 57% of these problems were resolved at the end of the case. Our estimate was that the LESFU SWAs spent about 18% of their staff time working on problems of this type. Our estimate of the total time spent on this type of problem divided by the number of problems reported resolved was about 17 hours per reported resolution.

The most common single problem was adult public assistance (MIS code 205): 56% of the client families had this problem, and 64% of the problems were reported resolved. This single problem area took up an estimated 8% of the total time spent by the LESFU staff with the families included in the study. The next most common type was "other" income and employment problems (code 206): 34% of the client families had such a problem, and 35% were reported resolved. The staff spent about 4% of its time dealing with adult education or vocational skills problems (code 204) and reported only 22% resolved.

Of clients who had at least one adult income and employment problem, 66% were referred to an external agency, reflecting the need to involve income maintenance staff of the public social services agency to resolve a problem. Problems that were referred to the external agency were either resolved quickly with relatively little contact or were so complex that they involved a high degree of contact with the external agency and a low rate of reported resolution. The external agency was most often the income maintenance staff at the New York City Human Resources Administration.

DEBRIEFING I RESULTS (A)

Table 4.1 is the index of the family's economic circumstances derived from the responses of the SWA at the first debriefing interview. It is a composite of four items and had an internal reliability of 0.71 as measured by Cronbach's alpha. Families with the mother and another adult present were the least well off according to this index, and families with both mother and father present were the best off ($p < .01$). Chinese families were somewhat better off as measured by this index ($p < .05$).

This index had a correlation of .43 ($p < .01$) with the Debriefing I housing index, showing the expected association of financial and housing circumstances. There were smaller correlations with the Debriefing I index describing father involvement ($r = .24$, $p < .05$) and with Debriefing II index of father's motivation ($r = 0.28$, $p < .01$). The correlations with the two father involvement indexes reflected the fact that families with fathers present were better off financially than families without fathers. There was also a positive correlation with the Debriefing I index describing agency involvement ($r = .26$, $p < .01$). The financial index had a small negative correlation ($r = -0.25$, $p < .05$) with the presence of a child behavioral difficulty in the Debriefing II interview.

As reported by the SWA in the first debriefing interview, financial need was the second most common area of client problems. It affected 26% of the families. An additional 26% needed to secure public assistance, to maintain their status receiving public assistance, to have their payment increased to meet their needs, or to secure Supplemental Security Income (SSI) benefits. Employment was a concern for 10% of the families, and chronic unemployment was a problem in 15% of the cases.

Table 4.2 presents the source of the client's income cross-tabulated by ethnicity. Almost half (49%) of the clients were receiving public assistance; more than a quarter (26%) were employed, and almost a fifth (19%) had "other" or unknown sources of income. Some of the "other" income may have been related to illegal employment of immigrants or underworld marketing. There were major differences in the patterns of income source ($p < .0001$). Chinese families were much more involved in the labor force, with 76% receiving wages and only one family receiving public assistance. Black families were less likely to have wages as a source of income and more likely to have "other" sources of income.

Table 4.3 shows the cross-tabulation of the SWA's assessment of the adequacy of the family's income by the family's ethnicity. More than a third (35%) were reported to have "very inadequate incomes," and 48% were reported to have incomes that were less than adequate. The table illustrates the extent to which the Chinese were better off than the other ethnic groups.

DEBRIEFING II RESULTS (B)

There were no indexes relating to financial issues derived from the analysis of the Debriefing II interview. After housing problems, financial difficulties were the most prevalent problem occupying the attention of the SWA. Overall, 30% of the clients had financial difficulties, down from 46% in the Debriefing I interview. Over 30% of the clients were receiving public financial assistance before contact with LESFU, with only one client described as receiving educational help. The SWAs established a connection with the New York City Income Maintenance Program for an additional 27% of the clients by the Debriefing II interview and helped secure food stamps and SSI benefits for another 8%.

The SWAs reported better material circumstances since the cases opened at LESFU in 33% of the cases covered in the Debriefing II interview. Specifically, employment was obtained in five cases and training in four cases. Other improvements included increased public assistance. The SWAs had plans to seek adult education or vocational training for 10% of the clients covered in Debriefing II and employment for 4% of the clients. The efforts of the SWAs to improve the preparation of their clients to enter the job marketplace were a conspicuous addition over and above what the clients were seeking for themselves.

CLIENT INTERVIEW RESULTS (C)

We derived two indexes from the client interview that dealt with financial issues. One dealt with the financial strain on the family, and the other with the participation of the family in the labor market.

Client Interview Index of Family Financial Strain

Table 4.4 displays an index defined by six items which taken together were descriptive of the strain in the client family's financial situation. The internal reliability of this index was .71 as measured by Cronbach's alpha, and the item-criterion correlations ranged from .62 to .30. The four family types were under essentially the same amount of financial strain on average ($p > .30$); the four ethnic groups had essentially the same amount of financial strain as well ($p > .35$).

There were only four correlations with absolute value greater than .2 among the indexes constructed from the first and second debriefing interviews. The SWA's estimate of the family's financial circumstances at the first debriefing interview and this index had a correlation of .23 ($p < .05$). Clients concerned with money problems tended not to be the same as those concerned with child behavioral problems ($r = -.26, p < .05$). This association was parallel to the association between the first debriefing index of the family's economic circumstances and the SWA's report of the presence of child behavioral difficulty in the second debriefing. The client's concern about finances was positively associated with the SWA's specifying at the first debriefing that the services of other agencies were required to meet the client's problems ($r = .22, p < .05$). Finally, the SWA's identification of money problems as occupying all or part of the service agenda in the second debriefing was positively associated with the client interview index of financial strain ($r = .26, p < .05$).

Almost half of the clients (48%) said that their need for help with their lack of money was an important reason for coming to LESFU, and 24% reported a financial crisis as the precipitating event in coming to LESFU. Almost a fifth (18%) of the clients felt that economic difficulty was a cause of current family problems.

Table 4.5 presents a cross-tabulation by ethnicity of the client's reports of the adequacy of their incomes. Almost half of the respondents (48%) defined their income as inadequate to raise their family decently. The pattern of their responses was consistent with the SWA's evaluations of their incomes shown in Table 4.3, but the SWAs felt that the client incomes were somewhat more adequate. The subjectiveness of the concept of "adequate" income complicated the interpretation of these responses. For example, even though the Chinese families reported about the same level of financial strain as other families, they reported themselves as much more liquid financially: 84% of Chinese families rarely ran out of money.

Over half (51%) of the respondents indicated that they ran short of money regularly. Only 37% found it easy to manage their incomes, and only 11% rarely worried about financial issues. When the clients ran out of money, they handled the problem with a range of approaches. Some borrowed from relatives or neighbors; some sought credit at the local bodega/store; and others ate rice and beans, did without any treats for the children, and "lived lean." The clients felt particularly oppressed by the high cost of living, unexpected expenditures such as medical bills, and the frustration of trying to feed growing, always-hungry children adequately.

The clients confirmed the positive reports of the SWAs in the MIS analysis. Of the 76 clients who reported an income problem, 72% ($n = 55$) felt that the problem was less serious, and 89% of those with an improvement ($n = 49$) regarded LESFU as helpful. During the course of the study, the phenomenon of "churning" in the public assistance system in New York City was ongoing. Clients were discontinued from assistance when they failed to deal adequately with more stringent demands for evidence relating to eligibility. Often the recipients lacked competence in dealing with the eligibility demands so that the help of the SWA was particularly welcome. Of the 13 clients with adult education and training needs as a problem, 46% ($n = 6$) felt the problem was lessened, and 67% ($n = 4$) of those with improvement felt that LESFU was helpful.

Client Interview Index of Family Dependence
on Public Assistance

The second index measured the extent to which the family's income was from public assistance rather than wages and is shown in Table 4.6. Its internal reliability was .76 as measured by Cronbach's alpha. It was composed of five items whose item-criterion correlations ranged from .71 to .28. The four types of family structures had essentially the same extent of dependence on public assistance as measured by this index ($p > .10$). The four ethnic groups differed in their dependence on public assistance ($p < .0001$). Chinese families were much less dependent on public assistance than other groups, and Hispanic families were somewhat more dependent than other groups.

The employment rate among those interviewed was 36%, with 23% never having been employed. This was mildly inconsistent with the 43% of clients who reported that they received their income from wages and the 26% who were reported as employed by the SWA in the first debriefing interview. Among Chinese families, 92% said that wages were the source of their income, compared to 76% reported by the SWA in Table 4.2. When the SWA's category of "other" was combined with wages, there was very good agreement: 90% from the SWA compared to 92% from the subjects. Among black families, 42% said that wages were their source of income. This was inconsistent with the SWA's report in Table 4.2, unless the "other" source of income was merged with wages. The combined figure was 39% from the SWAs.

Twenty-four mothers were employed (45% of families with employed persons), 16 fathers were employed (30%), nine fathers and mothers both were employed (17%), and four with relatives or relatives in the family household and parents were employed (8%). Eleven families (9%) were receiving other kinds of income, such as from renting a room, free-lance work, and occasional odd jobs.

Of those who had ever been employed (77% of those interviewed), the jobs held included garment worker (27%), clerical worker (11%), factory worker (11%), cook or waiter (10%), nurse's aide (7%), and child care worker (6%). Occupations of mothers included laborer or unskilled worker (13), skilled worker or sales clerk (13), seamstress (11), restaurant worker (9), maid (3), professional (1), and other (1).

Of those with a work history, 37% had not been employed within the past three years. About 46% of the interviewees intended to seek employment in the future. Their target occupations were secretary or clerk (25%), home attendant or child care worker (14%), seamstress (8%), technician (7%), waitress (5%), and beautician (3%). About 18% of the clients interviewed were out of the labor market entirely.

Almost three-fourths (73%) of the respondents indicated they would like to obtain more education for themselves, and more than half (53%) expressed an interest in job training. Sadly, 35% of the respondents expressed doubts about their chances of actually realizing their hopes.

More than half of the interviewees (51%) were receiving full support from public assistance, confirming the 49% figure reported by the SWAs and shown in Table 4.2. The SWAs confirmed the absence of Chinese families among those receiving public assistance. In addition, 12% of the families received partial support from public assistance so that almost two-thirds of the families (64%) were receiving some form of public assistance. Nineteen families (15%) were receiving support from Social Security.

For the 82 families receiving full or partial public assistance grants, 27% had been receiving support for one year or less, 23% for two to five years, 22% for six to ten years, 12% for 11 to 15 years, 12% for 16 to 20 years, and 4% for more than 20 years.

FACTOR ANALYSIS RESULTS (FA)

One of the factors extracted from the factor analysis of the major data sets dealt principally with financial problems and is shown in Table 4.7. There were six loadings with absolute value greater than .4. Four of these were indexes dealing with financial issues and confirmed the agreement of these measures. The largest loadings were on the Debriefing II report of working on financial problems (loading = .60), on the index of the client's report of financial stress (.59), on the client's report of agreeing to work on financial problems (.53), and on the first debriefing report of another agency being involved with the family (.52). The indication of the referral of the client family to another agency was consistent with the need for the involvement of public assistance officials. There was also a large loading on the Debriefing I identification of financial problems (.41).

A second theme that ran consistently through these results was that child behavioral problems tended to be disjointed from material problems like housing and finances. The client index of child behavioral adjustment had a large loading sign opposite to that of the financial variables (−.44). A similar pattern held for the second debriefing report of children's motivation to participate (−.31) and the client index of psychological pressures as motivation (−.30). The second debriefing report of medical and other services in the picture also had a loading with opposite sign (−.27).

The remaining two loadings had more substantive interest. The measures of financial problems were positively associated with the client's report of contact with the LESFU family worker (loading = .26). There was a negative association of the measures of financial problems with the highest stage of the LESFU model reached (−.29). This suggested that financial problems were not dealt with according to the protocol of the LESFU model and was consistent with other results demonstrating that dealing with public assistance problems followed a more specialized protocol requiring joint efforts with governmental employees in the social service income maintenance sector. There were no associations with case closing issues on this factor.

The measures of financial problems had large loadings on the factors dealing with father involvement, housing needs, adult health problems, family systems dealing with adult problems, and deteriorating family systems. These associations were consistent with the association of father presence and the financial security of the family, the use of additional income to buy better housing, and the inevitable association of financial strain with medical problems and a deteriorating family system. Mothers under emotional duress tended to have increased financial strain associated with the duress. It was more surprising that these measures of financial problems did not enter into the factors dealing with child behavioral adjustment, adult needs, evaluation of LESFU, or parent-child separation.

DISCUSSION AND CONCLUSIONS

Financial problems afflicted 74% of the client families. The LESFU staff devoted quite a large amount of its effort, about 18% of total staff time, to working on these problems and were considerably effective in dealing with the phenomena, especially in solving problems dealing with public assistance. Clients confirmed the SWA's reports in independent interviews.

There were serious problems of definition and measurement of employment, especially with regard to immigrant families. Both Chinese and black families appeared to have a different relationship in the economic structure of the Lower East Side than the Hispanic families and had "other" sources of income to a much greater degree. Nevertheless, the extent of unemployment and underemployment of the client families was considerable: 59% of the client families did not have an employed member, 37% had not been employed within the past three years, and 18% were out of the labor market entirely. In the case of single mothers caring for large families, there may not be much hope for removing the family from the public assistance roles. The wisest course may be to assist the mother in raising children trained and equipped to deal with the demands of a high-technology labor market.

The LESFU staff appeared to make efforts to involve the clients in education and training to a much greater extent than the clients would have sought on their own. These efforts had some success, but they required a very substantial expenditure of staff effort per problem reported resolved: our estimate was two weeks of time.

There was a wide range of skill among the clients in their ability to manage on very limited incomes. There is a double task facing preventive service workers: getting more dollars into the family's income and teaching survival skills to help clients more adequately deal with the oppressive circumstances. We were not able to document the amount of effort that the LESFU staff expended on training their clients to manage better with the resources available to them or its effectiveness. Counseling efforts aimed at increasing competence in "stretching a dollar" would seem promising in helping to diminish the recurrent financial crises that affected 51% of these families. These interventions could take the form of consumer counseling that seeks the enhancement of competence in such areas as meeting food budget requirements while tending to the nutritional needs of growing children, the purchase and maintenance of clothing, and managing the spending of income in a more controlled manner so as not to run completely short before receipt of the next check.

Implicit in this strategy is the assumption that there is stability in the paycheck or public assistance payment. Income maintenance in New York City's public social services as administered by the Human Resources Administration has been separated for several decades from social service delivery of the kind described here. The separation put an end to a mode of staffing that enabled a single social worker to deal with the eligibility of a client for public assistance and to minister to the personal and social needs manifested by family members. Agencies such as LESFU have come into being to help fill this void and serve a vital role in helping very vulnerable people to manage while being dependent upon a fragmented social service system. The welfare system in place for these clients had gross inefficiencies and appeared to increase the problems faced by these families. The lack of financial reserves of the typical family meant that any delay in receiving an assistance check or any layoff caused an immediate problem whose solution required a rather large expenditure of LESFU staff time and money. In the long run, a less fragmented and less specialized bureaucracy may be much more efficient and cost-effective.

Table 4.1
Debriefing I: Index of Family's Economic Circumstances

Item	Item-Total Correlation
A. How adequate is the family's income? (not adequate/ adequate)	.58
B. Was financial problem verbalized? (yes/no)	.53
C. Is change in material resources required? (no/yes)	.49
D. How well is the family managing to meet basic needs? (not managing at all/barely managing/ managing adequately/managing fairly well)	.48

Cronbach alpha coefficient = .71

Table 4.2
Sources of Income of Client Families, by Ethnicity

	Hispanic		Chinese		Black		White, Other		Total	
	No.	%	No.	%	No.	%	No.	%	No.	%
Public assistance	61	63.5	1	3.4	13	56.5	4	33.3	79	49.4
Wages	15	15.6	22	75.9	1	4.3	4	33.3	42	26.3
Relative's support	6	6.3	1	3.4	1	4.3			8	5.0
Other	13	13.5	4	13.8	8	34.8	4	33.3	29	18.1
Unknown	1	1.0	1	3.4					2	1.3
Total	96	100.0	29	100.0	23	100.0	12	100.0	160	100.0

Table 4.3
Social Work Associate's Estimate of Adequacy of Family Income, by Ethnicity

	Hispanic No.	%	Chinese No.	%	Black No.	%	White, Other No.	%	Total No.	%
Very adequate	6	6.3	2	6.9	2	8.7	1	8.3	11	6.9
Adequate	37	38.5	17	58.6	7	30.4	3	25.0	64	40.0
Neither	4	4.2	1	3.4	3	13.0			8	5.0
Somewhat inadequate	14	14.6	4	13.8	2	8.7	1	8.3	21	13.1
Very inadequate	35	36.5	5	17.2	9	39.1	7	58.3	56	35.0
Total	96	100.0	29	100.0	23	100.0	12	100.0	160	100.0

Table 4.4
Client Interview: Index of Family Financial Strain

Item	Item-Total Correlation
A. Has R had to worry about money matters? (never/ very often)	.62
B. How does R find managing on income? (easy/hard)	.53
C. Does income provide R with adequate money? (adequate/ inadequate)	.51
D. Does R ever run short of money or food stamps? (never/often)	.46
E. Did R want help with lack of money? (no/yes)	.31
F. Has R lost job or had assistance terminated during year? (no/yes)	.30

Cronbach alpha coefficient = .71

Table 4.5
Client View of Adequacy of Income and Money Management, by Ethnicity

	Hispanic [78]	Chinese [24]	Black [19]	White, Other [7]	Total [129]
			(percent)		
A. Income regarded as adequate to raise family decently*					
Adequate	28.6	12.0	5.3	14.3	21.1
Somewhat adequate	26.0	52.0	36.8	--	31.3
Inadequate	45.5	36.0	57.9	85.7	47.7
B. Ever run short of money?**					
Never/hardly ever	39.7	84.0	42.1	42.9	48.8
Sometimes	35.9	16.0	26.3	28.6	30.2
Often	24.4	--	31.6	28.6	20.9
C. Ease in managing income***					
Easy/fairly easy	43.6	16.7	36.8	28.6	36.7
Somewhat hard	35.9	54.2	26.3	57.1	39.1
Hard or very hard	20.5	29.2	36.8	14.3	24.2
D. How often worry about money matters?****					
Never/hardly ever	27.3	32.0	15.8	14.3	10.9
Sometimes	31.2	20.0	26.3	28.6	39.1
Often/very often	41.6	48.0	57.9	57.2	46.1

Questions posed to client:

Do you regard your income as providing you with an adequate amount of money to raise your family decently?

**Do you ever run short of money or food stamps so that you do not have the ability to buy food?*

***Some people are able to budget their income very carefully and "stretch a dollar" to make ends meet -- others find this hard to do. Would you say that you find managing your income is ...*

****During the past few months have you had to worry about money matters? Would you say...*

Table 4.6
Client Interview: Index of Client Employment Situation

Item	Item-Total Correlation
A. Source of income: wages? (yes/no)	.71
B. Income: public assistance full support? (no/yes)	.62
C. Are you employed? (yes/no)	.60
D. How long receiving public assistance? (low, never/high)	.48
E. How long have you worked? (high/low)	.28
Cronbach alpha coefficient = .76	

Table 4.7
Factor XIII: Financial Problems as the Focus of Service Effort*

Variable		Loading	
Debriefing I			
5. AOTHAGDN	Other agencies involved with family		.52
8. AMONEY	Financial problems identified		.41
Debriefing II			
21. BCHILDRN	Children's motivation to participate	(-)	.31
29. BMEDICAL	Medical and other services in picture	(-)	.27
35. BMONYATN	Financial problems being worked on		.60
Client Interview			
51. CMOTIVAT	Psychological pressures as motivation	(-)	.30
55. CFINANCE	Financial situation		.59
83. CWRKMONY	Agreed to work on financial problems		.53
85. CCONFWKR	Contact with LESFU family worker		.26
89. CHPROBM	Index of child behavioral adjustment	(-)	.44
LESFU MIS Data			
90. MHIMODLV	Highest stage of LESFU model reached	(-)	.29

*This table is Factor 13 from the factor analysis varimax rotation (14-factor solution).

Chapter 5

Housing Issues

INTRODUCTION

The absence of affordable housing for the poor in the Lower East Side was a condition the agency had identified early in its experience as a source of difficulty for most of its clients. The existence of housing subsidies and a city housing authority meant that LESFU clients had to deal with yet one more aspect of the bureaucracy. This chapter discusses LESFU's record in dealing with housing issues.

One of the most common types of housing problems was that of a "doubled up" family; that is, two family units in the same residence. Often, the second family was a young family using the parents' residence after the birth of a child to a teenage mother. In addition to crowding problems, inadequate housing took a steady toll on the quality of life these families experienced. Case Study V well reflected the impact of housing problems in adversely shaping the lives of clients.

Case Study V

Mrs. V is a 17-year-old mother of an 18-month-old infant. She is living with her husband and his family in a housing project. She approached LESFU because of her need for financial assistance, Medicaid, and the Women, Infants, and Children Nutrition Program (WIC). She also came because of dissatisfaction with her current circumstances. She wanted to get out of her husband's family's apartment and set up a household of her own so she could live independently with her child. She expressed strong attachment to the SWA with whom she says she relates easily because she is young, sympathetic, and Spanish speaking. LESFU helped her obtain public assistance and Medicaid. While she still feels pressed for necessities, Mrs. V is able to manage better. The situation with respect to the father of the child seems to be devoid of any positive features for the client. He assumes no responsibility for care or support of the child and she would like to leave him. So far, she has not been able to obtain public housing because she is underage—she will be 18 in four months and will again apply for housing.

Mrs. V is almost totally isolated. She never gets out of the home and has no social life. She claims she is cheerful, but her circumstances are clearly oppressive. She speaks of tearful encounters with her in-law family when her baby is hit for touching things. Emotional support from her worker appears very important to her. She feels later planning with LESFU will focus on housing, child care arrangements, and schooling and job training for herself. Mrs. V has a mother and father in Puerto Rico where she also has a sister. She last saw them a year-and-a-half ago. She can count upon them for child support if she becomes ill but otherwise gives no indication of wanting to return to her parental home.

Mrs. V comes across as a committed parent, concerned with the welfare of her child. She described the baby as faring well. Nevertheless, she clearly is quite immature and heavily burdened by the nonresponsiveness of the child's father and shows a strong sense of alienation from his parent's home. While not particularly verbal, she is open to counseling help.

MIS RESULTS

Marsters' analysis of the LESFU MIS reports found that 69% of the clients had at least one housing problem presented to the agency as a source of concern and that 37% of these problems were reported resolved at the end of the case. The most common specific problems were an apartment that was too small, eviction of family or no housing available, a utility shutoff, and an assortment of miscellaneous problems subsumed under the category "other."

We calculated that about 10% of LESFU staff time was spent on housing problems. The return on this expenditure was one reported resolution for about 15 hours of staff time. There were substantial contributions of efforts from other agencies in these cases. The MIS reports indicated that 42% of cases with housing problems involved a referral to an external agency.

Finding a larger apartment for a poor family in Manhattan was a legendarily difficult problem, and LESFU's modest success reflected this reality. The smallness of a family's apartment (MIS code 302) was a problem for 28% of the families and was resolved in only 20% of these cases. The agency had much greater success in dealing with the phenomenon of eviction or the fact of no housing being available. This was a problem for 23% of the client families. The rate of reported resolution was 54% with the SWA spending an average of five periods per problem of this type, accounting for about four hours of the SWA's time per problem. A utility shutoff was reported for six of the families, and LESFU was able to resolve this problem for 50% of these cases. This problem required an estimated 14 hours per case. The case closing information confirmed that there were some successes at finding new housing for the clients: a fifth of the cases were terminated because the client had moved out of the area served by LESFU.

DEBRIEFING I INDEX OF HOUSING NEED

The index of housing need combined five items from the first debriefing interview dealing with the client family's housing situation as shown in Table 5.1. The internal reliability of the index as measured by Cronbach's alpha was .85. The strongest item in terms of the item-total score correlation was the SWA's assessment that new housing was required. There was not a significant difference among the four family types with respect to this index, but there was a significant difference among the four ethnic groups ($p < .05$). The Chinese families showed much less of a need for new living quarters than the other families.

This housing index had a correlation of .43 with the Debriefing I index of money difficulties ($p < .001$), reflecting that money could be used to buy housing. It also had a positive correlation (.27) with the client's report of the nature of the employment situation in the family and a positive correlation (.21) with the client's report of the family's financial situation. Severe housing deprivation and child misbehavior problems had a correlation of $-.33$ ($p < .01$). This negative correlation appeared systematically throughout our results because there was a tendency for two subpopulations of clients to be identified: younger families with housing problems and older families with teenage children beginning to get involved in delinquency. Clients with high scores indicating psychological pressures associated with parenting responsibilities were less concerned about poor housing circumstances as reported by the SWAs in the Debriefing I interviews ($r = -.29, p < .01$).

For 15 of the 160 client families, a housing crisis was part of a precipitating event that led to the client's seeking LESFU's help. Housing problems were present in 46% of the cases ($n = 74$) and were the most commonly occurring problems. The clients most frequently cited housing as their highest priority problem (in 20% of the interviews). The SWAs felt that 27% (43 of 160) of the clients wanted advocacy for housing from LESFU.

Table 5.2 is the cross-tabulation of the SWA's assessment of housing adequacy by the client's ethnicity and illustrates the ethnicity finding on the housing index. None of the Chinese families had housing rated as very inadequate compared to 21% of the non-Chinese families.

Table 5.3 shows the SWA's judgment of whether new housing was required. Overall, they estimated that 51% of the families required new housing. Chinese clients were the least likely (28%) of the four ethnic groups to be regarded as needing new housing.

Table 5.4 shows the incidence of specific types of housing problems that the clients experienced at the time of case opening tabulated by the client's ethnicity. Overcrowding was a common problem with almost half of the client families (48%) afflicted. Chinese clients were less likely to be faced with deteriorated housing, the threat of loss of housing, or recent burnout of housing.

REPORTS FROM DEBRIEFING II ABOUT PROGRESS
ON HOUSING PROBLEMS (B)

We did not derive any indexes about housing issues from the second debriefing interview. The results of the interview confirmed the findings from the MIS that there was progress in dealing with housing problems. As shown in Table 5.5, the percentage of clients whose SWA mentioned housing as a problem in the second debriefing interview was 36%, a decline from the 46% reported in the first debriefing interview. Housing increased in priority between the two interviews. It was the first problem mentioned in 14% of the first debriefing interviews but was first mentioned in 23% of the second debriefing interviews.

The casework process to solve a housing problem necessarily required the involvement of outside agencies such as the New York City Housing Authority. In the second debriefing interview, the SWAs reported that 12% of the cases involved agencies sought by the clients themselves for assistance with housing problems. The SWAs referred 18% of the client families to the New York City Housing Authority and 4% to another housing agency. The SWAs also anticipated seeking housing services for another 7% of client families.

INDEX OF CLIENT'S CONCERN WITH HOUSING
SITUATION (C)

We consolidated five items from the client interview into an index reflecting the client's identification of housing problems as a motivating factor in seeking help from LESFU as shown in Table 5.6. The internal reliability of the index as measured by Cronbach's alpha was .76. The averages of this index for the four family types were not significantly different. Contrary to the earlier pattern in which the SWA's viewed the Chinese families as better off with regard to housing issues, the averages for the four ethnic groups were not significantly different.

The clients confirmed the reports of the SWAs in the MIS and the two debriefing interviews. They mentioned housing more frequently than any other problem. A majority of the clients (56%) said that their need for help with housing was important, and it was the main problem in 17% of the cases. Of the 129 clients interviewed, housing was mentioned as a problem in almost half of the cases (48%), compared to a prevalence rate of 69% computed from the MIS reports. A housing crisis was part of the precipitating event leading the client to seek LESFU's help in 23% of the cases.

The clients specified their problems as being homeless or evicted (12 cases) and being in overcrowded, inadequate, or unsafe housing (12 cases). Only 8% of the Chinese clients sought LESFU's help for a housing crisis, again demonstrating either their relatively better housing conditions or their acceptance of the housing that was available.

More than half of the clients (57%) reported that their housing conditions had improved since seeing LESFU, and more than a third (36%) said that LESFU had helped bring about the improvement in housing. Fifteen clients said their housing problems had been resolved. This often involved direct help to the client in searching for an available apartment on the Lower East Side with the SWA accompanying the client in approaching building superintendents, searching advertisements, and using informal networks to which LESFU had access. In 11 cases, the SWA helped the client to apply for public housing, and the client felt that chances for placement in an apartment had improved. The eviction of a family was prevented in two cases. The clients very much approved and appreciated this kind of personal attention.

About half of the respondents were dissatisfied with their current housing (39% "very dissatisfied" and 19% "fairly dissatisfied"). Only a third of the respondents had a positive opinion of their current housing (28% "very satisfied" and 8% "fairly satisfied"). Clients who were white/other or black were more likely to be dissatisfied with their housing.

Of the 74 clients who were dissatisfied with their housing, 34 did not have enough room, 26 were living doubled up, 26 had physically deficient housing (11 with lack of building maintenance, five rat or mice infested, five lack of heat or hot water, one roach infested, one lead paint, one building abandoned, one lack of elevator, one lack of bathroom), and ten lived in housing exposed to violence (five addicts in hall, three muggings or crime in building, two bad neighborhood).

Most of those dissatisfied with their housing were concerned about the effects of the housing conditions on their children. The most commonly reported effect (16%) was nervousness shown by the children, and 12% of the respondents cited limited playing areas for their children. The clients also saw fighting among their children, health problems and risk of contagion, depression in their children, and increased pressure. About 6% reported that a child was sleeping with someone of the opposite sex (three with adults, one with a child).

Table 5.7 presents the cross-tabulation of the interviewee's evaluation of the neighborhood as a place to raise children by ethnicity. The Chinese respondents had a more positive view of their neighborhoods than the others: 71% of the Chinese respondents had a positive impression compared to about 20% of the others. Only 12% of the Chinese had a negative view, compared to about half of the others.

Those who felt positive about their neighborhoods cited the presence of "good people" or "good neighbors" ($n = 25$, or 20%), the neighborhood being quiet or safe ($n = 8$), good buildings ($n = 6$), being among their own ethnic group ($n = 5$), schools, medical facilities, and other standard reasons for evaluating a neighborhood positively. They felt that their children could relate to good people and were happy in the area.

The most commonly cited reason for a negative view was the drug problem in the neighborhood ($n = 67$, or 54%). The crime problem and the frequent homicides were next most commonly cited ($n = 25$, or 20%). The respondents were also concerned about the poor neighborhood life and being surrounded by poverty, people (including drunks and prostitutes) hanging out on the streets, the dirtiness and noise in the area, and the constant fires. These respondents lived cautiously or were uneasy ($n = 28$), were afraid to go out of their apartments ($n = 20$), disliked their neighbors and had almost no friends ($n = 11$), regarded the neighborhood as a school for drug use ($n = 8$), were depressed ($n = 5$), and felt the need to be more protective of their children ($n = 4$). They felt that their children were negatively influenced because they were exposed to bad things and picked up bad habits and attitudes ($n = 23$), witnessed drug problems ($n = 21$), associated with children who were a delinquent influence ($n = 11$), had few friends and were depressed ($n = 6$), barely went out of the house ($n = 5$), had witnessed killings ($n = 5$), or were into the drug culture ($n = 4$).

FACTOR ANALYSIS RESULTS (FA)

One of the consistent factors in the factor analyses of the combined data sets related to housing and is shown in Table 5.8. The largest loading ($-.82$) was on whether housing problems were identified in the Debriefing I interview. The most obvious pattern in this factor was the consistency of housing reports in the data sets. Housing reported as being worked on in the Debriefing II interview had the second largest loading ($-.72$). The client interview provided a number of variables relevant to this factor. The client reported that there was agreement with the SWA to work on housing as an area of client need ($-.68$). The five-item housing index showed up strongly as expected ($-.66$). Further, housing condition as a cause of the family's problems had a large loading ($-.51$).

The second most obvious pattern was the positive association of financial problems and housing problems. Clearly, money could be used to obtain better housing. The loading on financial problems identified in the first debriefing interview ($-.35$) and the loading on the client wanting help with employment ($-.49$) reflected this predictable association.

There was a third pattern revealed by the factor analysis that had implications for the evaluation of LESFU's efforts to help its clients with housing problems. There was a negative association between a client with housing problems and the highest stage of the LESFU service model that a client reached as shown by the opposite signs of the loadings for the housing variables and the highest stage loading ($.34$). This suggested that housing problems require intensive but short-term investments of service and that housing problems were handled using a protocol other than the LESFU model. There was a positive association of housing problems with both the number of problems reported resolved in the MIS ($-.26$) and the ratio of the number of problems reported resolved to the number expected ($-.33$). There was also a positive association between a LESFU client's having a housing problem and the case closing because the client moved away ($-.38$). This association was quite understandable because finding housing outside of the Lower East Side placed the families outside the area of service permitted by the agency's contract with the New York City Human Resources Administration.

A fourth pattern was the negative association between the identification of housing as a problem and child behavioral problems. In the Debriefing II interview, child problems and associated risks being worked on had a loading opposite in sign to that of the housing problems (.37). The pattern was confirmed by the sign of the loading on the client's report of the child behavior as a cause of problems (.34).

MULTIPLE REGRESSION ANALYSIS OF THE CLIENT HOUSING INDEX

We ran a multiple regression analysis using the client housing index as the dependent variable and confirmed the consistency of the SWA's report on housing problems with the client's report and the negative association between housing problems and child behavioral problems. There were three significant associations with the client interview housing index that, taken together, explained 41% of the variance. The Debriefing I housing index was strongly and positively associated with the client interview housing index ($p < .0001$). The correlation between the two indexes was .55 and was an important consensual validation of the reports from the two parties to the service transactions. The second association was that focus of service activity on child behavioral problems in the Debriefing II interview was negatively associated with the client housing index ($p < .0001$). Apparently, there was a differentiation between a crisis around housing, such as pending eviction, as a motivating force for coming to an agency and a crisis related to the adjustment of children. The two motivating factors tended not to occur in the same cases. The third association was that an identified need for service by a hospital or other medical service was associated with the client housing index ($p < .01$), the problems tending to be raised together as issues for service.

OTHER REGRESSION RESULTS

In the multiple regression analysis of a measure of the frequency of contact between the clients and the SWAs, the Debriefing II variable indicating that housing was an issue occupying the attention of the SWA explained an additional 8% of explained variance ($p < .001$) and confirmed the association suggested by these factor loadings. The finding suggested that families beset by housing problems had more extensive service involvements with the agency. The problems associated with unmet housing needs apparently drew quick remedial attention.

DISCUSSION AND CONCLUSIONS

One of the many positive aspects of LESFU's work with these clients was its success at solving housing problems. Seeking to relieve the stress experienced by parents, working on relationship problems, and helping to enhance parenting skills must go hand in hand with the search for the material resources the families so obviously require.

Given that housing needs are a pressing issue for many of the clients in the study and given the lack of affordable housing for low-income people in New York City, what could an agency like LESFU be expected to do to solve clients' problems? The reason there were so many reports of actual improvement in housing was that New York City had some housing available to the poor. There was a lack of housing to be sure, but there was also public housing stock and housing under private ownership where many people lived. When space in the form of an apartment opened up, there was a scramble for the apartment among those who were homeless and those who were seeking to upgrade their housing conditions. The practical wisdom of the poor clearly defined that an apartment in a run-down building was better than living on cots in a huge armory for the homeless. Public housing projects were of course commonly seen as the major source of decent housing for the poor.

At the time of this study, gentrification of the Lower East Side continually threatened to deprive the poor of the small amount of private housing available to them. Community groups protested the destruction of private housing stock in order to build luxury housing. Given the stress caused by adverse housing circumstances, as brought out graphically in the client interviews, various forms of relief are required. Board of Education, library, church, settlement house, and storefront community programs should be seen as sources of important outlets during the day and evening for families living in crowded and otherwise distressed housing conditions.

In addition to assisting clients in securing new housing, it would be useful for theoreticians of social work practice to explore the development of interventions designed to make more tolerable the effects of crowding, doubling up of families, and deteriorated housing upon the parents and children who are compelled to live in these particularly adverse circumstances. Intervention strategies could include use of behavioral techniques to train individuals to better handle adult-adult, adult-child, and other interactions that lead to emotional blowups under stressful physical conditions.

A second strategy could be to develop counseling approaches that strengthen client abilities to enhance the physical attractiveness of their housing environments and to use space in a more versatile manner so that there is greater capacity to create private space and some sense of order in the midst of physical chaos. Practice theoreticians might also explore the ecology of the family living situation and examine the use of outside community facilities to relieve family pressures. Community groups could be encouraged to inventory the recreational resources of communities such as the Lower East Side and do needs assessment studies to insure that suitable recreational space is available to children and adults in crowded housing. It would also be useful to establish what relief might be attained when family members engage in visiting homes of relatives and friends as a way of increasing exposure to other environments. LESFU's after-school homework assistance program was an example of a program idea that provided a promising escape valve for children and parents.

Table 5.1
Debriefing I: Index of Housing Need of Client Family

Item	Item-Total Correlation
A. Is new housing required? (yes/no)	.81
B. How adequate is the family's housing? (very adequate/ adequate/inadequate/very inadequate)	.68
C. Other housing problems? (present/not present)	.67
D. Housing problem verbalized by client? (no/yes)	.64
E. Overcrowding of living quarters? (present/not present)	.58
Cronbach alpha coefficient = .85	

Table 5.2
Adequacy of the Family's Housing, by Ethnicity

	Hispanic No.	%	Chinese No.	%	Black No.	%	White, Other No.	%	Total No.	%
Very adequate	15	15.6	4	13.8	4	17.4	2	16.7	25	15.6
Adequate	35	36.5	16	55.2	11	47.8	2	16.7	64	40.0
Mixed	7	7.3	2	6.9					9	5.6
Inadequate	23	24.0	7	24.1	3	13.0	2	16.7	35	21.9
Very inadequate	16	16.7			5	21.7	6	50.0	27	16.9
Total	96	100.0	29	100.0	23	100.0	12	100.0	160	100.0

Table 5.3
Social Work Associate's Estimate of Whether New Housing Is Required, by Ethnicity

	Hispanic		Chinese		Black		White, Other		Total	
	No.	%	No.	%	No.	%	No.	%	No.	%
Not required	34	35.4	18	62.1	11	47.8	3	25.0	66	41.3
Unknown	7	7.3	3	10.3	2	8.7			12	7.5
Required	55	57.3	8	27.6	10	43.5	9	75.0	82	51.3
Total	96	100.0	29	100.0	23	100.0	12	100.0	160	100.0

Table 5.4
Problems of Clients Related to Housing, by Ethnicity ($N = 160$)

	Hispanic		Chinese		Black		White, Other		Total	
	No.	%	No.	%	No.	%	No.	%	No.	%
Overcrowding	48	50.0	13	44.8	8	34.8	8	66.7	77	48.1
Lacking own housing	33	34.4	6	20.7	3	13.0	4	33.3	46	28.8
Deteriorated housing	17	17.7	2	6.9	2	8.7	3	25.0	24	15.0
Threat of loss of housing	17	17.7	1	3.4	3	13.0	3	25.0	24	15.0
Recent burnout of housing	2	2.1			3	13.0			5	3.1
Other housing problem	14	14.6	1	3.4	7	30.4	5	41.7	27	16.9

Note: Each row shows the proportion of clients where the SWA identified the problem as present.

Table 5.5
Debriefing I and II: Housing Problems Facing Family

	1st Prob Mentioned		2nd Prob Mentioned		3rd Prob Mentioned		4th Prob Mentioned		Total	
	No.	%	No.	%	No.	%	No.	%	No.	%
Debriefing I: Housing problem	22	13.8	26	16.3	21	13.1	5	3.1	74	46.2
Debriefing II: Housing problem	31	23.0	11	8.1	4	3.0	2	1.5	48	35.6

Table 5.6
Client Interview: Index of Concern with Housing Situation

Item	Item-Total Correlation
A. Did agency's efforts help? (no change/changed)	.63
B. Did you want help with your housing? (not at all/ important)	.58
C. Did LESFU do as much as it could? (no/yes)	.56
D. Were you satisfied with your housing arrangements? (very satisfied/very dissatisfied)	.50
E. Did LESFU try to help with housing problem? (no/yes)	.49
Cronbach alpha coefficient = .76	

Table 5.7
Client View of Neighborhood as Place to Raise Family, by Ethnicity*

	Hispanic [78]	Chinese [24]	Black [19]	White, Other [7]	Total [128]
			(percent)		
A very good place	9.0	41.7	10.5	--	14.8
A fairly good place	10.3	29.2	10.5	28.6	14.8
Average	30.8	16.7	31.6	28.6	28.1
A pretty bad place	12.8	4.2	5.3	--	9.4
A very bad place	37.2	8.3	42.1	42.9	32.8

*Question posed to client:
How do you feel about this neighborhood as a place in which to raise your family?

Table 5.8
Saliency of Housing Problems Factor*

Variable			Loading
Debriefing I			
1. AHSINGPR	Housing problems identified	(-)	.82
8. AMONEY	Financial problems identified	(-)	.35
Debriefing II			
28. BCHPROBS	Child problems/risks worked on		.37
34. BHOUSATN	Housing problems being worked on	(-)	.72
Client Interview			
45. CEMPLOY	Wanted help with employment situation	(-)	.49
47. CFREQSRV	Frequency of contact with SWA		.39
48. CHOUSING	Wanted help with housing situation	(-)	.66
51. CMOTIVAT	Psychological pressures as motivation		.33
59. CQA09A11	Wanted help in dealing with an agency	(-)	.30
68. CEXPADVO	Expected advocacy help from agency	(-)	.27
76. CCAUHOUS	Housing cause of problems	(-)	.51
78. CCAUCHBH	Child behavior as cause of problems		.34
82. CWRKHOUS	Agreed to work on housing	(-)	.68
LESFU MIS Data			
90. MHIMODLV	Highest stage of LESFU model reached		.34
91. MNPRESEN	Number of problems reported resolved	(-)	.26
95. MENRATIO	Ratio of no. problems solved/expected	(-)	.33
Case Closing Information			
98. XFAMMOVE	Case closed because family moved away	(-)	.38

*This table is Factor 8 from the factor analysis varimax rotation (14-factor solution).

Chapter 6

Health Issues

INTRODUCTION

One of the most important features of a family's situation that determined the need for help from an agency such as LESFU was the extent of health problems that family members experienced. A high proportion of the case reports that we have provided here had as their originating problem a severe health crisis in the family. The rates of chronic childhood illness and mental retardation were strikingly high.

The results of the MIS analysis provided the most detailed information about the prevalence of specific health problems. The importance of health problems was so pervasive that the factor analysis results focused substantially on them. In retrospect, this problem area was not sufficiently elaborated in our interviewing instruments.

Case Study VI

Mrs. VI was a 46-year-old mother of seven. Her youngest child was eight years old and had been evaluated to need special education by the Committee on the Handicapped (New York City Board of Education). The child's problems were in the areas of learning and speech impairment. Mrs. VI lived with four of her children, her grandchild (oldest daughter's child), and her son's girlfriend in a five-room housing project apartment. She originally came to LESFU on the recommendation of her son's school guidance counselor who learned of the serious crowding problem faced by the family in its current housing. It was worse then because her oldest son, his girlfriend, and their infant also lived with them.

Mrs. VI described herself as "somewhere in the middle" in terms of general cheerfulness but felt bitter very often about the way life had turned out for her. Her firstborn was raised from age three by her mother in Puerto Rico, and Mrs. VI felt her life had not amounted to much because she had children too young (age 17). She described the children's father as an alcoholic lost to the streets. She wished to be trained as a nurse's aide. She was working in a nursing home as an orderly, which she enjoyed.

Mrs. VI described LESFU as a friendly place with a personal touch and had high praise for her SWA. With her son having been admitted to a special school and with somewhat less crowded conditions at home, Mrs. VI felt less nervous and less stressed. She credited LESFU with playing a helpful role in easing her situation and would recommend the agency to a friend in circumstances similar to her own.

SYNOPSIS OF OTHER CASE STUDIES

A medical problem was the initiating event in the problems experienced in many of the families already discussed. For example, Mrs. IVB underwent major surgery five years before she went on welfare. At that point, she and her husband separated. From then on, she and her family needed considerable assistance to get back on their feet. Other families—for example, Mrs. IVA's, were the victims of the death of the principal wage earner.

MIS RESULTS

There was at least one child health problem (code 900) reported for 56% of client families and at least one adult health problem (code 400) in 54% of client families. Of all health problems, 36% were reported resolved by the end of the case. Injuries or short-term illnesses had the highest rates of reported resolution: 60% of children's injuries or short-term illnesses (MIS code 907) were reported resolved, as were 50% of adult injuries or short-term illnesses (code 406). None of the ten cases involving adult drug dependency (code 402) and only one of the 11 cases involving adult alcohol dependency (code 401) were reported resolved. Of the seven cases involving child drug dependency (code 902), only one was reported resolved. There were child chronic or long-term illnesses (code 906) in 8% of the client families, child handicaps or physical disabilities (code 908) in 9%, and mental retardation (code 905) in 6%. The rates of reported resolution were under 20% for these three types of problems.

Child health problems took about 15% of LESFU staff time, and adult health problems took about 10%. The LESFU staff worker spent on the order of 60 hours per child health problem reported resolved and about 20 hours per adult health problem reported resolved. Problems related to child mental retardation and childhood chronic or long-term illnesses took considerable amounts of time. The greatest time allocations were to dealing with miscellaneous health problems (that is, health problems other than the ones categorized by the problem codes used in the MIS).

Of course, the total amount of time required to deal with health problems of the client families was much larger than that of the LESFU staff because of time investment from health service providers. Of clients with a child health problem, 51% were referred to an external agency. Of those problems that were referred outside LESFU, 82% of the referrals resulted in continuing service for the client. These tended to be serious, as shown by the low rate of reported resolution, 3%.

Of the clients with at least one adult health problem, 59% were referred to a health service provider. Of those problems referred, 72% resulted in continuing service for the client. The rate of reported resolution for problems requiring continuing contact with a health provider was 9%. The SWAs generally referred to hospitals, principally Bellevue (a municipal hospital), Beth Israel (a private hospital), and Gouverneur (another municipal hospital).

DEBRIEFING I RESULTS

Our index construction strategy did not extract any indexes dealing solely with health problems. Health problems were included in the six-item index shown in Table 6.1. The index covered a wide range of chronic problems, including criminal behavior, illiteracy, and adult behavior problems. The internal reliability of this index as measured by Cronbach's alpha was .52. The items in the index were more suggestive of the type of families called "multiproblem" in the 1950s and 1960s (Lagey and Ayres 1963). These families were beset with all kinds of problems and required a fairly extensive array of social services from a variety of service providers.

A family in which the mother was out of the home had a greater extent of these chronic problems on average than a family in which the mother was present either with the father or another adult ($p < .01$). Chinese families had less extensive chronic problems than other ethnic groups, especially the white/other families ($p < .01$). Table 6.2 shows that over 60% of non-Chinese families sought a solution to problems of the physical health of the family compared to 35% of Chinese families ($p < .01$).

The SWAs reported more specifically on the problems that the client most frequently identified as being of concern at the case opening. As shown in Table 6.3, 14% of client families said that they had an adult physical health problem, 11% a child physical health problem, 8% an adult mental health problem, 8% a health service problem, and 4% a teenage pregnancy problem. The total of 45% is somewhat less than the 58% of families with a health problem reported by the SWA shown in Table 6.2.

Health problems were involved in the events that stimulated the client to seek LESFU's help in 31 cases. Teenage pregnancy was the most common precipitating event and occurred in nine cases. Other pregnancy crises occurred in five cases. The hospitalization of the parent was a precipitant in five cases. A parent died in two cases, and a diagnosis of a terminal illness of a parent occurred in another two cases. There were six unspecified medical emergencies and problems, and two cases in which a developmental disability was part of the precipitating event. The SWAs felt that four (3%) of the health problems were life-threatening. They also reported that six of their clients wanted advocacy help with Medicaid.

DEBRIEFING II RESULTS

There was one index composed of three items from the Debriefing II interview that measured health problems. This index is shown in Table 6.4 and had internal reliability of .55 as measured by Cronbach's alpha. The four types of family structure had essentially the same level of dependence on medical service providers ($p > .75$), and the four ethnic groups had essentially the same average level of dependence on medical services ($p > .20$).

The reports of the SWAs suggested that modest progress had been made in dealing with health problems since the first debriefing interview. Adult health service needs were still present in 10% of the cases, down from 14% at the first debriefing. There was only a very slight reduction in child health service needs, from 11% to 10% as shown in Table 6.5. There was a large change in the ethnic distribution of health problems: 25% of Chinese families had a child health service need—the largest prevalence rate—and the Hispanic and black prevalence rates were very low. This was the complete reverse of the pattern shown in Table 6.2. There were slight reductions in the rate of health service problems and teenage pregnancy problems.

The SWAs specified the improvements: in 11 cases the client obtained health care, and in four the client obtained Medicaid. There were unspecified improvements in the child's health in three cases and in an adult's health in two cases. The SWA offered advocacy services in one case.

Of the 160 clients, 37 had found sources of medical help on their own without the intervention of the SWA. The vast majority of these clients (86%) used hospitals, primarily Bellevue and Gouverneur. The others had found a clinic (three used the Nina Clinic) or used private physicians (only two clients). Seven of the clients had sought these providers for pre- and postnatal health care.

When the SWAs sought out health providers, they had a very similar pattern of usage of service providers. Of the 44 health service providers sought out by the SWA, 39 were hospitals, three were clinics, and two were private practice physicians. The SWAs, however, went to private hospitals such as Beth Israel and St. Vincent's in 13 cases in contrast to the exclusive reliance of the clients on municipal hospitals.

CLIENT INTERVIEW RESULTS

Our index construction strategy did not yield any indexes exclusively related to health issues from the questions asked on the client interview. The most relevant variable was the number of stressful events experienced by the client's family in the past year. The events included were death in the family, sickness of a close relative, birth of a baby, and breakup with a spouse. The internal reliability of the index as measured by Cronbach's alpha was .36. The four family types had essentially the same average number of stressful events, and there was no significant difference among the four ethnic groups.

This variable was a highly significant predictor of the adjustment of the most troubled child index ($p < .001$), a result that will be discussed more completely in Chapter 9. As expected, there was a significant correlation with the client interview index measuring involvement with social and health service organizations. A family that had experienced a greater number of stressful events in the past year was involved with a larger number of social service and health services organizations on average ($r = -.26$, $p < .05$). Families that experienced more stressful events on average were more likely to have children identified by the SWA as experiencing school problems ($p < .05$).

Client responses to individual questions were much more informative about health-related issues. As shown in Table 6.6, 33% of the interviewed clients reported a serious illness. There was a surprisingly high rate of death in these families: 26% experienced the death of a family member in the past year. A somewhat greater fraction of black respondents, 37%, reported a death in the family in the past year, while only 12% of Chinese families reported a death. A baby being born to the family took place in 26% of the interviewed families, with the Chinese families reporting a rather low birth rate, 8%.

About a quarter of the clients regarded a health-related issue as a cause of their problems. There was an adult health problem, such as disability or accident, reported as the cause of the client's problems in 11% ($n = 14$) of the client interviews. The most common specific cause was an unwanted or unexpected pregnancy, and this occurred for 7% ($n = 9$) of the clients interviewed. There was an adult death—that is, spouse, mother, or father—for 4% ($n = 5$) of the clients interviewed. There was a birth defect or complication in pregnancy for 4% ($n = 5$) of the clients interviewed. With regard to how the clients reported telling the SWAs about their health problems, 12% ($n = 11$) told their SWAs that they needed Medicaid, 6% ($n = 8$) told their SWAs that one of their children had a physical health problem, and 2% ($n = 3$) told their SWA that they had a teenage pregnancy problem.

Of eight clients reporting an adult physical health problem for which they sought help from LESFU, 88% ($n = 7$) reported an improvement. The improvements reported were essentially generic: two reported their problem resolved, and three reported better physical health. One client reported having given birth to a healthy baby, and one reported an unspecified improvement. Of the seven reporting improvement, five credited LESFU as a source of help.

Of eight clients reporting a child physical health problem for which they sought help from LESFU, 63% ($n = 5$) reported an improvement. Three reported improvements were generic: two problems reported resolved and one child showed better physical health. One family had Medicaid eligibility established, and another changed health provider. The context of these reports was that 18% ($n = 23$) of the clients described ongoing connections with hospitals and other health providers. Services being received included family therapy and health care. The clients reported that the SWA had referred them to other agencies for health care in ten cases and for psychiatric evaluation in ten additional cases.

FACTOR ANALYSIS RESULTS (FA)

From the factor analysis of all data sets, there were three factors that dealt directly with health problems and a larger number of factors that included associations with health problems.

Adult Health Needs

One of the factors, the seventh in the 14-factor solution, is shown in Table 6.7 and dealt with adult health needs. The two loadings largest in absolute value were the SWA's identification of an adult health service need in the first debriefing (loading = $-.67$) and the SWA's statement in the second debriefing of a focus of work on adult health needs ($-.67$). There were no other large loadings.

There were loadings of intermediate strength on two client interview variables. There was a positive association between the two SWA statements of the existence of an adult health need and the increase of the client's fears of adult adjustment problems ($-.48$). This association seems to reflect the pattern that the SWA recognized psychiatric issues more commonly than the client. There was also a positive association between the SWA statements of the existence of adult health problems and the client's view that finances were a cause of the problems being faced ($-.40$). This association was quite natural in view of the high cost of medical care and the potential loss of adult income implicit in an adult health problem. There was also a positive association with the client-based index of the poorness of financial condition ($-.26$).

There were a number of weaker associations as well. When the SWA reported an adult health problem, the SWA was more likely to report that another social service agency was in the picture ($-.28$) and that medical and other services were in the picture ($-.27$). These associations reflected the need to involve Medicaid and other sources to finance health services for the poor and the need to involve a health care provider. The only surprise was that the association was as weak as it seemed to be. A client who had an adult health problem as indicated by the two SWA statements was less likely to participate in voluntary organizations ($.34$) and less likely to expect advocacy help from LESFU ($.27$).

A family that had an adult health service need tended either not to have or be concerned with child behavioral problems. There were three negative associations between the existence of an adult health service need and measures of child behavioral problems in the family. The client in a family that had an adult health problem reported lesser fears of child behavioral problems in the client interview ($.32$) and was less likely to see child behavior as the cause of the family's problems ($.27$). The SWA also reported in the second debriefing that the children were less motivated to work with LESFU ($.25$) when the SWA had reported adult health service needs.

Parental Health Need Requiring Family Worker Assistance

The fourth factor in the 14-factor solution focused on adult health problems associated with a need for relief assistance with parenting and is shown in Table

6.8. The two largest loadings in this factor were with the SWA's report in the first debriefing that the client was known to a hospital or medical services provider (loading = −.68) and with the client's report of being in contact with the LESFU family worker (−.68). In this section, we define the client profile to be that of a client with a health problem known to the LESFU family worker. This profile was negatively associated with the client's report of contact with other LESFU staff (.63) and with the degree of case activity (.55). This picture was completed by the positive association between the profile and the client's view that parenting circumstances were a cause of the family's problems (−.47). A client with this family profile was less likely to be known to other social service agencies as reported by the SWA in the first debriefing (.39).

It was more likely that, for a family with this profile, the SWA reported in the second debriefing that he or she was attending to adult service needs (−.40). There was a negative association between a client with this family profile and the client's evaluation of LESFU (.40).

It was less likely that a family with this profile had a child in placement at case opening (.28). It was also less likely that a client whose family had this profile reported that housing was a cause of the family's problems (.28) or that child behavior was a cause of the family's problems (.25).

The factor suggested an important type of case: A family with an adult member in the hospital needed assistance in parenting and was served by the LESFU family worker. The family had no need of any additional services as shown by its lack of involvement with social service agencies, lack of contact with other LESFU staff, a child not being in care at the start of the study, and housing or child behavior not a cause of the family's problems. The client's low evaluation of LESFU when the family worker had been involved was troubling. One hypothesis is that the use of the family worker represented a more intrusive level of intervention into the family's activities than the standard level of simply offering advice and counseling. The hypothesis would be that the interviewed parent was more resentful of the moment-to-moment interaction and the necessarily greater friction between LESFU and the client.

Child Health Needs

The tenth factor in the 14-factor solution had a substantial focus on child health needs and is shown in Table 6.9. The largest loading was on the number of children in the family (loading = .65), reflecting the necessary association that a family with more children was more likely to have a child with health problems than a smaller family. The second largest loading was on the SWA's report in the Debriefing I interview of a child physical health problem (.57). The next largest loading was on the SWA's report in the second Debriefing II interview that the family had problems not recognized by the client (.56). The profile suggested by the three largest loadings was that of a family with a large number of children including at least one with a physical health problem and with problems unrecognized by the family.

A family with this profile was less likely to have another social service agency in the picture as reported by the client ($-.42$). Such a family was more likely to have the mother being seen by the SWA ($.33$), to have a mother with greater motivation as reported in the Debriefing II interview ($.28$), and to have a client with greater motivation to work with LESFU as reported in the Debriefing I interview ($.32$). These associations suggested a picture of families that were motivated and worked hard to deal with child physical health problems.

A family with a greater number of children and problems unrecognized by the family was more likely to have a child in placement at case opening ($.29$). A family fitting the profile was more likely to have experienced a stressful event in the past year ($.29$). A family fitting the profile was less likely to come to LESFU for help in dealing with an agency ($-.26$) and less likely to have family relations identified as a problem at the Debriefing II interview ($-.27$).

On a positive note, a family fitting the profile—that is, with a large number of children, problems not recognized by the family, and at least one child with a physical health problem—had a greater number of problems reported resolved than expected at case closing ($.25$).

In the factor focused on the evaluation of LESFU (see Chapters 12 and 13), the SWA's report in the Debriefing II interview of focusing on child health care needs was positively associated with the client's evaluation of LESFU.

DISCUSSION AND CONCLUSIONS

We have portrayed the health factors that stimulated the request for help from LESFU. Over half of the client families had health problems. About 25% of LESFU staff time went to dealing with these problems. The most striking contributions of the SWAs were their ability to develop contacts for their clients with the private hospitals and their ability to develop a program with the Chinese parents to deal with children's health issues.

Because of the importance of the content and the simplicity of the measurement of the component items, we hypothesize that the number of stressful events experienced by a client family would have high reliability and validity in management information systems that routinely collect data monitoring the kinds of clients being served in agencies that offer child welfare preventive services such as LESFU.

The reports of the individual cases gathered in the client interviews documented the impact of a family being stricken by a serious health problem or death to a key family member. Families such as these did not have the reserves to survive a health crisis in one of the parents. Our data suggested that the model of a family without skills and resources accepting handouts from society did not fit these clients. An older model described these families more accurately: "the race is not to the swift, not the battle to the strong, neither yet bread to the wise, nor yet riches to men of understanding, nor yet favor to men of skill; but time and chance happeneth to them all." (Ecclesiastes, King James Version).

Table 6.1
Debriefing I: Index of Family Afflicted with Chronic Problems

Item	Item-Total Correlation
A. Were problems re: mental health of family identified? (yes/no)	.32
B. How long has the problem been going on? (more than 1 year/6 months to 1 year/ less than 6 months/less than 1 month)	.27
C. Was there criminal behavior in the family? (yes/no)	.26
D. Was there illiteracy in the family? (yes/no)	.26
E. Were adult behavior or adjustment problem identified? (yes/no)	.26
F. Were problems re: physical health of family identified? (yes/no)	.25

Cronbach alpha coefficient = .52

Table 6.2
Problems Reported by Clients for Which Solution Was Sought, by Ethnicity

	Hispanic		Chinese		Black		White, Other		Total	
	No.	%	No.	%	No.	%	No.	%	No.	%
Physical health of family	59	61.5	10	34.5	15	65.2	8	66.7	92	57.5
Total	96	60.0	29	18.1	23	14.4	12	7.5	160	100.0

Note: Row shows the proportion of clients where the SWA identified the problem as present.

Table 6.3
Problems Identified by Client at Case Opening

	1st Prob Mentioned		2nd Prob Mentioned		3rd Prob Mentioned		4th Prob Mentioned		Total	
	No.	%	No.	%	No.	%	No.	%	No.	%
Adult physical health problem	5	3.1	9	5.6	5	3.1	4	2.5	23	14.4
Child physical health problem	6	3.8	2	1.3	3	1.9	6	3.8	17	10.6
Health service problem			3	1.9	3	1.9	6	3.8	12	7.5
Teen pregnancy	5	3.1	1	0.6	1	0.6			7	4.4
Adult mental health problem	4	2.5	1	0.6	3	1.9	4	2.5	12	7.5
Child mental health problem	1	0.6	2	1.3			1	0.6	4	2.5

Table 6.4
Debriefing II: Index of Medical Service Providers in the Picture

Item	Item-Total Correlation
A. Were other agencies in the picture? (no/yes)	.42
B. Were services provided by hospital/medical provider? (no/yes)	.41
C. Was medical provider involved through LESFU? (no/yes)	.26
Cronbach alpha coefficient = .55	

Table 6.5
Problems Occupying Attention of Social Work Associate, by Ethnicity

	Hispanic		Chinese		Black		White, Other		Total	
	No.	%	No.	%	No.	%	No.	%	No.	%
Adult health service need	8	10.3	1	3.6			4	36.4	13	9.6
Child health service need	3	3.8	7	25.0	1	5.6	2	18.2	13	9.6

Table 6.6
Health-Related Stressful Events Experienced by Family during the Past Year, by Ethnicity

	Hispanic [78]	Chinese [24]	Black [19]	White, Other [7]	Total [129]
			(percent)		
A) Serious sickness within family?					
No	67.9	76.0	57.9	7.1	67.4
Yes	32.1	24.0	42.1	42.9	32.6
B) A death in the family?					
No	73.1	88.0	63.2	57.1	73.6
Yes	26.9	12.0	36.8	42.9	26.4
C) A baby born?					
No	66.7	92.0	78.9	85.7	74.4
Yes	33.3	8.0	21.1	14.3	25.6

Table 6.7
Adult Health and Social Service Needs*

Variable		Loading	
Debriefing I			
10. AADHLTH	Adult health service needs identified	(-)	.67
Debriefing II			
21. BCHILDRN	Children's motivation to work with LESFU		.25
29. BMEDICAL	Medical and other services in picture	(-)	.27
31. BAHELTHN	Focus of work on adult's health needs	(-)	.67
39. SOCSVCP	Social service agency in picture	(-)	.28
Client Interview			
55. CFINANCE	Financial situation	(-)	.26
56. CVOLORGS	Participation in voluntary organizations		.34
68. CEXPADVO	Expected advocacy help from agency		.27
73. CRSKCHBH	Fears increased child behavioral problems		.32
75. CRSKADAJ	Fears increased adult adjustment problems	(-)	.48
77. CCALMONY	Finances seen as cause of problems	(-)	.40
78. CCAUCHBH	Child behavior as cause of problems		.27

*This table is Factor 7 from the factor analysis varimax rotation (14-factor solution).

Table 6.8
Focus upon Adult Needs and Relevant Service Providers*

Variable		Loading
Debriefing I		
13. AHOSMEDK	Known to hospital/medical provider	(-) .68
17. ASOCSVCK	Client known to social service agency	.39
Debriefing II		
24. BACTIVTY	Case activity	.55
30. BADSERVN	Adult service needs being attended to	(-) .40
Client Interview		
44. CEVALAGY	Client evaluation of LESFU	.40
46. COTHRAGY	Other agency in the picture	.25
61. CQC06	Client contact with other LESFU staff	.63
76. CCAUHOUS	Housing cause of problems	.28
78. CCAUCHBH	Child behavior cause of problems	.25
80. CCAUPRNT	Parenting circumstances cause of problems	(-) .47
85. CCONFWKR	Contact with LESFU family worker	(-) .68
Case Closing Information		
99. XCHPLCOP	Child in placement at case opening	.28

*This table is Factor 4 from the factor analysis varimax rotation (14-factor solution).

Table 6.9
Large Families with Children Having Health Problems: Unmotivated Clients Not Recognizing Problems*

Variable			Loading
Debriefing I			
3. AMOTIVAT	Client's motivation to work with LESFU		.32
12. ACHHLTH	Child physical health problem identified		.57
Debriefing II			
19. BMOTHER	Mother's motivation to work with LESFU		.28
26. BFAMRELA	Family relations identified as a problem	(-)	.27
40. BQA03	Problems not recognized by client		.56
41. BOB05A	Mother being seen by LESFU worker		.33
Client Interview			
46. COTHRAGY	Other agency in the picture	(-)	.42
50. CINTVBEH	Client behavior during interview	(-)	.27
57. CSTRESCH	Stressor events and parenting		.29
59. CQA09A11	Wanted help in dealing with an agency	(-)	.26
64. CNCHDRN	Number of children in family		.65
LESFU MIS Data			
95. MENRATIO	Ratio of no. problems solved/expected		.25
Case Closing Information			
99. XCHPLCOP	Child in placement at case opening		.29

*This table is Factor 10 from the factor analysis varimax rotation (14-factor solution).

Part III

The Families and Their Problems

Chapter 7

The Mothers

In the third part of this book, we discuss the client family and how the LESFU effort affected them. We begin our discussion with the mothers and follow it with a chapter on family relations and chapters on the experiences of the older children and the younger children. The mothers were most often the primary caretaker of the children and the person who most often sought assistance from LESFU. Since the "client" in our interviews was usually the mother, we have included results about indexes describing the "client" in this chapter.

For 35% of the mothers interviewed, their first child was born when they were 18 or younger. Chinese mothers had their first child on average at 25, later than other mothers. Black mothers were the youngest on average (20 years) with Hispanic mothers intermediate at 21 years and white/other mothers at 23 years.

Case Study VII

Mrs. VII was youthful and attractive but quite volatile. She had a history of serious emotional problems. Her mother was an alcoholic, and her two brothers were addicts. Mrs. VII came to the agency on recommendation of a local hospital. Her husband's approach to her was to beat and harass her. He caused her to have serious health problems while pregnant, resulting in three months of hospitalization. She came to LESFU on the recommendation of her physician who hoped that the agency could get a more effective response from the police and courts in restraining her husband's assaults upon her. She divorced her husband prior to coming to LESFU.

She was quite caustic and negative in the interview about LESFU's lack of success in her case. She was particularly displeased with the way she was treated by two female SWAs but was laudatory about two male SWAs she dealt with. She was critical of being assigned to weekly sessions with a group of parents facing difficulties similar to her own. She did not want to hear about other people's problems. She just wanted her own specific needs met (i.e., relief from abuse from ex-husband, obtaining homemaker service to relieve her from child care so that she could go to school). She resented what she saw as the agency's disposition to steer her back to live with her husband because he had a job and could provide for her. She saw him as a drug addict who was highly disturbed and who was a danger to her. She was also negative about the family worker, whom she saw as uninvolved, nonworking, and useless to her ("just sat around watching TV").

She felt overwhelmed by her responsibilities but nevertheless firmly maintained that her love of her children was so strong she could see having another one. Her recent effort to obtain educational training was successful, and she hoped to go on with some program. On the whole, she was a dissatisfied client. There were no referrals or use of the LESFU model. From her standpoint, her problems were not adequately dealt with. Yet, she would refer a friend to the agency because she thought others might be able to get help with their kinds of problems even though she did not get help with hers.

SYNOPSIS OF OTHER CASE STUDIES

The other case studies presented so far have accurately reflected the centrality of the mothers in this study population. Mrs. V was a teenage mother living doubled up with her boyfriend's family. Mrs. IVA was a widowed mother of two who subsequently got involved with a man who abandoned her. Mrs. IVB was a mother of four who was abandoned by her husband when she faced major surgery. Mrs. VI was the mother of seven whose partner had also abandoned her.

MIS RESULTS

There were no problem codes that dealt solely with mother problems as such.

DEBRIEFING I RESULTS (A)

We extracted two indexes from the first debriefing interview: one measured the client's motivation to work with LESFU, and the other measured her role in keeping the family together.

Client's Motivation to Work on Problems with LESFU

Table 7.1 contains a six-item index that measured the motivation of the client to work with LESFU on the problems presented at case opening. The internal reliability of the index as measured by Cronbach's alpha was .73. There was not a significant difference among the various family configurations on this index ($p > .5$). Chinese families were measured as more resigned and less optimistic ($p < .05$).

Table 7.2 shows the degree of optimism, by ethnicity, of clients concerning their ability to overcome the difficulties that brought them to the agency. The SWAs characterized 63% of the clients as being quite optimistic and not at all overwhelmed by their circumstances. They rated 32% as being resigned and 5%

as being defeated. Hispanic and black clients were rated as slightly more optimistic than Chinese and white/other clients.

The client's resistance to ongoing involvement with LESFU by ethnicity is shown in Table 7.3. Only 14% of the clients were resistant to ongoing involvement. There were no differences by ethnicity on this variable. The finding on the index, therefore, mainly reflected a difference in the perceived acceptance of the client's condition rather than a difference in the client's conduct.

Mother's Role in Keeping the Family Together

Table 7.4 defines a three-item index that measured the mother's role in keeping her family together. The internal reliability of the index was .65 as measured by Cronbach's alpha. As expected, the SWA's rating of the mother's motivation in families with the mother out of the home was much lower than for other family structures ($p < .0001$). Mothers who were solely responsible for their families were rated as most motivated. There was a moderately significant difference among the ethnic groups ($p < .05$): black mothers were rated as most motivated, and white/other mothers as least motivated.

Table 7.5 shows the distribution of the SWA's rating of maternal responsibility by ethnicity. On the whole, the ratings were positive: 52% of the mothers were rated as responsible in carrying out their parenting roles, with only 8% seen as very irresponsible. The ratings of the black, Hispanic, and Chinese mothers were essentially the same.

With regard to the strengths of the mothers, the SWAs said that 43% of the mothers showed appropriate concern for their children's well-being. They commended 23% for fulfilling their maternal responsibilities and 23% as showing warmth, being caring, and being available to their children. Meeting the health care needs of their children, paying attention to their schooling, and good housekeeping standards were also among the more common characterizations. The maternal weaknesses most commonly mentioned were inadequacies in the use of discipline (16% of the mothers in the study), passivity (9%), immature behavior (9%), lack of understanding (8%), being overwhelmed (8%), showing poor parenting skills (7%), being emotionally unstable (7%), and being unable to provide for the children's material needs (7%). Other deficits included lack of maternal concern (6%), neglect of children (6%), alcohol or drug abuse (6%), and physical abuse of children (4%).

Debriefing II Results (B)

We extracted an index from the SWA's responses to questions in the Debriefing II interview that measured the quality of the mother's response to working with LESFU. As shown in Table 7.6, the index was based on seven items and had an internal reliability of .89 as measured by Cronbach's alpha. A mother who was out of the home had a lower measured motivation than a mother in other family groups ($p < .0001$). There was little apparent difference related to the various other family structures. There was also little apparent difference among the ethnic groups ($p < .2$). The first debriefing index of mother's motivation was strongly correlated with this index ($r = .53$). Both indexes contained similar content, and the strong association reflected consistent reporting from the SWAs.

Tables 7.7, 7.8, and 7.9 are cross-tabulations of the responses to three questions in this index by ethnicity. As shown in Table 7.7, 59% of the mothers never failed to keep an appointment. The Chinese mothers were somewhat more reliable in keeping appointments than other mothers. The variable in Table 7.8 is the mother's resistance to seeing the SWA: 66% showed no resistance compared to 12% showing considerable resistance. Finally, 57% of the mothers were able to discuss personal problems freely. The four ethnic groups had roughly the same distribution of resistance and ability to discuss personal problems.

CLIENT INTERVIEW RESULTS (C)

Our index extraction strategy developed two indexes from the client interview that were relevant to the issues of this chapter. The first index measured the psychological pressures on the client and the client's motivation to seek help. The second index measured the overall morale of the client.

Psychological Pressures on the Client and the Motivation to Seek Help

Table 7.10 contains the definition of an index that combined seven items from the client interview. The internal reliability of this index as measured by Cronbach's alpha was .73. Three of the items dealt with the client's concern and worry about her children, and three dealt with the client's own feelings. Chinese clients were under greater psychological pressures than the other ethnic groups ($p < .0001$). More specifically, they were measured as more anxious about their children.[1] Families with a mother and father together, who were more likely to be Chinese, were measured as under greater pressure and having more motivation ($p < .01$).

Table 7.11 presents the cross-tabulation of each question in the index by ethnicity. Obtaining advice on how to handle children was an important reason for coming to LESFU for 53% of the clients. Black clients were less concerned with getting advice on parenting: 47% did not want any advice. Fear that the children were not doing well in school or in the neighborhood was an important reason for 36% of the clients. A fear that the children would be sent away was an important reason for 26% of the clients. The Chinese clients were much more concerned about losing their children: 44% had this fear as an important reason for coming to LESFU.

Feeling upset or depressed was an important reason for coming to LESFU for 66% of the respondents. The four ethnic groups had the same patterns on this variable. Being fed up with how life was going was an important reason for coming to LESFU for 40% of the respondents. A desire to understand oneself better was an important reason for 42% of the respondents.

A multiple regression analysis using this index as the dependent variable found three associations that together explained 28% of the variation ($p < .0001$). First, the SWA's report of concern with money matters in the Debriefing I interviews was negatively associated with the index of psychological pressure and motivation ($p < .0001$). That is, a client with psychological pressure and high motivation to work with LESFU had less money worries reported at the first debriefing on average. The second association was that Chinese clients were under greater pressure and were more motivated to seek help ($p < .001$), a result consistent with our analysis of variance finding. The third association was that a client whose children had more reported contact with the SWA at the Debriefing II interview was under greater pressure and had more motivation as measured by this index ($p < .001$). The SWAs appeared to have been responsive to the concerns expressed by the client about her children.

Overall Morale and Satisfaction with Life

Table 7.12 contains the three items in the index extracted from the client interview that appeared to measure the overall morale and satisfaction with being a parent. The internal reliability of this index as measured by Cronbach's alpha was .71. The four family types had essentially the same overall average morale ($p > .95$), and there was no difference among the four ethnic types ($p > .50$). As discussed in more detail in Chapter 9, there was a significant association between this index and the indexes describing the behavioral adjustment of the client's children.

Table 7.13 is a cross-tabulation of the responses to two of the questions in this index by the ethnicity of the respondent. Overall, 25% of the respondents felt bitter very often about the way things had turned out. Only 8% of Chinese respondents felt bitter very often.

The respondents also reported whether their stress had been reduced: 89% reported that they felt changed for the better as a result of their involvement with LESFU. The changes reported were that 15% felt under less stress, 12% felt that they could cope better, 12% felt more secure, and 10% felt more tranquil. A few, however, still felt depressed and lonely.

FACTOR ANALYSIS RESULTS: MOTHERS IN SINGLE-PARENT HOUSEHOLDS (FA)

When all of the data sets were analyzed in a common data base, variables associated with the mother's role in seeking help from LESFU and working with its staff dominated the factor shown in Table 7.14. Measures of the mother's involvement with LESFU work had three of the four largest loadings in this factor. The largest loading was with the first debriefing index measuring the mother's motivation to work with LESFU (loading $= -.77$), and the fourth largest loading was on the Debriefing II index of the mother's motivation to work with LESFU ($-.66$). The size of the loadings on these two variables confirmed the consistency of the SWA's evaluation of the mother's motivation in the two debriefing interviews. The second largest loading was on the SWA's report in the second debriefing of the involvement of other family members ($-.73$). The magnitude of this association reflected the positive association between the measure of the mother's stress and the frequency of contact of the SWA with the children. The third largest loading was on the frequency that the mother was seen in the home by the LESFU family worker ($.72$). Since the sign of this loading was opposite to the sign of the other loadings, there was a negative association between frequency of seeing the family home worker and the motivation of the mother. This may have reflected the use of the home worker to monitor less-motivated mothers. There was also a positive loading on the client's report of contact with the LESFU SWA ($.29$): a less motivated mother reported seeing the SWA less frequently.

The factor structure indicated a positive association between these measures of the mother's motivation and whether the client viewed herself as changed for the better ($-.31$) and the SWA's report of improvement in the child's adjustment in the Debriefing II interview ($-.27$). These two results suggested that the mother's motivation was a positive indicator for a case with likely improvement in the mother's opinion of herself and improvement in the child's adjustment.

There was also a positive association between the mother's motivation and the number of family risk factors reported by the SWA in the Debriefing II interview ($-.28$). This association suggested that the mother's concern accurately reflected the problems she faced. A mother who was more motivated wanted more help in dealing with another agency ($-.33$). A mother who was more motivated tended to require less hospital and medical services according to the SWA's Debriefing I report ($.27$) and Debriefing II report ($.30$). These associations reflected the pattern of clients coming to LESFU for help in dealing with problems in a single area, either help with parenting or help with finances or with health problems.

DISCUSSION AND CONCLUSIONS

Clearly, these mothers occupied the lower rungs of the economic ladder, the "teenaged mothers" grown older, and they resided in the middle of a drug-infested area. The majority of these mothers were, on the whole, responsible parents who were motivated and cooperative in their efforts to work with LESFU. They kept their appointments and worked with the SWAs. They sought to parent their children better and to improve themselves. All were struggling under adversity. They tended to the needs of their children in one of the most hazardous areas in New York City. They were major actors in the war on drugs. It was their children who were at risk of becoming seduced into drug usage.

We developed five indexes that measured important aspects of the mother's psychological condition. Three indexes summarized the SWA's evaluation, and two summarized the client's responses. These indexes dealt with a central question faced by child welfare preventive service agencies. Many clients came on the urging of authorities—i.e., school, court, or police—rather than on their own initiative. Could they become engaged in the LESFU casework service process designed to help them? It was one thing to persuade a client to come to an agency and yet another to achieve positive results from the contact.

A major consideration in contemplating the tasks facing the agency in seeking to be helpful was whether the clients had the motivation and sufficient strength to grapple with their problems. If at a minimal level the client was unwilling to keep appointments made with the SWAs or to follow through on agreed-upon tasks—for example, going to an employment agency or visiting a child's school to obtain better treatment for him—resolution of the family's problems would be difficult. We hypothesized that these indexes would be important predictors of the course of the preventive service experience from the time of case opening.

Because the fate of children rested so heavily upon parents, particularly the mothers in poor, single-parent households, parental morale was a matter of concern. A demoralized mother who was overwhelmed by obnoxious circumstances was in danger of providing impaired parenting to her children, particularly in the ability to offer the emotional nurturance required by them.

The data examined in this chapter suggest that investment in social services to support parents in these difficult circumstances did not represent "money going down the drain" as some critics feared. There was reported improvement in 89% of the cases. These clients responded well to the support and counseling offered by the SWAs and showed a resilience that permitted them to overcome crises even though these often came in groups.

NOTE

1. See the Columbia University School of Social Work doctoral dissertation by Peter Li for more details about the problems of the Chinese clients.

Table 7.1
Debriefing I: Index of Client Motivation to Work on Problems with Agency

Item	Item-Total Correlation
A. How motivated is client now? (low/moderate/high)	.62
B. Is there a secure hold on client, committed to working with agency? (no/yes)	.49
C. How motivated was client to work with LESFU? (low/moderate/high)	.46
D. Client's attitude about possibility of solving problems? (defeat/resignation/optimism)	.44
E. Any client resistance to ongoing involvement with LESFU? (no/yes)	.44
F. How urgent does client feel about resolving problem? (hardly urgent/somewhat urgent/urgent/very urgent)	.37

Cronbach alpha coefficient = .73

Table 7.2
Attitude of Clients Regarding the Possibility of Solving Their Problems, by Ethnicity

	Hispanic No.	Hispanic %	Chinese No.	Chinese %	Black No.	Black %	White, Other No.	White, Other %	Total No.	Total %
Optimism	68	70.8	13	44.8	15	65.3	5	41.7	101	63.1
Resignation	25	26.0	14	48.3	5	21.7	7	58.3	51	31.9
Defeated	3	3.1	2	6.9	3	13.0			8	5.0
Total	96	100.0	29	100.0	23	100.0	12	100.0	160	100.0

Table 7.3
Client Resistance to Ongoing Involvement with LESFU, by Ethnicity

	Hispanic		Chinese		Black		White, Other		Total	
	No.	%	No.	%	No.	%	No.	%	No.	%
No	79	82.3	23	79.3	18	78.3	10	83.4	130	81.3
Undecided	4	4.2	2	6.9	1	4.3	1	8.3	8	5.0
Yes	13	13.5	4	13.8	4	17.4	1	8.3	22	13.8
Total	96	100.0	29	100.0	23	100.0	12	100.0	160	100.0

Table 7.4
Debriefing I: Index of Mother's Motivation

Item	Item-Total Correlation
A. How motivated is mother to keep family intact? (hardly motivated/moderately motivated/strongly motivated)	.59
B. How responsible is mother in meeting obligations? (very irresponsible/somewhat irresponsible/somewhat responsible/very responsible)	.43
C. Identification of client signing application form? (other/mother)	.40
Cronbach alpha coefficient = .65	

Table 7.5
How Responsible Mother Is in Meeting Parental Obligations, by Ethnicity

| | Hispanic | | Chinese | | Black | | White, Other | | Total | |
	No.	%	No.	%	No.	%	No.	%	No.	%
Very responsible	53	55.2	13	44.9	12	52.2	5	41.8	83	51.9
Somewhat responsible	23	24.0	7	24.1	5	21.7	1	8.3	36	22.5
Somewhat irresponsible	11	11.5	2	6.9	4	17.4	1	8.3	18	11.3
Very irresponsible	6	6.3	1	3.4	2	8.7	3	25.0	12	7.5
Unknown	2	2.0	2	6.9			1	8.3	5	3.2
Other	1	1.0	4	13.8			1	8.3	6	3.8
Total	96	100.0	29	100.0	23	100.0	12	100.0	160	100.0

Table 7.6
Debriefing II: Index of Mother's Motivation as LESFU Client

Item	Item-Total Correlation
A. Did mother fail to keep appointments? (no/somewhat/ very much)	.91
B. Is mother resistant? (no/somewhat/very much)	.85
C. Quality of the working relationship between mother and SWA? (good/fairly good/mixed/poor/very poor)	.79
D. Was mother late for appointments? (no/somewhat/ very much)	.71
E. Mother: level of motivation (high/moderate/low)	.64
F. Was mother unable to discuss personal problems? (no/ somewhat/very much)	.57
G. Mother: frequency seen (once a week or more/two or three times a month/once a month or less/no contact)	.49
Cronbach alpha coefficient = .89	

Table 7.7
Mother Failed to Keep Appointments, by Ethnicity

	Hispanic		Chinese		Black		White, Other		Total	
	No.	%	No.	%	No.	%	No.	%	No.	%
Very much	9	11.5			4	22.2	4	36.3	17	12.6
Somewhat	23	29.5	8	28.6	4	22.2	3	27.3	38	28.1
No	46	59.0	20	71.4	10	55.6	4	36.4	80	59.3
Total	78	100.0	28	100.0	18	100.0	11	100.0	135	100.0

Table 7.8
Mother Resisted Seeing the Social Work Associate, by Ethnicity

	Hispanic		Chinese		Black		White, Other		Total	
	No.	%	No.	%	No.	%	No.	%	No.	%
Very much	8	10.3	1	3.6	3	16.7	4	36.4	16	11.9
Somewhat	17	21.8	9	32.1	2	11.1	2	18.2	30	22.2
Not resistant	53	67.9	18	64.3	13	72.2	5	45.5	89	65.9
Total	78	100.0	28	100.0	18	100.0	11	100.0	135	100.0

Table 7.9
Mother Unable to Discuss Personal Problems, by Ethnicity

	Hispanic		Chinese		Black		White, Other		Total	
	No.	%	No.	%	No.	%	No.	%	No.	%
Very much	8	10.3	1	3.6			2	18.2	11	8.1
Somewhat	26	33.3	13	46.4	5	27.8	3	27.3	47	34.8
No	44	56.4	14	50.0	13	72.2	6	54.5	77	57.0
Total	78	100.0	28	100.0	18	100.0	11	100.0	135	100.0

Table 7.10
Client Interview: Index of Psychological Pressures and the Motivation of Client to Seek Help*

Item	Item-Total Correlation
A. Wanted advice on how to handle children (not at all important/important)	.59
B. Was fed up with how life was going (not at all/ important)	.49
C. Wanted to understand self better (not at all/ important)	.46
D. Afraid your children not doing well (not at all/ important)	.44
E. Came because people in authority urged (not at all/ important)	.43
F. Was afraid children would be sent away (not at all/ important)	.36
G. Was feeling upset or depressed (not at all/important)	.33
Cronbach alpha coefficient = .73	

*Question posed to the client:
Thinking back to when you first came to the Lower East Side Family Union, how important were the following considerations in seeking help? Would you say important, somewhat important, or not at all important as a reason for coming to the agency?

Table 7.11
Client Reasons for Seeking Help, by Ethnicity

	Hispanic [78]	Chinese [24]	Black [19]	White, Other [7]	Total [129]
			(percent)		
A) Wanted advice on how to handle children					
Not at all	38.5	20.0	47.4	42.9	36.4
Somewhat	7.7	20.0	15.8	--	10.9
Important	53.8	60.0	36.8	57.1	52.7
B) Fed up with how life was going - wanted more out of life					
Not at all	39.7	40.0	42.1	57.1	41.1
Somewhat	21.8	16.0	10.5	14.3	18.6
Important	38.5	44.0	47.4	28.6	40.3
C) Wanted to understand self better					
Not at all	32.1	28.0	42.1	42.9	33.3
Somewhat	25.6	28.0	15.8	28.6	24.8
Important	42.3	44.0	42.1	28.6	41.9
D) Afraid children not doing well in school or in neighborhood					
Not at all	61.5	52.0	52.6	42.9	57.4
Somewhat	5.1	4.0	10.5	14.3	6.2
Important	33.0	44.0	36.8	42.9	36.4
E) Urged to come by people in authority					
Not at all	57.7	64.0	78.9	42.9	61.2
Somewhat	14.1	4.0	5.3	28.6	11.6
Important	28.2	32.0	15.8	28.6	27.1
F) Afraid children would be sent away					
Not at all	67.9	56.0	68.4	85.7	66.7
Somewhat	9.0	--	10.5	--	7.0
Important	23.1	44.0	21.1	14.3	26.4
G) Was feeling upset or depressed					
Not at all	16.7	24.0	15.8	14.3	17.8
Somewhat	16.7	16.0	10.5	28.6	16.3
Important	66.7	60.0	73.7	57.1	65.9

Table 7.12
Client Interview: Index of Overall Client Morale

Item	Item-Total Correlation
A. Is R bitter about the way things have turned out? (yes, very often/no, hardly ever)	.46
B. How much satisfaction in being a parent? (none/ great deal)	.43
C. Is R generally a cheerful person? (not so cheerful/ pretty cheerful)	.42
Cronbach alpha coefficient = .71	

Table 7.13
Client Morale, by Ethnicity

	Hispanic [78]	Chinese [24]	Black [19]	White, Other [7]	Total [129]
			(Percent)		
A) Sees self as cheerful person?*					
Not so cheerful	20.5	20.8	10.5	14.3	18.8
Somewhat in middle	42.3	45.8	31.6	42.9	41.4
Pretty cheerful	37.2	33.3	57.9	42.9	39.8
B) Finds self feeling bitter about things?**					
Yes, very often	31.2	8.0	26.3	14.3	25.0
Yes, sometimes	36.4	72.0	47.4	42.9	41.4
No, hardly ever	32.5	20.0	26.3	42.9	29.7
C) How well getting along with people these days?***					
Better than usual	26.0	12.0	38.9	28.6	25.2
About the same	70.1	84.0	61.1	71.4	71.7
Not as well as usual	3.9	4.0	--	--	3.1

Questions posed to the client:

On the whole, would you say that you are generally a pretty cheerful person in your outlook on life these days, not so cheerful, or somewhere in the middle?

**Do you find yourself feeling bitter about the way things have turned out for you? Would you say...*

***In general, how well are you getting along with other people these days -- would you say better than usual, about the same, or not as well as usual?*

Table 7.14
Role of Mothers in the LESFU Service Effort*

Variable			Loading
Debriefing I			
7. AMOTHMOT	Mother's motivation to work with LESFU	(-)	.77
14. AHOSMEDR	Hospital/medical services required		.27
Debriefing II			
19. BMOTHER	Mother's motivation to work with LESFU	(-)	.66
27. BOFAMMEM	Other family members involved	(-)	.73
29. BMEDICAL	Medical and other services in picture		.30
32. BCHADJPR	Improvement in child adjustment	(-)	.27
38. BRISK	Number of family risk factors	(-)	.28
41. BOB05A	Mother being seen by LESFU worker		.72
Client Interview			
47. CFREQSRV	Frequency of contact with SWA		.29
50. CINTVBEH	Client behavior during interview	(-)	.26
59. CQA09A11	Wanted help in dealing with an agency	(-)	.33
65. CQE11A01	Self: change for the better	(-)	.31
67. CCFSEXM	Gender of child with most problems		.29

*This table is Factor 6 from the factor analysis varimax rotation (14-factor solution).

Chapter 8

Family Relations

INTRODUCTION

Family relations were a crucial aspect in the prevention of placement of children in foster care. The LESFU SWAs devoted considerable efforts to this area and achieved some notable successes. The case study discussed next had a more complex mix of problems facing the family than most and showed how challenging the service efforts could become.

Case Study VIII

Mrs. VIII was a grandmother who had custody of four of her grandchildren ranging in age from three to 13 years. The mother of the children had been in prison serving a two- to six-year sentence for a felony when Mrs. VIII came to LESFU. Both the mother and the father of her youngest child were drug addicts at the time. Mrs. VIII was referred to LESFU by the public service agency (SSC/HRA) so that she could secure help in the form of needed services for herself and the children. Mrs. VIII then lost her own husband about five months after coming to LESFU. She became depressed and suicidal. She was worried about the physical security of the children because of what was going on in the neighborhood and because of the distance the children had to walk to get to school. She felt overwhelmed by her child-rearing responsibilities and resented that the children's mother had not been in touch with them since she was put on parole. The oldest child had become a delinquent. She felt that something was wrong with the youngest child and was distressed by his hyperactivity. He had been born with signs of being drug addicted.

Her main problem was getting to and communicating with service providers. She needed medical services for herself and mental health services for the children. She also needed financial advocacy with the income maintenance people at HRA. Overall, Mrs. VIII expressed satisfaction with the services she received from LESFU. The mental health of the children had improved, and income was added from the public assistance budget. She was also able to get needed services.

MIS RESULTS (M)

The adult family relations code (O Problem Group) took about 14% of the total LESFU staff time. This problem area was extremely common: 74% of the cases had at least one problem in this area. The SWAs reported that 41% of these problems were resolved. Our model estimated that the staff spent from 16 to 18 hours per reported resolution. Nineteen percent of cases with at least one adult family relations problem were referred by the SWAs to external service organizations. The referred cases had multiple family relations problems and accounted for 28% of adult family relations problems. Ongoing contact with another agency was the result for 63% of the referred problems.

The most time-consuming and prevalent specific problem code in this group was adult conflicts between family members (MIS code 002). It occurred in 49% of the 160 cases and had a reported resolution rate of 30%. Our model estimated that about 10% of total staff time was spent on this problem. The next greatest amount of time allocated was to other adult family relations problems (code 007). An adult unwilling to cooperate (code 006) was also a problem that had a considerable amount of staff time allocated to it. An unwanted child or pregnancy (code 005) occurred in 6% ($n = 10$) of the cases, and problems associated with this phenomena were reported resolved in 50% of these cases.

Adult social relations problems (1 Problem Group) occurred in 31% of the families, and 25% of these problems were reported resolved. Our model allocated little LESFU staff time to these problems. Of those with at least one adult social relations problem, 11% (which generated 14% of the problems in this area) were referred to an external agency. Half of the referred cases reached an ongoing relation with the other agency. The SWA indicated that an ability to plan or structure time (code 105) was a problem for 11% ($n = 17$) of the cases, social isolation (code 101) in 8% ($n = 12$) of the cases, and uncontrollable adult emotions (code 102) in 8% ($n = 12$) of the cases. There were few reported resolutions for these three problem codes.

DEBRIEFING I RESULTS (A)

We created a five-item index that measured aspects of family violence and dysfunction. Table 8.1 contains the items in the index. The internal reliability of this index as measured by Cronbach's alpha was .52. There were no differences among the family types ($p > .50$) or among the ethnicities ($p > .50$) with respect to this index. This index was associated with the index of child behavioral adjustment as described in Chapter 9.

Many of the events that precipitated the client's seeking LESFU help were related to the issues covered in this index. Family violence was part of the precipitating event leading to the seeking of assistance from LESFU in 13 cases. Breakups and conflicts in the family were part of the precipitating event in eight cases. Death of the spouse was a precipitating factor in two cases. The SWA identified family relationship problems as an issue in 25% of the cases, spouse abuse in 21% of the cases, and adult behavior and adjustment in 13% of the cases.

DEBRIEFING II RESULTS (B)

Our index construction strategy extracted three indexes from the data of Debriefing II. These indexes measured the extent to which adult adjustment was the focus of the case, the extent to which family relations were the focus of the case, and the extent to which other family members were involved in LESFU's efforts.

Adult Adjustment as Case Focus

Table 8.2 displays a four-item index that measured adult adjustment problems as a focus of case activity. The internal reliability of the index as measured by Cronbach's alpha was .57. The four types of family structure had essentially the same average extent of adult adjustment as a case focus as measured by this index ($p > .40$). The four ethnic groups also had essentially the same average ($p > .35$). The correlation between the Debriefing I index of family violence and dysfunction and this index was .25 ($p < .01$).

Table 8.3 is a cross-tabulation of the prevalence of adult adjustment problems and family relation problems by ethnicity. Overall, there were adult adjustment problems in 14% of cases and family relations problems in 13%. The table confirms the similarity of the ethnic groups shown in the index, with the exception of the relatively low rate of adult adjustment problems in Chinese families.

Family Relationship Problems as Case Focus

Table 8.4 presents a two-item index that measured concern with family relationship problems as the case focus at Debriefing II. The internal reliability as measured by Cronbach's alpha was .43. The four ethnic groups had essentially the same averages for this index ($p > .25$). As measured by this index, family relations problems were more severe for mothers living alone than for others ($p < .05$). The correlation of this index and the Debriefing I index measuring family violence and dysfunction was .42 ($p < .0001$).

Table 8.5 presents the rates of risk for adult behavior and adjustment problems and for family relation problems by ethnicity. The overall risk of adult behavior or adjustment problems was 24%. The overall rate of risk of family relationship problems was 18%.

The SWAs reported that there were many unrecognized problems in this area. Specifically, lack of communication between spouses was not recognized in 5% of the cases. The spouse's impending release from prison was an unrecognized problem in 3% ($n = 4$) of the cases. On the positive side, the SWAs reported improved adult relations and family relationships in 22% of the cases. There were no differences in the rates of improvement among the four ethnic groups.

They reported improvements such as less family conflict (7%), more tranquility among the clients (7%), and improved marital relations (3%).

Involvement of Other Family Members

Table 8.6 presents a two-item index that measured the involvement of other members of the family in the case. The internal reliability of this index as measured by Cronbach's alpha was .63. The four ethnic groups had essentially the same average family case involvement as measured by this index ($p > .10$). Families in which the mother was absent had a much greater involvement of other family members than families with other structures ($p < .0001$). The correlation of this measure with the Debriefing I index of the mother's role was .59 ($p < .0001$).

In 32% of the cases, it was relevant for the oldest child in the family to have contact with the SWAs; 61% had no difficulty in keeping appointments. Of the 135 families, 26% had family members who ought to have been involved with the efforts at LESFU but were not. These included three mothers; 15 fathers, putative fathers, or boyfriends of the mother; one parental pair; nine children; three grandparents; three relatives; and two other significant persons. Resistance to involvement was frequently cited in these cases. The Hispanic families and the black families showed the highest proportion of family members who ought to have been involved in working with LESFU but were not: 46% of Hispanic families and 52% of black families had a member who was not involved, compared to only 7% of Chinese families.

In addition, other agencies than LESFU were involved. For example, nine cases (7%) received therapy, adult counseling, or family therapy from an external agency.

CLIENT INTERVIEW RESULTS

We extracted two indexes from the data collected in the client interview. These indexes measured the frequency of the social contacts that the client had and the client's involvement with activity in voluntary organizations. The association of a measure of social isolation and problematic behavior has been one of the oldest and most continuing themes in social research, dating back to Durkheim's work on suicide (1971). We were especially interested in describing the client's social life since many of the families were single-parent households at high risk of social isolation of the parent.

Frequency of Social Contacts

Table 8.7 is a six-item index that measured the social relations of the parents. The internal reliability of the item as measured by Cronbach's alpha was .72. The four family types had very similar averages for this index ($p > .40$); the four ethnic groups had essentially the same average as well ($p > .90$). There were no significant associations of this index with any of the Debriefing I and Debriefing II indexes. It was associated with the child adjustment index in a multiple regression analysis ($p < .01$).

The level of isolation was quite high: 30% knew no families in the neighborhood that they could visit, 16% knew only one family, 30% knew two or three, and 24% knew four or more families. The level of friendships followed the same pattern: 26% had no close friends, 23% had one close friend, 35% had two or three friends and 16% had four or more friends. There was somewhat more visiting reported in the interviews: 16% were totally isolated and had never visited anybody, 21% had between one and ten visits, 37% had contacts more than once a month but not weekly, and 26% had weekly contacts. The extent of receiving visitors was very low: 44% had not had a visitor in the previous month, 23% had at least one visitor in the month but were not visited weekly, and 32% had visitors at least once a week.

Activity in Voluntary Organizations

Table 8.8 defines a two-item index that measured the extent to which the clients participated in voluntary organizations in their neighborhood. The internal reliability of this item as measured by Cronbach's alpha was .71. The four family groups had essentially the same level of participation in voluntary organizations ($p > .70$). Chinese families had much higher involvement in voluntary neighborhood organizations, and white/other families had much lower participation ($p < .01$).

There were only three minor correlations of this index with other Debriefing I and II indexes. At Debriefing I, clients who were more active in organizations were on average not coming to LESFU because of concern about behavioral problems of their children ($p < .05$). A family in which the father lived in the home and carried responsibility for financial support of the family was more extensively involved in the activities of voluntary organizations ($p < .05$). At Debriefing II, a client who was involved with medical service providers about health problems was more extensively involved in voluntary organizations ($p < .05$). Finally, the index had a correlation of 0.22 ($p < .05$) with the index measuring the client's frequency of social contact.

Anecdotal Information about Family Relations

The clients interviewed reported that a family relationship crisis was involved in the precipitating event bringing them to LESFU in 16% of the cases and that an adult adjustment crisis was present in 7% of the cases. These rates were less than, but consistent with, the rates the SWA reported in the debriefing interviews. Black families reported family relationship crises as part of the precipitating event more often (32%) than other families. The clients mentioned family relationship problems in 11% of the interviews, adult mental health problems in 9%, conflicts with spouse or romantic friend in 5%, loneliness in 4%, and family violence in 2%. The most commonly cited cause of their problems (19%) was family problems or marital conflict. An unwanted or unexpected pregnancy was a cause in 6% of the cases, and a death in the family was cited in 3%.

In the interviews, 16% of the clients said that they had a family relationship problem, and they reported improvement in 57% of these cases. The improvements ranged from less conflict and the elimination of physical abuse to effecting a marital separation. The efforts of LESFU were credited as being helpful in bringing about the improvement in 52% of the improved cases.

The clients identified adult behavior or mental health problems in 15% of the cases and reported improvement in 74% of these cases. They regarded LESFU's efforts as helpful in 68% of the improved cases. The nature of the improvement ranged from "easing of condition" to getting a child safely out of state.

FACTOR ANALYSIS RESULTS (FA)

Two of the factors in the rotated solution had themes related to family relations and are discussed here. The first dealt with a family system under pressure; the second dealt with a deteriorating family system involving children at risk of placement in foster care.

Family System under Pressure

Table 8.9 presents a factor that reflected a family system operating under pressure. The SWA's identification of family problems in the first debriefing had the largest loading (loading = −.65). The client's expectation of emotional support had the second largest loading (−.58) followed by the SWA's report of failure of the family system in Debriefing I (−.50). These three variables were positively associated. The next largest loading was on the SWA's report in Debriefing II of working on adult adjustment problems (−.43). These loadings suggested a latent variable that reflected a client family that was close to failure due to problems with adult adjustment with a mother reaching out for support. This latent variable was positively associated with the SWA's report of treatment progress in Debriefing II (−.31) and of working on parenting problems (−.31). This latent variable was positively associated with the client's report of how long the problem had been going on (−.29), with the number of problems reported in the MIS (−.26), with the client's report of wanting help with her employment situation (−.25), and with the client's report of having agreed to work on relationships (−.25).

There were some negative associations with the latent variable suggested by the larger loadings. The suggested latent variable was negatively associated with the client's report of expecting advocacy help (.35) and with the client's report of herself changing for the better (.33). It was also negatively associated with the highest stage of the LESFU model reached (.27).

The loadings suggested an important pattern in dealing with the failure of a family system. The reported progress did not extend to improvement of the client or formal progression through the LESFU model. There were no associations with the problem resolution variables from the MIS data base or variables from the case closing data base.

Deteriorating Family System Involving Children at Risk of Placement in Foster Care

Table 8.10 presents the 14th factor in the 14-factor solution. The largest loading was on the client's fear that family problems were worsening (loading = $-.70$). This was positively associated with the SWA's report in Debriefing I of a failure of the family system ($-.49$). A client who was fearful of worsening family problems experienced less satisfaction with life ($-.41$), had an SWA who reported in Debriefing II of working on family relations problems more ($-.40$), and also reported that family conflict was more the cause of her problems ($-.38$). These loadings suggested a latent variable measuring the client's fear of worsening problems and a view that family conflict was the cause of her problems. These views were confirmed by reports from the SWA of failure of the family system and work on family relations problems. The client was correspondingly dissatisfied with how her life was going on.

The smaller negative loadings in this factor suggested some important associations with variables measuring the children's condition. When the client was more fearful of worsening family problems, she reported that the SWA was seeing the children more frequently ($-.33$), that the children had poorer behavioral adjustment ($-.32$), that there were more likely to be children in the family with a problem ($-.26$), and that she was under psychological pressure as a motivation for seeing LESFU ($-.25$). When the client was more fearful of worsening family problems, the placement of a child in the family at the end of the study was more likely ($-.25$), and the case was more likely to be closed because the family moved out of LESFU's catchment area ($-.31$).

There were some inconsistent associations suggested as well. When the client was more fearful of worsening family problems, the SWA reported working less on child school-related problems (.28). A client more fearful of worsening family problems also had a more stressful financial situation ($-.34$), but the SWA reported less extensive financial problems in Debriefing I (.27). These inconsistencies may reflect the SWA's focusing on the conflict in the family to the exclusion of school and financial problems.

On balance, the factor suggested some important associations. The variables with loadings greater than .40 in absolute value confirmed the consistency of client and SWA report. The association between the client's fear of worsening family problems and the placement of a child at the end of the study confirmed the validity of the fears. More important, it suggested the importance of taking the client's evaluation of her situation at face value in the initial stages of work. The SWAs were responsive to the seriousness of the family's problems and made appropriate efforts to deal with the problems of family conflict. Their efforts were apparently not sufficient to avoid entirely the placement of children in foster care.

DISCUSSION AND CONCLUSIONS

Overall, there was a report of a change for the better with respect to improved adult adjustment and family relations in 22% of the cases and improved parent-child relations in 16% of the cases. Family relations problems and the client's fear of worsening family problems were associated with increased behavioral difficulty in the family's children and with a greater risk of placement of the children in foster care at the end of the study.

There was considerable social isolation of the parents in these families: 30% knew nobody in the neighborhood that they could visit, 26% had no close friends, and 16% visited no one else.

The "LESFU model" of explicit contracts with the client to deal with specific problems was not well adapted to this type of family relations problem. The LESFU conception was of a "managerial function" that gathered information and established procedures, planning, and specification of tasks (Weissman 1978). The needs of these client families for help in dealing with family conflict seemed to require a different social work approach than the LESFU model supported. The SWAs, in fact, appeared to use a different strategy in these situations than the formal structure of the LESFU model.

Table 8.1
Debriefing I: Index of Family Violence-Dysfunction

Item	Item-Total Correlation
A. Family relation problem? (no/yes)	.25
B. Problems re: family violence? (yes/no)	.37
C. Risk of parent failure? (low/high)	.36
D. Chronic unemployment in family? (yes/no)	.25
E. Is change in client's behavior required? (no/yes)	.19
F. Parental performance (very irresponsible/responsible)	.19
Cronbach alpha coefficient = .52	

Table 8.2
Debriefing II: Index of Adult Adjustment Problem as Case Focus

Item	Item-Total Correlation
A. Adult adjustment problem occupying attention of social worker? (no/yes)	.49
B. Risk of adult behavior and adjustment breakdown? (no/yes)	.34
C. Improvement in adult adjustment and family relations? (no/yes)	.32
D. Adult education -- employment to be sought? (no/yes)	.27
Cronbach alpha coefficient = .57	

Table 8.3
Problems Occupying Attention of Social Work Associate, by Ethnicity

	Hispanic		Chinese		Black		White, Other		Total	
	No.	%	No.	%	No.	%	No.	%	No.	%
Adult adjustment problems	12	15.4	2	7.1	3	16.7	2	18.2	19	14.1
Family relation problems	10	12.8	3	10.7	5	27.8	0	0.0	18	13.3

Table 8.4
Debriefing II: Index of Family Relationship Problem as Case Focus

Item	Item-Total Correlation
A. Risk of family relationship breakdown? (low/high)	.27
B. Family relationship problem occupying attention of SWA? (no/yes)	.27
Cronbach alpha coefficient = .43	

Table 8.5
Risks Facing the Family and Its Members, by Ethnicity

	Hispanic		Chinese		Black		White, Other		Total	
	No.	%	No.	%	No.	%	No.	%	No.	%
Risk of adult behavioral/adjustment problem	20	25.6	3	10.7	7	38.9	2	18.2	32	23.7
Risk of family relation problem	15	19.2	4	14.3	4	22.2	1	9.1	24	17.8
Total	78	100.0	28	100.0	18	100.0	11	100.0	135	100.0

Table 8.6
Debriefing II: Index of Case Involvement of Other Family Members

Item	Item-Total Correlation
A. Other family members seen? (no/yes)	.46
B. Caretaker of children at Time II? (mother & father or mother/other family member)	.46
Cronbach alpha coefficient = .63	

Table 8.7
Client Interview: Index of Frequency of Social Contacts in the Life of the Client

Item	Item-Total Correlation
A. How often had friends to home in past month? (not at all/every day)	.55
B. How often get together with friends? (never/every day)	.52
C. How often visited friends in their home in past month? (not at all/every day)	.45
D. How many families in neighborhood known well enough to visit in homes? (none/one or more)	.42
E. How many close friends at ease with, can talk to? (none/one or more)	.41
F. How often telephone close friends, relatives? (not at all/every day)	.37
Cronbach alpha coefficient = .72	

Table 8.8
Client Interview: Index of Activity in Voluntary Organizations

Item	Item-Total Correlation
A. How many voluntary organizations does R belong to? (none/one or more)	.75
B. How active in these organizations, clubs? (not active/very active)	.75
Cronbach alpha coefficient = .71	

Table 8.9
Family System Dealing with Adult Problems

Variable			Loading
Debriefing I			
4. AFAMFAIL	Failure of family system	(-)	.50
9. AFAMPROB	Family problems identified	(-)	.65
Debriefing II			
22. BCHANGE	Treatment progress	(-)	.31
23. BADADJUS	Adult adjustment problem worked on	(-)	.43
26. BFAMRELA	Family relations identified as a problem	(-)	.25
36. BPARENTN	Parenting problems being worked on	(-)	.31
Client Interview			
45. CEMPLOY	Wanted help with employment situation	(-)	.25
58. CQA03	How long had the problem been going on?	(-)	.29
65. CQE11A01	Self: change for the better		.33
68. CEXPADVO	Expected advocacy help		.35
69. CEXPESUP	Expected emotional support	(-)	.58
84. CWRKTHER	Agreed to work on relationships	(-)	.25
LESFU MIS Data			
90. MHIMODLV	Highest stage of LESFU model reached		.27
93. MNUMBRPR	Number of problems observed in case	(-)	.26

*This table is Factor 12 from the factor analysis varimax rotation (14-factor solution).

Table 8.10
Deteriorating Family System under Pressure on Many Fronts*

Variable			Loading
Debriefing I			
4. AFAMFAIL	Failure of family system	(-)	.49
8. AMONEY	Financial problems identified		.27
Debriefing II			
25. BSCHOOL	Child school-related problem worked on		.28
26. BFAMRELA	Family relations problem being worked on	(-)	.40
Client Interview			
50. CINTVBEH	Client behavior during interview		.28
51. CMOTIVAT	Psychological pressures as motivation	(-)	.25
54. CSATISFY	Satisfaction with life	(-)	.41
55. CFINANCE	Financial situation	(-)	.34
62. CQD06	Were children ever seen by the SWA	(-)	.33
63. CANYCHPR	Any child in family with problem?	(-)	.26
74. CRSKFAMR	Fear family problems get worse	(-)	.70
79. CCAUFAMR	Family conflict cause of problems	(-)	.38
89. CHPROBM	Index of child behavioral adjustment	(-)	.32
Case Closing Information			
98. XFAMMOVE	Family moved away	(-)	.31
100. XCHPLEND	Child placed when study ended	(-)	.25

*This table is Factor 14 from the factor analysis varimax rotation (14-factor solution).

Chapter 9

Problems of Older Children

INTRODUCTION

In this chapter, we document the extent to which older children were at risk of placement in foster care or of developing antisocial careers. The results provide valuable insights into the nature of the problems of preventive services and force consideration of a broader approach to preventive services. The experiences of these children illustrated that the development of criminality or drug usage were outcomes whose prevention should have a higher priority than the prevention of placement in foster care.

Children were at the center of the concerns of an agency such as LESFU. The service program came into being because there was a determination on the part of child welfare advocates and community-based professionals to prevent the unnecessary placement of children in foster care and to promote the general well-being of children living in an environment replete with social problems. The specific mandate given to LESFU by its funding sources was to act to prevent the placement of children in foster care. Although many children experienced separation from their families because their parents could not function adequately and failed to meet community standards, the children themselves could behave in such a way that required their placement away from home because the misbehavior could no longer be tolerated within the community.

Case Study IXA

Ms. IXA was a strikingly attractive, well-spoken woman who seemed to understand the research questions easily and who was responsive throughout the interview. Her story was stark and filled with personal and family disasters. She had her first child, a daughter, at age 14 and her second child, a son, within fifteen months. She said both were of the same father. She currently lived with another man who had fathered her third child, now six years old.

The case opened at LESFU when the two oldest children were suddenly released from foster care in a different city and shipped to her. They had been in placement for eight years. Ms. IXA was given no preparation for their return and was put under great pressure by this turn of events. Her health was not the best because she had experienced drastic surgery some years ago leaving her very vulnerable. She suffered from several chronic illnesses over this period. Her current housing in a project was secured through the help of the hospital social service staff when there was no further justification for her occupying a hospital bed.

LESFU quickly assisted in making arrangements for the arrival of the children. Unfortunately, things did not work out happily even though the mother tried her best. Almost immediately, the children got into "bad company" and became active in the streets. The daughter was now a street person, sleeping almost anywhere including a men's shelter, and she was on drugs. Ms. IXA was afraid her daughter would be killed someday soon. She saw this as almost inevitable. The older son was recently placed in a residential treatment institution. There was no contact between the two older children and Ms. IXA.

Ongoing service contact between LESFU and Ms. IXA was important to her in her effort to stabilize her living situation with her youngest child. LESFU took initiative to get a public assistance grant awarded for the child (she was on SSI). The case was active in many ways, and the client frequently called her worker in emergencies. Ms. IXA said she highly valued her relationship with her SWA, seeing her as very available, concerned, and active on her behalf. Referral to an agency offering psychological treatment was carried through, and Ms. IXA was receiving counseling from this source. However, she expressed many negatives about this agency even though she insisted upon rating their services as "good." Ms. IXA highly valued foster care and felt the local New York City agency had provided her youngest child with an excellent foster home during the six months she was hospitalized for her surgery.

Case Study IXB

Family IXB was a stable family consisting of husband, wife, and three children living in a housing project. The oldest child, now 16 years old, was the husband's child from his first marriage. The first wife abandoned her son as an infant while the father was in the military. The child was placed in foster care in Puerto Rico. The father gave up his military career to remove his son from foster care and arranged for his mother, the child's paternal grandmother, to care for him. Unfortunately, she was harsh and primitive in rearing him.

Mrs. IXB met the child when he was four years old and assumed care of him when he was six years old, at the time of her marriage to his father. She adopted the child. He was difficult from the beginning although she felt she tried hard to connect with him in a positive way. The son was 14 years old when his teacher at a special school in a settlement house referred the family to LESFU. He had been a serious runaway since fourth grade. He was absent from school for days or weeks at a time. When he was older, he would miss school months at a time. He was associating with unsavory characters and was increasingly out of control. He stole money from his family and continued his truancy. There were indications that he used drugs and alcohol. Efforts to involve the son in direct counseling contact with the SWA were not successful, although he did have several meetings with the SWA. For a time, the SWA and family considered foster care as a possible solution to the son's problems, but this never happened because he would disappear.

The situation was relatively quiet in the six months prior to the interview. The son had been staying at home and behaving. He was thrown out of his girlfriend's apartment and had no place to go. He still was a frequent truant and was not doing well at school. There was still a long-term risk in his situation although there was some lessening of its crisis character. The situation remained touch-and-go.

Mrs. IXB was quite glowing in describing LESFU and reported that she found her SWA most helpful in his sympathetic understanding, willingness to listen, and the manner in which he extended himself on the family's behalf. He went to family court five times when a school referral source made allegations of neglect against the family. He defended Mrs. IXB and was able to provide essential input to convince the court that she was an attentive, caring mother.

MIS RESULTS (M)

There were no MIS codes that specifically related to the problems of older children that we are discussing in this chapter. The closest classifications were those subsumed under "7. Child Educational and Vocational Training," "6. Child Social Relations," and "8. Child Life Skills."

The prevalence rate of families identified under child educational and vocational training was 69%, with 49% of the problems reported resolved. The most common specific problem of this type was the catchall "other" category (MIS code 708) with a prevalence rate of 41% and a resolution rate of 56%. The next most common was child truancy from school (code 706) with a prevalence rate of 24% and a resolution rate of 25%. LESFU had good success in enrolling a child in school: of the 18 problems of this type, 61% were reported resolved. The agency had little success dealing with the problem of a child with no skills or training for a job (code 703): only one of eight problems of this type was reported resolved.

Overall, our calculations were that the SWAs devoted about 18% of their reported time to working on child educational and vocational training problems and that this problem area received the largest amount of staff effort. There was an investment of about 20 hours per reported resolution of a problem. Our estimate was that the SWAs invested relatively little effort in the problems of truancy from school (code 706) and a child whose behavior was disruptive in school (code 705). A child who was not enrolled in school (code 704) required an expenditure of about 30 hours per reported resolution.

By their nature, child educational and vocational training problems required interaction with other agencies: 62% of families with these problems were referred to an external agency. Of problems referred, 74% reached a level requiring substantial interaction with the agency to which a referral had been made. Those problems requiring a deeper involvement with another agency had a lower rate of reported resolution, presumably because they were more complex and harder to solve.

Child social relations problems occurred in 37% of the client families, and the reported resolution rate was modest, 36%. Of the ten families in which the child had a sex-related problem (code 604), 70% were reported resolved. The problem of child juvenile offenses was more common. Of the 18 cases with this problem, 50% were reported resolved. The agency had less success dealing with the 19 cases in which child behavior was inappropriate for the child's age (code 601). Only 15% of these were reported resolved. The miscellaneous category (coded as "other") of child social relations problems (code 607) was equally problematic: only 17% of the 17 cases were reported resolved. This category of problem also included children engaging in criminal activities (code 602).

Our estimate was that the SWAs spent about 6% of their reported time dealing with problems in the various child social relations areas identified above. Our calculations showed that they invested relatively little time dealing with child sex-related problems (code 604) and child social isolation problems (code 605). About 2% of their total effort went to dealing with juvenile offenses and related court dates (code 603), and another 2% of their total effort went to dealing with child age inappropriate behaviors.

The SWAs handled 81% of the problems involving a child's social relations problems internally and referred only 19% of such cases. Of those that were referred to an external service organization, 80% reached a substantive interaction with the agency to which the case had been referred. There was a very low rate of reported resolution (12%) among these child-related problems referred to an external agency and receiving substantive attention from the external agency.

Child life skills problems were the least prevalent problem group and were reported in only 17% of the cases. Overall, the rate of reported resolution was 30%. The rate of reported resolution of a child refusing household responsibility (code 802) was 16%. The most common problem in this area was an indication that the child was not using time constructively (code 804), with a prevalence rate of 11%. Our estimate was that the SWAs devoted about 1% of their total effort to problems in this group. Very little external effort was devoted to these problems: the SWAs reported referring only 11% of cases to outside agencies. Of those that were referred, however, all reached a substantive involvement with the external agency. None of these were reported resolved.

Finally, 8% of client families worked with LESFU on the problem that a child had run away from home (code 504). In the client interviews, 12% of families reported that a child had run away from home within the past year. The percentage of black families with this experience was higher: 21% of 19 black families.

DEBRIEFING I RESULTS (A)

We extracted one index based on three items from the Debriefing I interview. It is shown in Table 9.1. It measured the misbehavior of the children in the client family as a source of concern. Its internal reliability as measured by Cronbach's alpha was .54. The four family structures had essentially the same average on this index ($p > .50$); the four ethnic groups had essentially the same average as well ($p > .05$).

The SWAs reported child behavioral problems in 26% of these cases ($n = 41$), school problems in 18% ($n = 28$), and educational or vocational training problems in 6%. Although the index did not have any ethnic differences, Chinese families had a much lower prevalence of child behavioral problems, 7%, compared to about 30% among non-Chinese families.

Child truancy was a precipitating event in 6% ($n = 9$) of these cases, teenage pregnancy in 3%, and acting out behavior in 3%. In 4% of the cases, the clients were worried about peer influences upon their children and the effects of the pervasive drug problems in the neighborhood.

DEBRIEFING II RESULTS (B)

We extracted three indexes from the Debriefing II interviews that measured aspects of problems of older children. The first index measured the motivation of the oldest child as a LESFU client. The second measured the extent to which child problems were a focus of the case. The third measured the extent to which a child's school problems were part of LESFU's work with the client.

Oldest Child's Motivation as LESFU Client

Table 9.2 displays the seven items in the index that measured the oldest child's motivation as a LESFU client. The internal reliability of this index as measured by Cronbach's alpha was .88. The average of each of the four family structures was essentially the same for this index ($p > .25$), and there were no significant ethnic differences ($p > .25$).

Child's Behavioral Problems as Reported in Debriefing II

Table 9.3 shows the two items in the index that measured whether child behavioral problems were at issue in the case. The internal reliability of this index as measured by Cronbach's alpha was .69. The average of this index was roughly the same for the four family structures ($p > .15$) and for the four ethnic groups ($p > .20$).

There were three statistically significant associations with the indexes from Debriefing I. First, a family with a child behavioral problem at the second debriefing had a less serious housing problem at case opening ($p < .0001$). Second, a family that had child behavioral problems as a source of concern in Debriefing I had more extensive child behavioral problems as a case focus at the second debriefing ($r = .54, p < .0001$). Finally, a family that had more extensive child behavioral problems as the case focus at the second debriefing had less serious economic problems as reported at the Debriefing I interview ($r = -.21$, $p < .05$).

A family with the father out of the picture had children's problems as the focus of the case more extensively ($p < .05$). The presence of children's problems was associated with early positive changes in a case ($p < .01$).

The SWAs reported that 18% of the cases had a child behavioral problem at Debriefing II compared to 26% at Debriefing I. Even though there were no significant differences in the averages of this index by ethnic group, only 7% of Chinese families had child behavioral problems compared to 28% of black families. The Hispanic families had a lower rate at Debriefing II, 21%, compared to the 30% reported at Debriefing I. The SWAs reported that 23% of the cases were at risk of a child behavioral or adjustment problem. There were no significant differences among the four ethnic groups on the rate at risk.

Child's School Problem as Part of LESFU Client Work

Table 9.4 shows the two items in an index that measured the extent to which a child's school problems were a focus of the case. The internal reliability as measured by Cronbach's alpha was .63. There were no significant differences by either family group ($p > .90$) or ethnic group ($p > .25$). School problems occupied the attention of the SWA at the Debriefing II interview in 26% of the cases. As expected, there was a significant correlation ($r = .36$) between this index and the Debriefing I index of concern about a child's behavior ($p < .0001$). This correlation supported consistency of case information provided by the SWAs over the two debriefing interviews. A case that had a child's school problems as focus of the case had a higher measured level of oldest child's motivation ($p < .05$) and had a higher level of case activity ($p < .01$).

CLIENT INTERVIEW RESULTS (C)

Table 9.5 presents the 13 items in an index that measured the parental concern about the behavioral adjustment of a child. The internal reliability as measured by Cronbach's alpha was .84. There were no differences by ethnicity for the index of the oldest child's behavioral adjustment ($p > .90$), and there were no significant differences by family structure.

As shown in Table 9.6, 37% of the children were a source of concern as expressed in the parent interview. On average, the parents were most concerned about the oldest child, with 49% of oldest children often causing worry, and the parents were less concerned about the younger children. There were no strong ethnic differences in the proportion of children that were sources of concern to the responding parent.[1]

In the main, the responding parents expressed pride in their children as shown in Table 9.7. Overall, they felt "good" about 63% of their children.

Table 9.8 shows the percentage of children showing problems listed in the index controlling for the parity of the child. As expected, the frequency of problems diminished with the parity of the child because parity was negatively correlated with the age of the children. That is, older children had more adjustment problems on average than younger children.

The parents reported that 24% of their children were sources of concern because of their refusal to accept parental guidance. A child behavioral crisis was part of the precipitating event for 29% of interviewed parents. The parent interviewed showed concern for about 20% of oldest children having a school-related problem (that is, problem B, C, or D). Cumulatively, 36% of the parents interviewed regarded their children's problems in the school or neighborhood as an important consideration in seeking out LESFU's help. A school-related crisis was part of the precipitating event that led the client to LESFU for 19% of the interviewed parents and was part of the problem for 25% of parents interviewed.

About 14% of the parents were concerned that their oldest child was having a problem with the police or the courts, and 9% of parents interviewed were concerned that their oldest child had a drug abuse problem. Parental concern about the moodiness or depression of the oldest child was reported by 34% of parents interviewed.

The overall rates reported in Table 9.8 understated the extent of problems in the children because the rates were based on all children, even including those who were too young to be at risk. The prevalence rates were much higher for children who were 11 or over. As expected, a child's refusal to accept parental guidance occurred more frequently for older children ($p < .0001$): 37% of children 11 or over were reported to have this problem compared to 11% of children five or under. Similarly, 39% of children 11 or over were reported to have school attendance problems. The same association held for motivation to learn and to do schoolwork ($p < .0001$): 31% of children 11 or over had a low motivation to learn compared to 3% of children five or under. Boys were more likely than girls to have a low motivation to learn ($p < .05$) and were more likely to fail to do homework ($p < .05$).

Children over 11 were likewise more likely to be involved with the police or courts ($p < .0001$): 23% of children 11 or over had trouble with the law, and 24% of children 11 or over stayed out overnight without permission. The responding parents reported that 15% of their children 11 or over were drug abusers. They also reported that 22% of children 11 or over rejected their values.

The age of onset of child moodiness and depression was between six and ten and nearer to six than to ten: only 11% of children five or under were moody or depressed compared to 32% of children between six and ten and 33% of children 11 or over.

Interviewed Parents' Reports of Improvement in Child Behavior

The client interview asked whether there was improvement in the problems that the clients faced and what the nature of the improvement was. Of the 32 clients with children having a behavioral or mental health problem, 63% ($n = 20$) reported an improvement, and 50% credited LESFU as a source of help. Sixteen reported "improvement" without detailing the nature of the improvement. Two improvements were due to the placement of the child, one to the return of a runaway child, and one to the entrance of the family into therapy.

Of the 32 clients whose children had school problems, 75% reported improvement, and 63% credited LESFU as a source of help. The improvements were that eight clients reported that the child was attending school regularly or doing fine, seven reported that educational needs were addressed, two clients had a child placed in an appropriate class, and one client had a child who received remedial aid. The other six clients reported generic "improvement."

The clients reported that 49% of the oldest children had changed for the better since they had first come to LESFU. The specific improvements were better conduct, better school performance, improved psychological state, more tranquility, and better communication and attitude. The percentage of younger children who improved since the client had first come to LESFU was progressively lower: 44% of second children, 39% of third, 38% of fourth, and 25% of fifth. The specific improvements followed the pattern of improvement shown by the oldest child. There were no significant differences by ethnicity.

Multiple Regression Analyses of Index of Child Behavioral Problems of the Child Reported to Show the Most Difficulties

The dependent variable of these analyses was the index of child behavioral problems for the child showing the most problems. The independent variables included the client interview index scores as a way of shedding light upon the context in which the child was being reared. Since the child behavioral adjustment index came from the responses of the same informant as the other client interview indexes, the results of the analysis could simply be a "halo effect." That is, the respondent showed a tendency to be unduly influenced by a single overall quality of a situation in making an assessment of a single trait (Bostwick and Kyte 1988). Consequently, we asked the respondent questions about quite specific behaviors to make this effect as small as possible.

There were five independent variables that together explained 55.1% of the variance ($p < .0001$). The age of the child was the variable most strongly correlated with this index ($r = .56$) and by itself explained 32% of the variance ($p < .0001$). This finding replicated our findings in the Casey study (Fanshel, Finch, and Grundy 1990) that as children grow older their capacity to become involved in acting out behaviors expanded significantly. The second most important association was the positive correlation with the measure of the interviewed parent's morale or life satisfaction ($p < .001$). A respondent who did not have much satisfaction in being a parent and was bitter about the way things had turned out reported that the family's most poorly adjusted child showed more behavioral problems than the most poorly adjusted child of a respondent who was less demoralized but otherwise similar. A client who reported more stressful events happening in the family during the past year, such as a death in the family, serious illness, or loss of employment, described the most poorly behaved child as showing more problems ($p < .001$). A parent who felt under strong psychological pressure as shown by the client interview index reported that the most poorly adjusted child had greater problems ($p < .001$). A mother whom the SWA felt was highly motivated to seek help in the first debriefing interview reported that her most poorly adjusted child was in greater difficulty than a mother who was less motivated but who was otherwise similar ($p < .01$).

There were other associations whose significance was less clear. Although some of the associations were plausible, the reader should regard them as more tentative. When the most troubled child was a boy, there were more extensive behavioral problems than when the most troubled child was an otherwise similar girl ($p < .05$). After accounting for the associations with the child's age, responding parent's morale, number of stressful events taking place in the family in the past year, respondent's psychological pressure, and the SWA's perception of the mother's motivation, a family whose most poorly adjusted child showed more problems had greater perceived case progress ($p < .05$). There was a positive association between the extent of behavioral problems shown by the most poorly adjusted child and the SWA's perception of risk of family breakdown at the second debriefing ($p < .05$). The most poorly adjusted child tended to show somewhat more problematic behavior when the father was absent ($p < .10$).

Statistical Analyses of Index of Child Behavioral Problems of the Oldest Child

The dependent variable in these statistical analyses was the index of child behavioral problems of the oldest child in the client family. Based on a three-way analysis of variance, the adjustment of the oldest child was the same on average for the four family structures. The four ethnic groups had essentially the same index of child adjustment for the oldest child in the family. Those oldest children who were boys had poorer average adjustment as measured by this index than oldest children who were girls ($p < .05$). Older children had poorer adjustment as measured by this index than younger oldest children ($p < .001$).

The independent variables in a multiple regression analysis were the Debriefing I indexes, the Debriefing II indexes, and the client interview indexes. The analysis found four significant associations that together explained 48% of the variance ($p < .0001$). As in the analysis of the index describing the behavioral problems of the most problematic child, the age of the oldest child had the largest correlation with the oldest child's behavioral adjustment index, .47 ($p < .0001$). As before, a respondent who was in psychological distress as a parent and had as a reason for seeking help from LESFU concern about children reported that the oldest child had more extensive behavioral problems ($p < .005$). The third significant association was that a child who reported being faced with more pressing financial problems reported more severe problematic behaviors being shown by the oldest child ($p < .01$). The fourth significant association essentially validated the SWA report in the Debriefing I interview. The index descriptive of child behavioral problems from the Debriefing I interview was positively associated with the index of child behavioral problems in the oldest child based on the client's report ($p < .001$).

We ran other multiple regression analyses and found some noteworthy associations. There was a significant association between the index descriptive of family violence and dysfunction and the oldest child's behavioral problem index when only the Debriefing I indexes were the independent variables. When the SWA evaluated a family as more afflicted with violence and dysfunction, the respondent reported that the oldest child had more problematic behavior ($p < .05$).

In a multiple regression analysis including indexes from both the Debriefing I and II debriefings, when the SWA reported that family relationship problems were being worked on at the second debriefing, the respondent reported that the oldest child had more extensive behavioral problems ($p < .01$). The SWA reported less improvement in child adjustment and parent-child relationships in a family whose oldest child showed more behavioral problems ($p < .05$).

When the independent variables only included the client interview indexes, the respondent's report of the number of stressful events experienced in the past year, the respondent's report of morale, the respondent's report of extent of social visiting, and the respondent's report of housing problems were associated with the oldest child's behavioral problem index in the expected directions. A respondent who reported experiencing more stressful events in the preceding year reported more extensive behavioral problems in the oldest child ($p < .001$). A respondent who was more demoralized reported that the oldest child in the family had more extensive behavioral problems ($p < .01$). A respondent who reported less visiting of friends and more social isolation reported that the oldest child showed more extensive behavioral problems ($p < .01$). A respondent who reported poorer housing conditions reported more extensive behavioral problems in the oldest child ($p < .05$).

Statistical Analyses of Index of Child Behavioral Problems of the Second Oldest Child

Of the 106 second-born children, 82% were old enough for the calculation of the index of child behavioral problems to be meaningful. Based on a three-way analysis of variance, second-born children who were older showed more extensive behavioral problems based on this index ($p < .001$). There were no statistically significant differences based on ethnicity or sex.

The independent variables in a multiple regression analysis were the Debriefing I, Debriefing II, and client interview index scores. The analysis found nine significant associations that together explained 58.4% of the variance ($p < .0001$). The most significant association was again with the age of the child studied: older second children showed more extensive behavioral difficulties than younger second children ($p < .0001$). A family that participated less in the organized life of the community had a second child with more extensive behavioral problems ($p < .01$). A client who had greater psychological distress reported that the second child showed more extensive behavioral problems ($p < .01$). There was an association between the SWA's report of treatment progress in the Debriefing II interview and the extent of behavioral problems in the second child ($p < .01$). A client who reported greater social isolation reported that the second-born child showed more extensive behavioral problems ($p < .01$).

There were a number of marginally significant associations. The SWA's report of child problems in the Debriefing I interview was associated with more extensive behavioral problems in the second-born child ($p < .05$). A respondent who reported that the family had experienced a greater number of stressful events in the past year also reported more extensive behavioral problems in the second-born child ($p < .05$). There were also associations between the extent of behavioral problems in the second born-child and the SWA's evaluation in the second debriefing that the mother was the main client ($p < .05$) and the client's evaluation of LESFU ($p < .05$).

Consistency of Results in the Three Sets of Analyses

The age of the child being studied had the most significant association with the extent of child behavioral problems as measured by this index in each of the three analyses. The number of stressful events reported experienced by the family and the extent of psychological stress reported were also associated with the index of child behavioral adjustment in all three analyses. That is, children who were described as suffering from a high degree of behavioral difficulty were embedded in family situations in which the adult caretaker was coming to LESFU under great emotional stress with child problems being an important feature of that distress. The families in which these children were embedded had also suffered stressful events in the form of death and illness of family members, separation of spouses, conflict with the law, or loss of employment. This picture was very much in accord with the experience of social workers employed in economically distressed urban areas.

For the child showing the greatest extent of behavioral problems, the other significant associations were with measures of the parent's psychological state, such as the parent's morale and the SWA's perception of the mother's motivation. Financial condition or quality of housing were not significantly associated with the extent of behavioral problems of the most troubled child. In contrast, financial condition and quality of housing were associated with the extent of behavioral problems in the oldest child. There were hints that classic sociological variables such as the extent of social isolation of the family were associated with the extent of child behavioral problems.

FACTOR ANALYSIS RESULTS (FA)

The factor dealing with children as the focus of the case appeared consistently in all solutions with two or more factors extracted. The pattern of this factor was the clearest and most consistent set of associations found in the data. The factor presented in Table 9.9 and discussed here was the first factor in the 14-factor solution.

The largest loadings were on the client's report of the age of the child with the most problems (loading = $-.77$) and the SWA's report at the Debriefing II of seeing children in the family ($-.76$). There were five variables with loadings greater than .50 in absolute value, and each dealt with child problems: the client's report of a child in the family with problems ($-.68$), the SWA's Debriefing I report of a child behavioral problem ($-.64$), the client interview–based index of child behavioral adjustment of the family's oldest child ($-.61$), the Debriefing II index of child problems or risks being worked on ($-.60$), and the SWA's Debriefing II report of working on child school-related problems ($-.56$).

The variables with substantial loadings consistently reflected a larger latent variable measuring a child having problems and being worked with by the LESFU SWA. There were eight lesser associations. Six of these associations were intuitively obvious. There was a positive association between the larger child behavioral variable and the client's report of agreeing to work on relationship problems ($-.45$). There was a positive association between the larger child behavioral variable and the client's reported expectation of a change in child behavior ($-.44$). There was also a positive association of the larger child behavioral variable and the client's report of the child's behavior as a cause of problems ($-.43$). There were positive associations between the larger child behavioral variable and the client's report of stressor events and parenting ($-.40$), between the larger child behavioral variable and the client's report of the number of children in the family ($-.37$), and between the larger child behavioral variable and the client's identification of risk in the child's behavior ($-.37$).

Two associations did not have a direction that supported an optimistic view of progress with the child. There was a negative association between the larger child behavioral variable and the SWA's report in the Debriefing II interview of the child's motivation to participate (.41); that is, children with a greater extent of problems were less motivated to participate with the SWA. There was also a negative association between the larger child behavioral variable and the SWA's report in the Debriefing II interview of improvement in the child's adjustment (.37).

There were four weaker associations that were in the expected or hoped for direction. The larger child behavioral latent variable was positively associated with the SWA's Debriefing II assessment of the number of factors that put the family at risk ($-.30$), with the client's report of psychological pressures as motivation to seek help from LESFU ($-.28$), and with the client's report of a change for the better in any family member ($-.28$). The last of these associations may reflect the client's grasping for silver linings more than real improvement in the family's condition. A family in which the client reported less frequent social visiting (.28) had a greater extent of child behavioral difficulty.

Finally, there were three relatively small negative associations that reflected a specialization and focus in LESFU casework. The extent of child behavioral difficulty in the larger latent variable was negatively associated with the SWA's report of working on adult adjustment problems in the Debriefing II interview

(.31), with the client's report of agreeing to work on financial problems (.30), and with the SWA's identification of a need for child care in the Debriefing I interview (.21).

These factor analysis findings were consistent with the multiple regression analyses reported above that linked social and psychological characteristics of the parents with the child's behavioral adjustment.

DISCUSSION AND CONCLUSIONS

The pervasiveness and seriousness of the behavioral problems of the older children were striking and were powerful reminders that there were many outcomes for children worse than placement in foster care. About 8% of the families had at least one child run away. Of children 11 or over, 39% were reported to be truant from school, 15% were reported to use drugs, and 23% were already involved with the law. This sequence seemed to start with a very early onset of childhood moodiness and depression, with 32% of children between six and ten years old showing this symptom.

Our estimate is that the LESFU staff spent about 25% of its time dealing with problems related to the behavior of older children. This commitment seemed quite reasonable in view of the manifest seriousness of these children's problems. Since foster care was a possible response to problems such as these, LESFU's efforts in treating these problems were consistent with its mandate to prevent foster care placement. Nevertheless, incarceration was a much more probable outcome for some of these children than foster care. On a more realistic level, we feel that a wiser course of action would be to expand the mandate of the preventive services to include the prevention of children reaching adulthood without job skills, the prevention of children beginning criminal careers, and the prevention of drug involvement.

An index composed of 13 items of information secured from the client interview was useful in providing an overall measure of child behavioral problems. Across a number of statistical analyses, age emerged consistently as a very strong factor in accounting for problematic behavior in the children. This finding suggested that, as the children in these families matured, greater proportions of them would exhibit the troubled behavior shown in the study by their older siblings. Gender occasionally emerged as having some predictive value, with boys more likely to exhibit acting out, aggressive behavior than girls, but the variable did not emerge as strongly as in the Casey study (Fanshel, Finch, and Grundy 1990). This too was disturbing because the finding suggested that females might display the same extent of drug involvement and criminal conduct as males in contrast to past experiences in which females showed less criminal behavior and drug involvement.

Social and psychological factors in the attitudes and circumstances of caretakers, often single female parents, were strongly associated with reports of child behavioral adjustment problems. Clients who came to LESFU because they were feeling depressed and wanted to get more out of life and who were feeling upset about their children had more acting out and dysfunctional child behaviors to report. Respondents in families where death, illness, loss of a job, breakup of a marriage, or birth of a baby had occurred during the past year also reported more difficult behavior on the part of their children. There was also a suggestion that severe financial problems and housing difficulties were significantly associated with problematic child behavior in the oldest child.

The problem of cause and effect could not be disentangled here. Was a mother's depression brought on by a child's behavioral difficulties, or was the child reacting to the mother's discontent and emotional unavailability? There was much in the concatenation of forces in the lives of oppressed and depressed families that was likely to be the seeding ground for child protest and abandonment of suitable life goals. It was likely also that there was a reverberation of forces with unhappy parents beset by economic deprivation and social isolation, emotionally unavailable, and sometimes rejecting their children who in turn become unmanageable and antisocial as a way of responding, causing more depression and low morale in their unhappy parents. In any event, the stress experienced by the parents was too clearly linked to the behavioral adjustment problems of the children to ignore this area as one of high priority in the delivery of preventive services.

These findings were clearly suggestive of the possibility of developing a social epidemiological approach to case outreach in areas of urban stress so that children at high risk of developing deviant careers could be identified based upon the personal characteristics and social conditions of their families.

NOTE

1. In Chapter 3, we gave information on the location of 391 children we had identified among the 129 families represented in the client survey. In the material of this chapter, the size of the group of children we refer to varies somewhat depending upon the question being addressed. Omissions of children are for the following reasons: (1) 39 children were not living at home; (2) we did not inquire about child No. 6, 7, or 8 for some questions; (3) three respondents were the children themselves and one was an aunt; if a parent was not the respondent, some questions did not apply; (4) some specialized circumstances resulted in responses that had to be classified as "other"; and (5) some parents did not reply to certain questions.

Table 9.1
Debriefing I: Index of Child Behavioral Problem as Source of Concern

Item	Item-Total Correlation
A. Risk of child behavioral problem? (no/yes)	.49
B. Child behavioral or adjustment problem identified? (no/yes)	.32
C. Child school problem identified? (no/yes)	.27
Cronbach alpha coefficient = .54	

Table 9.2
Debriefing II: Index of First Child's Motivation as LESFU Client

Item	Item-Total Correlation
A. Did child fail to keep appointments? (very much/ somewhat/no)	.79
B. Is child resistant? (very much/somewhat/no)	.77
C. Was child late for appointments? (very much/ somewhat/no)	.72
D. Child: level of motivation (high/moderate/low)	.70
E. Quality of the working relationship between child and SWA? (good/fairly good/mixed/poor/very poor)	.64
F. Child: frequency seen (low/high)	.56
G. Was child unable to discuss personal problems? (very much/somewhat/no)	.53
Cronbach alpha coefficient = .88	

Table 9.3
Debriefing II: Index of Child Behavioral Problem as Case Focus

Item	Item-Total Correlation
A. Child behavior as problem occupying attention of SWA? (no/yes)	.53
B. Risk of child behavioral-adjustment breakdown? (low/high)	.53
Cronbach alpha coefficient = .69	

Table 9.4
Debriefing II: Index of Child School Problem as Case Focus

Item	Item-Total Correlation
A. School problem occupying attention of SWA? (no/yes)	.46
B. School involved through LESFU? (no/yes)	.46
Cronbach alpha coefficient = .63	

Table 9.5
Client Interview: Index of Child Behavioral Adjustment

Item	Item-Total Correlation
A. Refusal to accept guidance or discipline? (concern not indicated/concern indicated)	.69
B. Failure to do homework? (concern not indicated/ concern indicated)	.60
C. School attendance problems, truancy? (concern not indicated/concern indicated)	.58
D. Low motivation to learn? (concern not indicated/ concern indicated)	.52
E. Staying out overnight? (concern not indicated/ concern indicated)	.52
F. Problems with police or courts? (concern not indicated/ concern indicated)	.51
G. Reason to worry about how child is doing? (none/one or more reasons)	.50
H. Rejection of parents, parental values? (concern not indicated/concern indicated)	.48
I. Does parent often feel good about child? (often/sometimes/hardly ever or never)	.48
J. Drug abuse problem? (concern not indicated/ concern indicated)	.47
K. Child moodiness; often not happy? (concern not indicated/concern indicated)	.40
L. Alcohol problem? (concern not indicated/ concern indicated)	.29
M. Girl/boyfriend problems? (concern not indicated/ concern indicated)	.21
Cronbach alpha coefficient = .84	

Table 9.6
Client Reports about Whether Having Reason to Worry about Child*

	Child No. 1 [124]	Child No. 2 [104]	Child No. 3 [58]	Child No. 4 [37]	Child No. 5 [16]	Total** [339]
	(percent)					
Reason to worry about child						
Never	33.1	43.3	41.4	51.4	75.0	41.6
Hardly ever	4.0	9.6	8.6	2.7	--	6.2
Sometimes	13.7	12.5	24.1	13.5	12.5	15.0
Often	49.2	34.6	25.9	32.4	12.5	37.2

Question posed to client:
For each child, please tell me whether during the past year you have had reason to worry about how your child is doing.
**Six families reported about a sixth child, three families about a seventh child, and three families about an eighth child.*

Table 9.7
Is Parent Feeling Good about How Child Is Doing?*

	Child No. 1 [121]	Child No. 2 [97]	Child No. 3 [56]	Child No. 4 [32]	Child No. 5 [10]	Total** [316]
	(percent)					
Feeling good about child						
Often	64.4	62.9	67.9	53.1	60.0	63.3
Sometimes	18.2	21.6	17.9	21.9	10.0	19.3
Hardly ever or never	17.4	15.5	14.3	25.0	30.0	17.4

*Question posed to respondent:
We know that raising children is not always a matter of having problems. Parents often think positive things about their children -- their talents, their personal qualities, ability to work, and so forth. For each of your children, please tell me whether you have had such feelings and what they are. Say for _____(CHILD NO. 1), how often do you feel good about how he/she is doing? Would you say often, sometimes, or hardly ever or never?
**We have omitted eight children where the response was coded as "other" and 12 children whose ordinal position in the family was No. 6, 7, or 8.

Table 9.8
Children Showing Problems in Specific Behavior Areas*

	Child No. 1 [124]	Child No. 2 [104]	Child No. 3 [58]	Child No. 4 [37]	Child No. 5 [16]	Total [339]
	(percent showing problem)					
A. Refusal to accept parent guidance	29.8	23.1	17.2	21.6	6.2	23.6
B. Failure to do homework	20.2	17.3	15.5	16.2	6.2	17.4
C. School attendance problem--truancy	25.0	13.5	15.5	18.9	6.2	18.3
D. Low motivation to learn	21.0	16.3	6.3	18.9	6.2	18.0
E. Staying out over- night	13.7	8.7	5.2	5.4	--	9.1
F. Problem with police, courts	13.7	7.7	6.9	10.8	6.2	10.0
H. Rejects parents or their values	20.2	15.4	6.9	10.8	6.2	14.7
J. Drug abuse problem	8.9	5.8	5.2	5.4	6.2	6.8
K. Moodiness--child often not happy	33.9	23.1	15.5	16.2	6.2	24.2
L. Alcohol problem	3.2	4.8	1.7	--	6.2	3.2
M. Girlfriend/ boyfriend problems	6.5	3.2	1.7	2.7	--	4.1
X. Other problems	16.9	12.5	1.7	2.7	--	10.6

*Question posed to respondent:
During this past year have you had concern about any of your children because of the following kinds of problems?
Percents shown reflect the child who the respondent says manifests the problem.

Table 9.9
Behavioral Adjustment of Children in Client Families*

Variable			Loading
Debriefing I			
6. ACHLDPR	Child behavioral problem identified	(-)	.64
11. ACHCARE	Child care need identified		.21
Debriefing II			
21. BCHILDRN	Children's motivation to participate		.41
23. BADADJUS	Adult adjustment problem worked on		.31
25. BSCHOOL	Child school-related problem worked on	(-)	.56
28. BCHPROBS	Child problems/risks worked on	(-)	.60
32. BCHADJPR	Improvement in child adjustment		.37
38. BRISK	Number of factors putting family at risk	(-)	.30
43. BOB05C	Children being seen by LESFU worker	(-)	.76
Client Interview			
51. CMOTIVAT	Psychological pressures as motivation	(-)	.28
52. CVISITN	Frequency of social visiting		.28
57. CSTRESCH	Stressor events and parenting	(-)	.40
63. ANYCHPR	Any child in family with problem	(-)	.68
64. CNCHDRN	Number of children in family	(-)	.37
67. CQE11A08	Any family member change for better	(-)	.28
70. CEXPCHCH	Expected child behavior change	(-)	.44
73. CRSKCHBH	Identified risk of child behavior	(-)	.37
78. CCAUCHBH	Child behavior as cause of problems	(-)	.43
83. CWRKMONY	Agreed to work on financial problems		.30
84. CWRKTHER	Agreed to work on relationship problems	(-)	.45
88. CCFAGEM	Age of child with most problems	(-)	.77
89. CHPROBM	Index of child behavioral adjustment	(-)	.61

*This table is Factor 1 from the factor analysis varimax rotation (14-factor solution).

Chapter 10

Parenting Problems and Issues Related to the Care of Young Children

INTRODUCTION

The last aspects of our study of these families were the young children in the family. They were the ones most at risk of extended foster care placement. We hypothesized that parenting skill and capacity would be important exogenous variables in the determination of the need for foster care. In this chapter, we discuss the results obtained from our analyses relevant to this issue. Our concerns were to identify the vulnerabilities of the children of the study families as seen by the SWAs and to document the concerns of the parents with regard to their children.

SYNOPSIS OF OTHER CASE STUDIES

Many of the study families had young children who were at risk of placement in foster care. Mrs. III was a teenage mother who was having trouble living with her husband's family and who might have trouble establishing herself in her own apartment. Mrs. VI's youngest child needed special education. Mrs. VIII was an unstable mother with young children.

MIS RESULTS (M)

Several of the problem codes in the MIS dealt with parenting problems. In 9% ($n = 14$) of the families, there was an abused child (MIS code 002), and the rate of reported resolution was 35%. In 8% ($n = 12$) of the families, the SWA reported the problem that an adult neglected a child's physical needs (code 003), and 50% of these problems were reported resolved. Our analysis of the time records indicated that very little time was allocated to this problem area. In 7% of the cases ($n = 11$), an adult neglected a child's emotional needs (code 004), and 36% of these problems were reported resolved. Our time analysis also indicated that very little LESFU staff time was allocated to this problem. In 6% ($n = 10$) of the cases, an adult had an unwanted child or pregnancy (code 005), and the SWA reported that 50% of these problems were resolved. Our analysis of SWA reports of time expenditures indicated that substantial effort was allocated to this problem when it occurred. In 18% ($n = 29$) of the families, a child had a learning disability (code 702), and in 31% this problem was reported resolved. Our analysis of time records indicated that between 4% and 5% of LESFU staff time was allocated to this problem. In 6% of the families, one or more of the children was regarded as mentally retarded, and 11% of the problems related to this condition were reported resolved.

DEBRIEFING I RESULTS (A)

There was no Debriefing I index that reflected parenting problems as its principal focus. Parental performance appeared as an issue in the index of family violence and dysfunction discussed in Chapter 8. The index combined issues of parenting with family violence and family relations.

In the first debriefing, the SWAs identified a failure of parental performance as an area of staff concern in 27% of the 160 cases. They reported that 16% of the clients said that their problems were in the area of parenting skills and responsibilities and that 3% ($n = 5$) reported a problem with child abuse. The event that precipitated the client's seeking help from LESFU often included parenting issues. The precipitating event was reported child abuse in six cases and suspected child abuse in another. It was reported child neglect in five cases, suspected child neglect in three, parental rejection of the child in one, and a failure of the parent to send the child to school in one. The precipitating event was a mandate from a court or Special Services for Children in one case. Incest was part of the precipitating event in two cases. The SWAs reported that the clients wanted assistance with dealing with parental responsibilities in nine cases.

The SWAs reported a need for help with child care arrangements in 16% of the cases. A problem with child care arrangements was part of the precipitating event in only three cases, a result to be expected since child care was usually not an immediately crucial problem to a family. It was the main problem the client wished to resolve in 7% of the cases in total and the main problem for 42% of the cases with a child care problem. The SWAs reported that the clients wanted help in advocacy for child care in ten cases and help in finding child care in eight cases and homemaker services in six cases.

There were four families with retarded or developmentally disabled children who needed help with school placements. There were ten clients whom the SWA reported were seeking advocacy help with the school system's Committee on the Handicapped, and there were another five families that wanted generic advocacy help dealing with the school system.

DEBRIEFING II RESULTS (B)

None of the indexes extracted from Debriefing II had a focus on the quality of parenting issues despite the fact that there was considerable anecdotal information and concern about parenting problems in the interview results. Problems in parenting occupied the attention of the SWAs in 13% of the cases active at that point. There was no difference in this percentage among the four ethnic groups.

The specific problems that the SWAs reported working on were the need for child care in ten cases, the need to improve parenting skills and responses in nine cases, dealing with child abuse in five cases, and dealing with child neglect in one case. The SWAs reported some overall improvement in 70% of the cases and improvement of parent-child relationships in 16% of the cases. Some improvements specific to child care and parenting were that ten families had been connected to child care providers, seven families had their educational needs addressed, six families had improved parent-child relations, five had their parenting skills improved, four clients were less neglectful of their children, two families had obtained an educational evaluation of their children, two families had improved housekeeping, one parent had learned to cope with a child better, one parent had accepted a child's developmental needs, and one parent had accepted a child's condition.

In 39% of the cases, the SWAs reported that there was a problem either not recognized by the client or not on the client's agenda with LESFU. The specific unrecognized or ignored problems that involved parenting issues were five clients with poor parenting skills, three families with mother-child conflicts, three mothers exhausted by their responsibilities, two mothers showing lack of maternal feelings, one child who needed summer camp, one mother who was not looking out for her own needs, one family with a need for day care, one parent who preferred one child to another, and one child with emotional problems.

Many of the families had obtained help with parenting issues without LESFU's intervention. In order of their frequency, ten families had arranged for child care with a social service agency without LESFU's assistance, seven families had arranged pre- and postnatal health care, seven families had dealt with their children's educational needs, four families had obtained therapy or counseling for their children, and one had arranged for a home attendant.

The LESFU SWAs had connected the client families with service providers to help the parents deal with parenting issues. These included the neighborhood public school in 20 cases, the Board of Education's Committee on the Handicapped in 15 cases, day care centers in ten cases, the City's Special Services for Children Agency in four cases, an educational agency in three cases, and a summer program for youth in two cases. The SWAs' plans included seeking therapy and counseling for parents in 12 additional cases, child care in ten cases, additional services to meet a child's educational needs in six cases, providing a home attendant in four cases, therapy and counseling for children in four cases, and training in parenting skills for an additional three cases.

The LESFU family worker was an important component of the agency's staffing for service delivery. In theory, the family worker was a part of the community and helped the agency's outreach efforts. There was to be a "partnership with the parent," and the family worker was to have a higher and more realistic expectation of the client family than a middle-class professional would have. Much of the family workers' time went to escorting clients to service providers, interpreting for them when they could not speak English, engaging in parent education, organizing the households to be better managed, and engaging in child care if the parents were absent from the home on a temporary basis. The family workers were also used to monitor the performance of the parents.

Table 10.1 contains the percentage of families by ethnic group that had a LESFU family worker participating. The family worker participated with 39% of the client families overall. The fraction of black families that had a family worker participating was only 22%, much less than the others ($p < .01$).

CLIENT INTERVIEW RESULTS (C)

Our index construction strategy did not find any indexes that focused principally on parenting issues. In Chapter 7, we discussed two indexes that included parenting issues as an important component. The index of the client's psychological pressures and motivation to seek help included the client's seeking advice on how to handle the children, the client's fear that the children were not doing well, and the client's fear that the children would be sent away. Parenting issues were combined with issues about the client's morale and need for self-understanding. The index of the client's overall morale included the client's satisfaction in being a parent. It also included measures of the client's bitterness and positiveness of approach to life.

There was a considerable body of results from the interview itself that was not included in the index analysis. Of the 129 clients interviewed, 53% sought advice on how to handle their children, and 33% had a parenting problem as part of the event that precipitated their seeking LESFU's help, as shown in Table 10.2. Black clients placed somewhat less emphasis on this need ($p < .01$) and were less likely to have a parenting crisis as part of the event precipitating seeking LESFU's aid ($p < .05$).

The clients, in general, did not regard parenting issues as the main problem for which they sought help. A child care problem was the main problem for 6% of those interviewed and was identified as a problem of lesser urgency for 23% of the interviewees. A need to develop additional parenting skills was the main problem for 2% of those interviewed and was a less central problem for 5%. Child neglect was the main problem for 2% of the clients interviewed. In 11% of the interviews, the clients reported that the cause of the problems for which they sought help was that child care responsibility was problematic. In 5% of the interviews, the client thought that problems with child care arrangements were the root cause. In 2% ($n = 2$) of the interviews, the clients thought that the root cause was their neglect of their children.

Of the 30% ($n = 32$) of clients who said that their problem was that they needed resources or other help in their parenting role, 77% reported that the problem had improved since they started work with LESFU, and 62% with this problem regarded LESFU as a source of help. In 13 cases the child was placed in day care, in two cases the parent became better at coping with children, and in two cases the parent learned parenting skills. Four clients reported generic improvement: two reported their problem resolved, one reported improved child behavior, and another said the child no longer had the problem. There were a range of additional specific improvements cited in individual cases: child maintained at home, better coping with service providers, improved adult health, better coping with personal problems, improved mental health, Medicaid obtained, parent training obtained, help from a home attendant.

Of the 25% of clients who said that their problem was a child school problem, 75% reported an improvement since they started working with LESFU, and 62% of those with a child school problem regarded LESFU as a source of help. Many child school problems took the form of truancy and were discussed in Chapter 9. Of those relating to parenting and nurturing issues, seven clients reported that the educational needs of the child were addressed, two clients reported that a child was placed in an appropriate class, and one reported that the child was getting remedial aid. Of the three clients who reported that their problem was their relations with one of their children, two reported an improvement, and both regarded LESFU as a source of help. One client reported that the child's behavior had improved and the other that the client's coping had improved. Issues similar to this were sometimes classified as family relationship problems. There were two clients who reported better relationships with their children under this category.

Table 10.3 shows the distribution by ethnicity of the clients' views on four questions about their parenting experiences. Except for Hispanic clients, the clients thought that their experiences raising children were somewhat harder than that of their friends and relatives. The clients reported considerable satisfaction in being a parent. Chinese clients reported somewhat less satisfaction in being a parent than other clients. The muted responses of the Chinese respondents may have reflected cultural norms about how one expressed feelings about intimate areas of life. The majority of clients, 55%, felt that they had first become parents at the right age. The vast majority of clients, 85%, were satisfied with the number of children they had.

FACTOR ANALYSIS RESULTS (FA)

Although many of the factors included variables that reflected the parenting and nurturing issues that were the focus of this chapter, no single factor consolidated the issues discussed in this chapter. In Chapter 8, we discussed a factor that considered a family dealing with adult problems. This factor was the one closest to the issues of this chapter. The largest loadings were on the Debriefing I identification of family problems, the client's expectation of emotional support from LESFU, and the Debriefing I identification of failure of the family system. These variables were positively associated with the Debriefing II work on parenting problems and the client's report of agreement to work on relationships. These variables in turn were positively associated with the number of problems observed in the case and negatively associated with the highest stage of the LESFU model reached.

Multiple regression and correlation analyses confirmed the patterns suggested by the factor. The index of psychological pressures and motivation to seek help included several parenting issues, namely whether the client reported wanting advice on how to handle the children, reported being afraid the children would be sent away, and reported being afraid that the children were not doing well. This index was positively correlated with the first debriefing index of family violence and dysfunction ($p < .05$), with the first debriefing report of parental concerns about problems the children were showing ($p < .05$), and with the client's report of wanting help dealing with employment problems ($p < .05$).

DISCUSSION AND CONCLUSIONS

The interview schedules as a group failed to gather information about parenting issues that could be usefully summarized using our index construction strategy. We recommend that researchers attempting to replicate our study supplement the interview schedules with additional questions dealing with parenting such as the Magura-Moses Child Well-Being Scales (Magura and Moses 1986).

Child abuse and neglect were serious problems in this population and had a prevalence rate of slightly under 10%. Unwanted pregnancy was an issue for 6% of the client families and drew considerable effort from the SWAs. The parenting problems that these families faced were far more difficult than ordinary: 18% of the client families had at least one child with a learning disability, and 6% had at least one child who was mentally retarded. The SWAs reported some success in dealing with problems related to these conditions.

Obtaining child care was a problem for 16% of the client families, and both SWAs and clients reported success in dealing with this issue. Of the 129 clients interviewed, 53% reported seeking advice on parenting. Parenting issues were a large part of the problems of these families and were part of the precipitating event leading to the clients' beginning to work with LESFU for 33% of the clients interviewed. While there were indications that the parenting problems these families faced were, in fact, more severe than usual, 67% of the clients interviewed reported receiving great satisfaction from parenting.

The large picture from our findings was that there were clear areas of progress made in dealing with these problems and that many of the clients could report very specific improvements in dealing with parenting issues. The majority of the clients credited LESFU as a source of help.

Table 10.1
Is LESFU Family Worker Participating, by Ethnicity?

	Hispanic		Chinese		Black		White, Other		Total	
	No.	%	No.	%	No.	%	No.	%	No.	%
Not participating	44	56.4	19	67.9	14	77.8	5	45.5	82	60.7
Yes, Participating	34	43.6	9	32.1	4	22.2	6	54.5	53	39.3
Total	78	100.0	28	100.0	18	100.0	11	100.0	135	100.0

Table 10.2
Client Reasons for Seeking Help, by Ethnicity*

	Hispanic [78]	Chinese [25]	Black [19]	White, Other [7]	Total [129]
			(percent)		
Wanted advice on how to handle children					
Not at all	38.5	20.0	47.4	42.9	36.4
Somewhat	7.7	20.0	15.8	--	10.9
Important	53.8	60.0	36.8	57.1	52.7
Parenting problem as precipitating event					
None	69.2	60.0	78.9	42.9	67.4
Parenting crisis	30.8	40.0	21.2	57.1	32.6

Table 10.3
Client View of Parenting Experience, by Ethnicity

	Hispanic [78]	Chinese [25]	Black [19]	White, Other [7]	Total [129]
			(percent)		
Raising children compared to friends, relatives*					
Easier	37.3	21.7	22.2	14.3	30.9
Same	28.0	30.4	27.8	28.6	28.5
Harder	34.7	47.8	50.0	57.1	40.7
How much satisfaction in being a parent?**					
Less satisfaction	11.5	16.7	11.1	--	11.8
Some satisfaction	15.4	41.7	22.2	14.3	21.3
Great satisfaction	73.1	41.7	66.7	85.7	66.9
Feelings regarding age when first became parents***					
Too young or old	40.3	43.5	52.6	85.7	45.2
Just right	59.7	56.5	47.4	14.3	54.8
Feelings regarding number of children****					
Feels negative	11.5	12.0	15.8	57.1	14.7
Feels satisfied	88.5	88.0	84.2	42.9	85.3

Questions posed to client:

*When you consider the experiences you have had raising your children, and compare them with the experience of friends and relatives, would you say yours have been easier, about the same, or harder?

**How much satisfaction do you experience these days in being a parent to your children? Would you say ...

***Do you have any feelings, positive or negative, about the age at which you first became a parent? For instance, do you think that you became a parent at too young an age, or too old, or just right?

****Do you have any feelings, positive or negative about the number of children you have had?

Part IV

Outcome Issues

Chapter **11**

Foster Care Issues

In this last part of the book, we discuss the outcome measures of our study and our conclusions. In this chapter, we summarize the information we collected about foster care placement and parental attitudes toward foster care. Since the principal purpose leading to the creation of LESFU was to prevent foster care placements, this chapter has fundamental importance in the overall evaluation of the organization. The primary justification advanced by New York State legislators for a hundred-million-dollars-a-year appropriation for child welfare preventive services, such as those offered by LESFU, was that placement of children in foster care could be forestalled.

We started with rather basic questions: What experiences with separation of children from parents had the families experienced before coming to LESFU? How many children were previously placed in foster care, placed in foster care at the time of intake, and placed while the case was open? What was the attitude of parents regarding the acceptability of foster care as an arrangement for their children in time of need?

The creation of LESFU anticipated the promulgation of a national policy regarding child welfare services that made "permanency planning" for children the avowed goal of service interventions on behalf of beleaguered families. As defined in the Adoption Assistance and Child Welfare Act of 1980 (Public Law 96-272), child welfare services should prevent the unnecessary separation of children from their families by identifying family problems, assisting families in resolving their problems, and preventing breakup of the family where the prevention of child removal was desirable and possible (Maluccio, Fein, and Olmstead 1986).

The threat of dismemberment of families and the placement of children in foster care were two of the central concerns of any child welfare agency offering preventive services. Our overall experience with this phenomenon in our study of 160 families led us to two conclusions about the realities the families faced in this regard. First, the actual number of the children placed was relatively modest. Second, the risk of placement was cited differentially in the various data-gathering occasions, and a substantially larger proportion of cases stood on the abyss of separation than actually experienced it.

Case Study XI

Family XI was an intact Chinese family with five children from three years old to 14 years old. They were living in a two-bedroom apartment in a nice neighborhood in Brooklyn. The apartment appeared a bit small for such a big family. However, the family could not afford to move to other places because of the high rental costs. The family appeared to be living together harmoniously. The children were very appealing and were friendly to one another during the interviewer's visit.

Among the five children, the oldest daughter was the only one born in mainland China. She had been separated from her parents for eight years. When they reunited, both parties had difficulty in relating to one another, and each expected something different from the other. Most important, the parents felt it was acceptable to use corporal punishment to discipline their children.

One time, the mother physically punished the older daughter who later reported the incident to her school teacher. The daughter said her mother was abusing her and not paying any attention to her affairs. The school teacher reported the matter to the police who, in turn, reported the case to Child Protective Services (CPS). Meanwhile, the teacher arranged for her to be examined for her bruises in a nearby hospital. Her disappearance greatly worried her parents who tried to locate her in various places (school, police department, etc.).

Not too long after this, a LESFU SWA called upon the family to inform them that SSC had sent them a directive to become active in the situation. The oldest daughter had to be placed in a foster home immediately to prevent further physical abuse by the parents. The parents were furious at SSC, but the agency insisted upon the child's placement. LESFU's staff gave the parents several options. Finally, the parents placed the daughter in a group setting for a period of time and then worked with LESFU to secure her return home. While she was away, LESFU constantly informed the parents of her condition.

LESFU staff worked on parenting skills with the parents as well as counseling them about the daughter's rebellious behavior. The parents accepted the advice offered by staff and gradually changed their attitudes. The daughter also changed her view of her parents and came to behave more cooperatively. She was able to rejoin her family after about three months, and they got along better.

The family had financial problems because of a younger child's serious illness and the costs related to this. The family also suffered from overcrowding. Despite such conditions, they appeared to be living together harmoniously. In general, the father was a quiet-spoken, rational man while the mother was impulsive and emotional. They expressed appreciation of LESFU's help.

MIS RESULTS (M)

There were no codes in the monthly MIS Forms that dealt directly with foster placement issues.

FAMILY RECORDS (F)

In Chapter 3, we reported a census of the children in the study population. There were 3% of the children in some component of the child care system: four children were in foster family care, four in congregate child care programs, three in emergency shelters, one in correctional care, and two in hospitals. There were other undesirable outcomes: one child was reported homeless, two children were reported as runaways, and four children had whereabouts unknown to their parents. Additionally, 6% of the children under 18 had commenced independent living.

Table 11.1 contains the percentage of families that experienced foster care placement of a child while the case was open for each of the ethnic groups. The information was based on a complete review of case folders and reports submitted by staff to the LESFU MIS. Overall, 14% of the families ($n = 21$) had a child in foster care at the time of case opening or had a child placed while the case was open.[1] There were no statistically significant differences among the four ethnic groups ($p > .20$).

There was considerable flux in the foster care placement history: 9% ($n = 14$) of the families had a child in foster care at case opening; 5% ($n = 7$) of the families had a child placed in foster care while the case was open. Of the 14 families with a child in foster care at case opening, two had the child returned from foster care and subsequently replaced in foster care.[2]

DEBRIEFING I RESULTS (A)

Our index construction strategy did not isolate an index relating to foster care placement from the Debriefing I data base. The SWAs reported that five families (3%) came with an expressed desire to place their children in foster care while three (2%) came in an effort to secure the release of children from care. The SWAs reported that four families (3%) had children living with relatives and were seeking reunion with them. In two cases (1%), a reconstituted family involving children who had returned from foster care were in a situation where parents and returned children were not getting along. Additionally, the SWAs reported a relatively large number of cases where there was a precipitating event that had increased the risk of placement of a child in foster care: there were two families that had a parent who died, two families with a terminally ill family member, two families with incest problems, one court- or SSC-mandated family, one pregnant teenager living at home, one suspected child abuse case, one child abandoned by the mother, and one rejection of the child by a parent. In all, 6% of the mothers ($n = 10$) were out of the picture.

The SWAs said that 53% of the families were likely to have at least one child placed in foster care if the problems were not resolved. This evaluation should be placed in the context that LESFU's mandate was to prevent the placement of children in foster care. The SWAs reported two families with children where the possibility of having to put them up for adoption had been raised by the parents.

The SWA's assessment that the family was at risk of having a child placed was positively associated with the use of other services as reported by the client ($p < .001$). This finding suggested that the LESFU staff was attentive to its principal mission of child welfare preventive services and was effective at influencing the clients to obtain services from other agencies in ongoing efforts to prevent the placement of the family's children in foster care.

DEBRIEFING II RESULTS (B)

Our index construction strategy also failed to extract an index that focused on foster care issues from the Debriefing II data. The SWAs identified a large number of problems facing the families that characteristically increased the risk of a foster care placement for the children in the family: 4% ($n = 6$) of the mothers had a drug or alcohol abuse problem, 3% ($n = 5$) of the families had a child abuse problem, and 3% ($n = 4$) had a reported need to place the children. Another two families were at risk of having a child placed, one family had a neglected child, and one family had a child whose living arrangement with the parents had been interrupted.

The SWAs identified a number of improvements that reduced the risk of the placement of children in foster care. Three clients were in drug treatment and were reported to be improved; two clients had avoided the separation of a child from the family, and the child was at home; one child was returned from foster care; one child who had been a runaway returned home; and in one family the grandparents had assumed care of the children.[3]

At the second debriefing, the SWAs regarded 12% of the families as being at risk of having one or more children placed in foster care. Table 11.2 presents the percentage of families by ethnic group viewed as at risk of having a child placed. These percentages were not significantly different and were much more in line with the historical record than the percentages reported in the Debriefing I interviews.

Negotiations had been initiated, without LESFU's involvement, that might have led to placement in 13 cases at the time of the second debriefing: 6% ($n = 8$) of the client families were involved with the family court, 3% ($n = 4$) with Special Services for Children, and 1% ($n = 1$) was involved with a private agency that provided foster care. The placement of a child was the issue in five of these cases. Additionally, the SWAs reported plans to involve agencies in the future in planning the placement of a child in foster care in five families. The SWAs planned to involve the family court in 4% ($n = 6$) of the cases, to involve the city agency dealing with foster care and other child welfare agencies in 3% ($n = 4$) of the cases, and to involve private child welfare agencies in another two cases.

CLIENT INTERVIEW RESULTS (C)

Our index construction strategy extracted one measure based on three items, as shown in Table 11.3, that dealt with the history of parental separation from the family's children. The internal reliability of the index was .74 as measured by Cronbach's alpha. A family in which the mother alone was caring for her children or one with the mother out of the home had more extensive separation history as measured by this index ($p < .01$). Chinese and Hispanic families had less extensive separation from their children than did black or other white/other families ($p < .05$).

A family that had experienced more separation from its children received more extensive services from social service agencies as measured by a client interview–based index ($p < .05$) and the SWA's Debriefing I report ($p < .05$), had less extensive contact with the LESFU SWA as measured by a client interview–based index ($p < .05$), had experienced more stressful events in the past year as measured by the client interview–based index ($p < .01$), was more fearful that the children would be separated from the family ($p < .05$), had children who were reportedly seen more often by the SWA ($p < .01$), and did not have working on financial problems as part of its LESFU agenda ($p < .01$). Clients with prior family separation experiences were more likely to have children in foster care placement at the time of approaching LESFU ($p < .01$) and more likely to have children in placement at the time of case closing ($p < .05$).

A family that had experienced a greater degree of separation from its children was evaluated by the SWA at the Debriefing I interview as more violent and dysfunctional ($p < .05$). At Debriefing II, a family that had experienced a greater degree of separation from the children had children regarded by the SWA as more motivated to work with LESFU ($p < .05$).

As shown in Table 11.4, of the 129 clients interviewed, 48% had experienced a separation from their children. Black clients were more likely to have experienced a separation than other clients ($p < .01$), confirming the results of the comparison of the ethnic groups using the separation index. For parents who were separated from one or more of their children, 52% reported that the separation was for a year or longer. Black clients reported a shorter separation period than other clients, especially Chinese and white/other clients. This was due mainly to immigration circumstances that made it difficult for Chinese families to arrive in the United States intact.

Table 11.5 contains a tabulation of the circumstances surrounding a total of 113 reported experiences of separation. Of the 57 first separations involving the oldest child, 16% ($n = 10$) involved a placement in foster care or another aspect of the child welfare system. Overall, 21 separations involved foster care placement or another aspect of the child welfare system: nine separations were voluntary placements, six were court-mandated foster care placements, and five were placements in special schools or institutes. Separations of child and parent were reported as a family matter in 45 incidents: 19 separations were of the child to grandparents, ten separations were the result of parental court problems or substance abuse, nine separations were reported generically as "sent away," three separations involved sending the child to the father, three separations were the result of severe marital conflict, and one separation was the result of the child running away.

Circumstances associated with the immigration of the family to the United States occurred in 18 separation incidents, and health issues were involved in 17 separations. The family's economic circumstances were involved in 12 separations. The homelessness of the mother was the circumstance for seven separations, and the family's being destitute accounted for three separations.

One of the indexes extracted from the client interview data that was discussed in Chapter 7 partially dealt with foster care concerns. This was the seven-item index that described the psychological pressure on the mother resulting from her concerns that her children were not doing well. The items included her seeking advice on how to deal with her children, her coming to LESFU because those in authority had directed her to, her fear that her children would be sent away, and her fear that her children were not doing well. As measured by this index, Chinese clients were under more stress about their children than others ($p <$ .01). Among the Chinese clients, 44% feared that their children would be taken away, compared to 26% of clients overall. Perhaps, as new immigrants unfamiliar with the American scene, the Chinese parents felt less able to guide their children and control their behavior in their new environment.

There was substantial additional data about issues related to foster care that were not captured in the indexes. Of the 129 families, covered in the client interview, 7% ($n = 9$) had one or more children in a foster care placement when the parent came to LESFU to get help in having the child returned to the family. The proportion of these cases that the client reported as improved was 78% ($n = 7$). The clients regarded LESFU as a source of help in 56% ($n = 4$) of these cases. The improvements were the return of the child from foster care in five cases, the sustaining of the child's return in one case, and the improvement of family relationships in another. The threat of placement of a child in foster care was a problem for three clients when they came to LESFU. None of the three families had a child placed, and each client credited LESFU as a source of help. Four clients came to LESFU for assistance in placing a child in foster care. In one case the child was placed and subsequently returned to the family. The clients with this request reported a very low rate of improvement, only 25%. That is, LESFU did not assist in the placement of the children in foster care in three of the four cases when this was requested.

There were a number of problems that were often associated with the placement of a child in foster care: three families came to LESFU for help with a teenage pregnancy, two for help with child neglect, one for help with dealing with the drug abuse of the caretaker of the children, and one for help dealing with the drug abuse of a family member. Among the 129 clients interviewed, 12% reported that a child had been a runaway within the last year.

The clients felt that the root cause of their families' problems were the separation of the child from the mother in 5% ($n = 6$) of the cases, the death of a parent in 4% ($n = 5$), the birth defect of a child in 3% ($n = 4$), the parent's neglect of the children in 2% ($n = 2$), and problems associated with the return of children from foster care in 2% ($n = 2$).

There were resolutions of other problems associated with foster care issues: in one family a runaway child returned, in one family a child was sent safely out of state, and in three families the grandparents assumed care of the child.

Client Views on Foster Care and Giving up Parental Responsibilities

We asked the respondents their views about foster care for their children should health reasons prevent them from being able to care for their children. As shown in Table 11.6, only 29% had a positive opinion of foster care, and 67% had a negative view. Of 24 Chinese clients, 62% said that they had a positive view of foster care, a much higher percentage than for the other ethnic groups. The black and white/other groups were somewhat more negative about foster care than the Hispanic clients.

When asked if they knew any relatives, friends, or neighbors who had the experience of having their children placed in foster care, 33% responded positively, and there were clear differences among the ethnic groups. None of the Chinese respondents had any friends or relatives who had experienced children being placed in foster care, compared to 53% of the black respondents and 38% of the Hispanic respondents. We are skeptical of our results that the Chinese views of foster care were so positive and speculate that the views they expressed were a reflection of a culturally based response set to the interviewing situation. Further, there was an association between the extent that an ethnic group had direct experience with foster care and their negative opinion of it.

Among those clients who said they had a friend or family member who had a child placed in foster care, 21 reported that the experience was negative for the child and family. They reported that the child did not prosper in the placement in 11 cases. The problems were that four children were not happy in their placements, two children felt unloved, two children became estranged from their parents, one child became bitter as the placement continued, one child felt like an orphan, and one child increased drug use while in foster care. There were five clients who reported that the child was treated cruelly in the placement. There were three clients who reported that the parents had difficulty getting the child back, and two clients reported that the parents then abandoned the child. There were only nine clients who reported that the experience was positive: six clients reported that the child had a good placement, two reported that the placement helped the mother, and one reported that the problem was resolved and the child returned home. In two of the good placements, the children reached adulthood and were doing well as adults.

The respondents were asked about potentially positive aspects of a foster care placement. Their fundamental negativism about foster care appeared in their responses, which are tabulated in Table 11.7. Of the 129 respondents, 36% did not cite a positive aspect, and 2% ($n = 2$) gave a conditional aspect, that the quality of the foster mother determined whether the placement could be positive.

The most frequently cited positive aspect of a foster care placement was the material benefits to the child: needed care for the child, security, shelter, nutrition, stability of living arrangement, and clothing. Another 9% cited advantages to the natural parent as the most positive aspect of a foster care placement: the last resort for help to the parents. Only 14% of the respondents cited advantages to the child's well-being as the most prominent positive aspect of a foster care placement. These included guidance and education, the opportunity to grow and develop, more professional care, and keeping the children in a family together. Only two respondents felt that the child in a foster care placement would receive love.

The specification of negative aspects of foster care brought forth a larger number of responses from the clients, and these are shown in Table 11.8. The most commonly cited first fear were issues related to the maltreatment of the child in the foster care placement, such as the foster child being treated more poorly than the natural children, being maltreated, not being loved, living in a home of uncertain quality, and being subjected to multiple placements. These were the first cited concerns for 36% of the respondents. The psychological damage inflicted on the child was the first cited concern for 17% of the respondents. Finally, 11% of the respondents first cited damages inflicted upon the parents, including the difficulty of getting their children back and being unable to see them while they were in the placement.

In the event of the illness of the parents, the vast majority, 86%, wanted their children to be cared for by a family member; another 6% wanted their children to be cared for by someone in their extended family. Only a small minority, 19%, would have planned for their children to be cared for by the child welfare system. When questioned, the clients seemed optimistic that the arrangements they specified as their preferences could be carried out. In only five cases were there indications from the client that the desired living arrangements were actually not possible.

As shown in Table 11.10, 64% of the respondents said that they had not considered in the past year the idea that someone else take on the care of their children. Chinese respondents were particularly emphatic about caring for their children with 88% saying that they had not considered giving up the care of their children in the past year. Among the 45 respondents who had considered giving up the care of their children, the most common reasons were serious illness or hospitalization (67%) or death (31%). There were two respondents who regarded divorce as a possible cause of giving up the care of the children, two if job requirements forced it, two if the health needs of the child forced it, one if they were homeless, and one if an emergency trip had to be made.

FACTOR ANALYSIS RESULTS (FA)

Two of the factors in the 14-factor solution dealt with the issues of this chapter. The first related the amount of agency staff time spent on a case that had a high risk of child placement. The second dealt with the client's fears of separation from her child.

Agency Staff Time and Risk or Fact of Child Placement

Many of the factors included important relations on issues related to the placement of the children in the family in foster care. One of these, the third factor extracted from the 14-factor solution, combined MIS-derived information about staff time with both the risk and fact of foster care placement. It is shown in Table 11.11.

The MIS report of the time spent on a case had the largest loading in absolute value (loading $= -.80$), and the second largest was on the MIS report of the number of months the case was opened (loading $= -.64$). These two variables were positively associated, as expected, and suggested a larger variable reflecting the extent of involvement of the LESFU staff in a case both in the total hours and in the length of time the case remained active with the agency.

The variables with the next largest loadings were the case closing form record indication of whether a child was in placement at the end of the study ($-.51$), the SWA's assessment at the Debriefing I interview that there was a risk of placement of the children ($-.50$), and the case closing form record of a child in placement at case opening ($-.44$). These three variables suggested a latent variable of risk or fact of child placement. These three variables were positively associated as expected.

The major association suggested by this factor was that a family that had a child in placement or was at greater risk of having a child placed received more time from the LESFU staff on average and was involved with LESFU for a greater length of time. The two latent variables, LESFU effort and risk of child placement, were positively associated.

The other loadings confirmed this basic pattern. The SWA's Debriefing II report of case activity (.42) was associated both with the SWA's report of time in the MIS and the risk or fact of placement. A case that received more LESFU time and with greater risk or fact of placement advanced farther on average into the LESFU model ($-.41$) and had a greater number of problems reported ($-.40$). Both the SWA's report at the Debriefing I interview of the risk of placement ($-.36$) and the report that the client was known to other agencies ($-.35$) were positively associated with the latent LESFU effort and the latent risk of child placement. The client's report of the number of stressful events ($-.34$), the client's report of being involved with other agencies ($-.32$), and the MIS number of problems reported resolved ($-.31$) were also positively associated with the latent LESFU effort and the latent risk of child placement. There were weaker positive associations with the SWA's Debriefing II report of school-related problems ($-.30$), of involvement with other agencies ($-.29$), and of the number of risk factors ($-.25$). Additionally, a case that received more LESFU time and was at greater risk or fact of placement was more likely to have the respondent indicate fear that a child would be placed (−.24).

As a whole, the factor indicates that the organization did marshal resources in time and was able to involve families at greater risk of placement or who already had a child in placement. Some of this work was effective, as indicated by the positive association of time reported spent with problems reported resolved. There was also a positive association between the time reported spent and whether the child was placed at the end of the study.

In Chapter 6, one of the factors focused on adult needs and relevant service providers (the fourth factor in the solution discussed here). Its associations also suggested that there was a positive association between whether a child was in placement at the opening of the case and the SWA's Debriefing II report of case activity, the index of the client's evaluation of LESFU, and the client's report of contact with other LESFU staff.

A second factor discussed in that chapter (the tenth factor in the solution extracted) provided an additional complimentary association. A family with a child in placement at the case opening had a greater case success ratio as measured by the ratio of the number of problems reported resolved to the number of problems expected to be resolved on the basis of the agency's total experience.

In Chapter 8, one of the factors (the 14th in the solution used) dealt with a deteriorating family system under pressure on many fronts. Whether a child was in placement when the study ended was positively associated with the SWA's Debriefing I report of the failure of the family system, with the SWA's Debriefing II report of working on family relations problems, with the client-based index of child behavioral adjustment, and strongly with the client's fears that family problems would get worse.

Fear of Parent-Child Separation

A second factor, the ninth in the solution extracted here, had a principal focus on the issues discussed in this chapter. The largest loading in absolute value (−.54) was on the index of past separation of children and parents based on the responses from the client interview defined earlier in this chapter. The next largest loadings were on the respondent's fear that a child in the family would be placed (−.51) and on the respondent's view that family conflict was the cause of the problems that led to seeking LESFU's assistance (−.47). These three measured variables suggested a larger latent variable concerning past separation from children and continuing fears of family disruption.

A respondent who had been separated from the children and who had a continuing fear of family separation and dissolution was reported as more motivated to work with LESFU by the SWA in the Debriefing I interview (−.25) and more likely to have adult service needs being attended to as reported by the SWA in the Debriefing II interview (−.33). The case of such a client had on average more problems reported resolved (−.27).

The remaining loadings suggest that the respondent's fears of having a child placed were a stimulus for more intensive service effort. There was a negative association between a family with a past history of separation from children and continuing fears with the SWA's Debriefing II report of the children's motivation to participate in the LESFU work (.42), with the SWA's Debriefing I report of involvement of other agencies with the family (.39), with the SWA's Debriefing II assessment of the risk of child placement (.36), and with the SWA's Debriefing I assessment of requiring aid from other social service agencies (.32).

On balance, the factor suggested that the LESFU workers were particularly responsive to a client who had a past history of separation from children by helping to resolve a larger number of problems, that the client's continuing fears of separation were a motivation to work hard and well on problems, and that the workers responded sensitively to the client's needs by addressing adult problems.

DISCUSSION AND CONCLUSIONS

Our data supported the view that the organization was meeting its mandate. The families in this study included many who were at high risk of having a child placed in foster care. Of the 129 respondents interviewed, 48% said they had been separated from one of their children, with over half of the separations for a year or longer. Of the 160 families in the study, 14% had at least one child in foster care placement before the end of the study. At the opening of the case, 9% had a child in placement. At the Debriefing II interview the SWAs reported that 12% of the cases had a continuing risk of placement. The prevalence of factors putting a family at risk of having a placement was extremely high. For example, 6% of the mothers were out of the picture.

The workers made focused and extensive efforts to deal with the problems putting the family at risk. There was a very high association between the time spent on a case and variables measuring the fact or risk of placement. In addition, the workers reported substantive improvements and reductions in risk factors in the second debriefing. More important, the LESFU results compared very favorably with much more extensive and expensive interventions to prevent foster care placement. Wells and Biegel (1990), in a recent review of research dealing with the results of family preservation services, reported placement rates that varied from 12% to 16% with lengths of service contacts up to a year.

The majority of the respondents conveyed a caring attitude about their children and sought to avoid their placement in the child welfare system. The vast majority would consider placement only in the event of the parent's severe illness or death. They had extremely negative views about the foster care system: 36% could not or would not cite any positive aspects to foster placement. The majority of positive responses cited material advantages to the child: food, clothing, shelter, and so on. The negative views about foster care voiced by the clients, representing a group whom the SWAs thought were at risk of a placement if the family problems were not resolved, were echoes of the criticisms of foster care

voiced over the years by study groups, child welfare advocates, and other interested community groups (National Commission for Children in Need of Parents 1979).

Implications for Practice

Policy discussions about publicly supported kinship foster homes should incor-
porate these strong statements of parental hostility to assigning the care of their
children to strangers. These views take on a special significance given the re-
markable growth in the use of kinship foster homes: New York City witnessed a
marked growth in 1989 in the use of kinship foster homes, some 14,000 children
being placed in such arrangements.[4]

A foster care placement is not necessarily an undesirable outcome. Some
children will thrive better in a placement than with their family if their parents are
sufficiently impaired in their functioning. Nevertheless, there is widespread support for the major emphasis of national policy that seeks to assist families living
under adverse conditions in areas of urban disaster in order to forestall foster care
placements. Policies leading to major social expenditures, such as paying for a
foster care placement, could more profitably start with sustaining families who
are in high-risk neighborhoods.

A foster care placement is essentially an effort to replace the environment of
the natural family: replacement will usually be more expensive than repair of the
condition causing parent-child separation. The largest cost of the foster care
placement is the hidden emotional costs to the parents and child. Our recent
research on foster children in five western states showed that increased number
of living arrangements was associated with an increased anger and hostility in the
child. This increased anger and hostility was associated with subsequent increased delinquency in foster care, poorer adaptation while in foster care, and
poorer condition at discharge from the placement. These undesirable results were
associated with poorer adaptation as an adult, including greater involvement in
criminal activities. The child in foster care typically makes tremendous efforts to
get back to the natural family. Overall, the most humane and efficient plan is to
support the natural parent, even in many cases where the parent's capacities are
limited by an involvement with drugs or alcohol, and to restrict foster care
placement as a response of last resort.

Although many children fare relatively well in foster care (Fanshel and Shinn
1978), the fears of bad outcomes in foster placements that the respondents cited
are real and accurate. Quality foster parents are an increasingly scarce resource in
this era of the two-career family, and a policy of unrestrained foster care placement would only send the costs soaring. Further, there are no guarantees that the
foster home is itself desirable, particularly when the supply does not meet the
demand and standards are lowered in foster parent selection. When we interviewed adults who had been in foster homes in the western program, 24% of the
women reported that they had been sexually molested in their last foster home

(8% of the men reported being molested), and 25% reported severe corporal punishment in the foster placement (Fanshel, Finch, and Grundy 1990).

Practitioners need to spell out the criteria that define the appropriateness of the placement of children in foster care. The direct financial costs of a foster care placement are extremely large, and the hidden and indirect costs are usually even larger. On balance, the wiser course of action is to support the natural families, to repair their functioning, and to develop the parenting capacities of natural mothers, especially when they are young and alone. Child welfare preventive service agencies such as LESFU should be assigned the responsibility to work routinely with families whose children are in foster care. The results presented here suggest that these parents were often highly motivated, that the fears of the parents about being separated arbitrarily from their children and ultimately losing them were a major obstacle when foster care would be appropriate, and that work with families like this was highly productive. These arrangements might include supervision of children who are visiting their families and would make available service provision to the parents by an agency that is better integrated with the community. The separation of foster care services from child welfare prevention services ought to be overcome because it makes no sense and, in fact, may hinder the return of children to their families.

NOTES

1. This tabulation covers 156 families. There were four cases where we could not establish the facts.

2. Case Study IXA was one of these two families.

3. At the time of the study it was not the policy of the public social service agency to consider accepting grandparents as foster parents.

4. "Treating Kin Like Foster Parents Strains a New York Child Agency," *New York Times*, October 20, 1989, pp. 1, 4.

Table 11.1
Foster Care Placement, by Ethnicity

	Hispanic [94]	Chinese [29]	Black [22]	White, Other [11]	Total [156]
			(percent)		
Child ever placed?					
No placement	86.2	93.1	77.3	90.9	86.5
Placement experienced	13.8	6.9	22.7	9.1	13.5

Note: Data derives from a systematic review of all data sets and the case folders maintained at the agency. Of the 21 families where child placement was indicated, there were 12 cases where a child was in care at the time the case opened at LESFU: seven cases where the child was placed while the case was open; two cases where a child was in care when the case opened, returned home, and reentered care while the case was open. Four cases are not reported for lack of information.

Table 11.2
Percentage of Families at Risk of Placement, by Ethnicity

	Hispanic No.	Hispanic %	Chinese No.	Chinese %	Black No.	Black %	White, Other No.	White, Other %	Total No.	Total %
Risk of placement	12	15.4	2	7.1	1	5.6	1	9.1	16	11.9

Table 11.3
Client Interview: Index of History of Separation from Child

Item	Item-Total Correlation
A. Ever been separated from oldest child? (no/yes)	.74
B. How long was separation? (low/high)	.70
C. Were there other separations? (no/yes)	.38
Cronbach alpha coefficient = .74	

Table 11.4
Family Experience with Separation of Child, by Ethnicity

	Hispanic [78]	Chinese [25]	Black [19]	White, Other [7]	Total [129]
			(percent)		
A. Oldest child ever separated from mother?*					
No	57.7	60.0	21.1	42.9	51.9
Yes	42.3	40.0	78.9	57.1	48.1
B. Length of separation:					
Less than one year	48.5	25.0	69.2	25.0	48.3
One year or more	51.5	75.0	30.8	75.0	51.7

*Question posed to client:
Have there been any times since your oldest child was born when you were separated from him/her for a month or longer -- either because you were away or because he/she was away from home?

Table 11.5
Circumstances of Past Separations of Children from Families

	Child No. 1 (First Separation)	Child No. 1 (Other Separations)	Other Children	Total Incidents
		(N = 129)		
Child Welfare System Involved	10	7	4	21
Parental Personal or Family Problems	20	5	20	45
Immigration Experience	13	1	4	18
Health Problem	7	4	6	17
Parental Economic Circumstance	7	1	4	12

Table 11.6
Client View of Foster Care if Circumstances Prevented Own Care of Children, by Ethnicity*

	Hispanic [69]	Chinese [24]	Black [17]	White, Other [5]	Total [115]**
			(percent)		
Positive, for such a plan	5.8	41.7	5.9	--	13.0
Somewhat positive	18.8	20.8	--	--	15.7
Neutral	2.9	8.3	--	20.0	14.3
Somewhat negative	13.0	8.3	41.2	--	15.7
Negative, against such a plan	59.4	20.8	52.9	80.0	51.3

*Question posed to client:
How do you feel about foster care -- where an agency places children with a family not related to the children? For example, if you had a health problem and could not take care of your children, how would you feel about placing them in foster care?
**Fourteen clients not included where parent was not the caretaker.

Table 11.7
Respondent View of Positive Aspects of Foster Care

	First Reasons No. %	Second Reasons No. %	Total Reasons No. %
	(N = 129)		
No Positive Response	46 35.7		
Conditional Response	3 2.3		
Provides Basic Child Needs	39 30.2	16 12.4	55 42.6
Provides for Parents	11 8.5	2 1.6	13 10.1
Provides Supplement to Child's Welfare	18 14.0	8 6.2	26 20.2
Other	1 .8		

Table 11.8
Respondent View of Negative Aspects of Foster Care

	First Reasons No. %	Second Reasons No. %	Total Reasons No. %
	(N = 129)		
Maltreatment or Neglect	47 36.4	10 7.8	57 44.2
Psychological Damage to Child	22 17.1	8 6.2	31 24.0
Damage to Parent	14 10.9	2 1.6	16 12.4
Nothing Good	2 1.6	1 .8	3 2.3

Table 11.9
Preferred Arrangement for Care of Children if Parent Became Physically Ill*

	No.	%
	(N = 129)	
Family	102	79.1
Child Welfare System	24	18.6
Unknown	3	2.3

*Question posed to respondent:
   What if a parent like yourself cannot take care of his/her children, say, because of physical illness? What would be the best arrangement a parent could secure for the care of the children?

Table 11.10
Client View of Relinquishing Care of Children, by Ethnicity*

	Hispanic [77]	Chinese [24]	Black [17]	White, Other [7]	Total [125]
		(percent)			
Ever have the idea that you would like to stop caring for the children?					
No	57.1	87.5	64.7	57.1	64.0
Yes	42.9	12.5	35.3	42.9	36.0

*Question posed to client:
   In recent years, have you ever had the idea that you would like to totally stop taking care of your children by having someone else do this?

Table 11.11
Agency Staff Time—Risk of Placement of Children and Placement History*

Variable		Loading	
Debriefing I			
15. APLACRSK	Risk of placement of children	(-)	.50
16. ARISKPLC	Risk of placement of children	(-)	.36
17. ASOCSVCK	Client known to social service agency	(-)	.35
Debriefing II			
24. BACTIVTY	Case activity		.42
25. BSCHOOL	School-related problems	(-)	.30
38. BRISK	Number of family risk factors	(-)	.25
39. SOCSVCP	Social service agency in picture	(-)	.29
Client Interview			
46. COTHRAGY	Other agency in the picture		.32
57. CSTRESCH	Stressful events in family life	(-)	.34
72. CRSKPLCM	Fear child would be placed in foster care	(-)	.24
LESFU MIS Data			
90. MHIMODLV	Highest stage of LESFU model reached	(-)	.41
91. MNPRESEN	Number of problems reported resolved	(-)	.31
92. MSUMTIME	Sum of all time spent on case	(-)	.80
93. MNUMBRPR	Number of problems observed in case	(-)	.40
94. MNUMOFMO	Number of months case remained open	(-)	.64
Case Closing Information			
99. XCHPLCOP	Child in placement at case opening	(-)	.44
100. XCHPLEND	Child placed when study ended	(-)	.51

*This table is Factor 3 from the factor analysis varimax rotation (14-factor solution).

Table 11.12
Fear of Parent-Child Separation

Variable		Loading	
Debriefing I			
3. AMOTIVAT	Client's motivation to work with LESFU	(-)	.25
5. AOTHAGDND	Other agencies involved with family		.39
18. ASOCSVCRZ	Service required from social agency		.32
Debriefing II			
21. BCHILDRN	Children's motivation to participate		.42
30. BADSERVN	Adult service needs being attended to	(-)	.33
37. PLCRISK	Risk of child placement		.36
Client Interview			
53. CSEPCHILD	Past separation of children and parents	(-)	.54
72. CRSKPLCM	Fear child would be placed	(-)	.51
79. CCAUFAMR	Family conflict cause of problems	(-)	.47
LESFU MIS Data			
91. MNPRESEN	Number of problems reported resolved	(-)	.27

*This table is Factor 9 from the factor analysis varimax rotation (14-factor solution).

Chapter 12

The LESFU Model and Case Flow Patterns: SWA Results

The essence of LESFU's mission was to be a community-based child welfare agency comprised of teams of professionals and neighborhood residents acting as a "general practitioner in social welfare" to guarantee service integration. The possibility of the agency subcontracting with other agencies for certain services and acting as an intermediary between the public and private sector was specifically indicated (Young 1985). In this chapter, we present our findings from the reports of the SWAs about the flow of a case through the LESFU model and a summary of our measures of LESFU's effectiveness. The model has been described in Chapter 1.

MIS RESULTS

Overall, the SWAs reported that at least one problem was resolved by the end of the case in 77% of the 160 cases. The median number reported resolved was two, with one case having 13 problems reported resolved. Of the 1,309 problems reported for the 160 cases, 35% ($n = 455$) were reported resolved. When we tested whether the four teams had equal rates of reported resolution, we found no difference ($p > .05$).

The SWA's identification at the Debriefing I interview of housing problems as a reason for coming to LESFU had a correlation with the number of problems reported resolved of .23 ($p < .05$). Similarly, there was a significant correlation ($r = .26$) of the number of problems reported resolved with financial problems as a reason for seeking help ($p < .01$). The identification in the Debriefing I interview of a risk that a child would be placed had a correlation of .33 ($p < .001$) with the number of problems reported resolved.

The client's report of more frequent contact with the SWA had a significant correlation ($r = -.24$) with the number of problems reported resolved ($p < .05$). A client family with a larger number of children had fewer problems reported resolved ($r = .22, p < .05$).

The total time expended by the SWAs for all cases in the study as reported in the MIS data was 11,000 hours. A multiple regression model to allocate the time into the various problem groups resulted in the findings measuring the distribution of staff time in the 160 cases shown in Table 12.1. This table represents our estimate of where the LESFU staff actually invested its efforts.[1]

Figure 12.1 shows the distribution of the highest level of the LESFU model that the SWA reported for the case. Only 44% of the cases reached or passed the contract stage, and only 21% of the cases reached the closure point of the follow-up stage.

As shown in Table 12.2, the indirectly standardized ratio of number of cases reported resolved was extremely low for cases that did not progress past the work agreement stage (stage 2) of the model ($p < .0001$). There was little difference in the indirectly standardized ratio for cases that reached the goals stage or subsequent stages. Our interpretation was that a client who was able to work with the SWA well enough to define goals would naturally be more successful in the mutual effort. This finding was partial support for the efficacy of the LESFU model as a positive factor in the agency's operation.

The indirectly standardized ratio of the number of problems reported resolved to the number of problems expected to be resolved was potentially a strong measure of the success of handling a case. Of the 26 SWAs who handled the 160 cases, some SWAs had a higher average indirectly standardized ratio than others ($p < .001$). One worker had an average indirectly standardized ratio of 1.84 for the clients handled, while another had no problems reported resolved among his cases. Our multiple regression analysis of the number of problems reported resolved in a case identified three workers who were associated with a lower number of problems reported resolved once the difficulty of the case as measured by the number of problems expected to be resolved and the stage of the LESFU model that the client had reached were controlled for.[2]

Finally, using multiple regression analysis, we found an association between the number of problems reported resolved and the indirectly standardized time ratio for a case ($p < .01$). A case that had 10% more time expended on it than expected had 2.2% more problems reported resolved than an otherwise similar case that received the expected amount of time. The result supported the hypothesis that a greater expenditure of effort on a case would lead to greater results, although the magnitude of the improvement compared to the effort suggested that a point of diminishing returns would be quickly reached.

A major component of the LESFU philosophy of case management was that it should have a role in referring clients to agencies that could provide additional, more specialized services. While we have reported the prevalence and resolution rate for each problem group in the preceding chapters, we repeat for our reader's convenience these statistics in Table 12.3 along with the fraction of cases with a problem in the area that were referred to external agencies.

The most prevalent problems identified in Table 12.3 reflected the working poor and the long-term poor clientele of an agency such as LESFU. They had more income, employment, and housing problems than a middle- or upper-class clientele. LESFU's mission of preventing foster care placement was reflected in the high prevalence of adult family relations problems, 74%, and the high prevalence of child educational and vocational training problems, 69%.

The referral rate is high for adult income and employment problems (66%), child education and vocational training problems (62%), and adult health problems (59%). These were problem areas that required the coordination of services with the economic assistance systems, school system, and health care systems. The high referral rates suggested that LESFU was effective at advocacy and maintained lines of communications with service organizations in these areas.

The referral rate was less than 30% for problem areas that were within the social work areas of expertise. For example, the referral rate was 28% for problems in adult family relations. These data suggested that LESFU was invested in establishing communication with external agencies in areas such as income and education, where coordination was essential, and that it used its internal resources for problems that fell within the expertise of social work.

The large picture that emerged from these analyses was that of staff using external agency resources for problems in groups that were beyond the expertise of a social work staff and that of a staff dealing internally with problems in areas of its own capability. Further, given that the staff sought an external agency, there were indications in the data of investment of effort in establishing at least ongoing work with the external agency or in resolving the problem with minor external assistance.

CASE CLOSING INFORMATION (X)

Table 12.4 is the cross-tabulation of the nature of the case closing by the ethnicity of the client for the LESFU study population. A planned or anticipated closing occurred in 51% of the cases. Almost a third of the closings (31%) were not planned. The public agency monitoring these cases (Special Services for Children) ordered the closing of 5% of the cases because it had been determined that another plan for dealing with the family's situation was in order. Another 9% of the cases were closed because the family was no longer eligible for service, usually because the family had moved out of the geographic area served by LESFU.

There was little difference in the patterns of closings by ethnicity. Chinese clients were somewhat more likely to have a planned case closing (62%) and somewhat less likely to have an unplanned case closing (21%) than other clients ($p < .05$). This pattern was consistent with our other results suggesting a more orderly process in casework with the Chinese clients. Black and white/other clients were more likely to have their cases closed on the basis of not meeting eligibility requirements (14%) than Hispanic or Chinese clients (3%).

As shown in Table 12.5, 53% of the cases were closed based upon the mutual decision of both worker and client, and in 30% of the cases the client was the source of termination. Chinese clients were more likely (74%) to terminate on the basis of a mutual decision than other clients and less likely (19%) to initiate the closing on their own. For Hispanic clients, 54% terminated on the basis of a mutual decision with the SWAs; this was true of 39% of the black clients. As shown in Table 12.4, black and white/other clients were more likely than Chinese or Hispanic clients to have their cases terminated by the public agency for reasons out of their control.

Table 12.6 contains the percentages of clients with various status indications by ethnicity. There were no important ethnic differences for the various status indicators. Service had been recorded as completed for 53% of the clients. A move out of the LESFU catchment area occurred in 20% of the cases. Often this reflected evidence of a positive effect of the agency's work: needed housing was secured.

Continuance and discontinuance of clients in treatment has long been of interest to social work researchers (Ripple 1957). Almost two-fifths of the LESFU clients were unwilling to continue, usually in the face of service not being completed. Sometimes, however, service had been completed, but the SWAs felt that more work could be done. Ethnic differences in regard to this variable were slight.

Finally, it should be noted that there was a turnover of SWAs at LESFU during this period. A single SWA handled 75% of the cases, and there were two or more SWAs in 25% of the cases.

DEBRIEFING I RESULTS

Alcabes and Jones (1985) observed that researchers and practitioners fail to distinguish between "true clients," those who are receiving treatment, and those who are being socialized to the client role but have not become engaged as participants in the helping effort. They argued that "this failure accounts for the discrepancy between research findings and practice wisdom as to the efficacy of treatment" (p. 53). Their perspective has relevance for the findings reported here.

Debriefing I Index of SWA's Assessment of Need for External Agencies

Table 12.7 defines an index that summarized the SWA's assessment of the need for external agencies to meet the client's problems. The component items were whether a first, second, or third external agency would be needed. The internal reliability as measured by Cronbach's alpha was .67.

There was a quite weak finding that families in which the mother was alone or the mother was out of the home needed more help than families in which the mother had either the father or some other adult ($p < .10$). There were no statistically significant differences among the ethnic groups with respect to the average level of this index ($p > .50$).

Anecdotal Reports of the SWAs from Debriefing I

As reported by the SWA, the welfare of one of the family's children was the most common class of events that precipitated the client's coming to LESFU and was part of the precipitating event in 45% of the cases ($n = 72$). These included school placement issues or other school-related problems (12 cases), the truancy of a child (nine cases), teenage pregnancy (eight cases), child neglect or suspected neglect (eight cases), a child with a specific service need (seven cases), child abuse or suspected abuse (seven cases), a child running away (five cases), a child acting out (four cases), child care needs (three cases), incest (two cases), and a child developmental disability (two cases). There were three cases in which the precipitating event was the parent's desire to have a child returned from foster care and two in which the precipitating event was the return of the child from foster care.

The second most common theme to the events that precipitated the client's seeking LESFU's help was a financial or housing crisis. A housing crisis was the precipitant in 12% ($n = 19$) of the cases, and a financial crisis was the precipitant in 16% ($n = 25$) of the cases.

Health-related crises were the third most common theme to the precipitating event and occurred in 19% ($n = 30$) of the cases. These problems included an unspecified medical problem (seven cases), the hospitalization of a parent (four cases), the terminal illness or death of parent (four cases), a pregnancy crisis (three cases), and mental health problems (two cases). Of course, the eight teenage pregnancies and the two children with developmental disabilities also have to be considered as causing a health-related crisis.

The fourth most common theme was family violence and conflict. It occurred in 13% ($n = 20$) of the cases. Generic family violence was the precipitant in eight cases, breakup of the adult partnership in five cases, wife battering in three cases, and family conflicts in four cases.

Overall, the SWAs reported that 46% of their clients reported that they faced a housing problem, 26% a financial problem, and 21% a child behavioral problem. The SWAs reported that 20% of their clients regarded their housing problem as the one with the highest priority, while 13% identified a child behavioral problem and 11% a financial problem. Table 12.8 presents a summary of the incidence rates by type of problem and repeats information presented in earlier chapters. The table shows a rather striking transformation of problem types that were part of the event that precipitated the client's coming to LESFU to a rather different mix of problems that the SWAs recorded as being of concern at case opening.

Table 12.9 is an enumeration of the SWA's perception of the client's expectation. It provides more documentation of the SWAs' transformation of their clients' problems into the resources and skills that they had at the moment. The

SWAs reported that 58% of their clients sought advocacy, principally with public assistance, housing, and school. They thought that 10% of their clients wanted the SWA to help secure homemaker or child care services. They reported that 8% wanted traditional social work child or family therapy with another 1% seeking vocational or consumer help. They felt that 8% of their clients wanted emotional support and that 4% of the clients wanted the SWAs to deal with the foster care system, primarily to place a child.

DEBRIEFING II RESULTS

We were able to extract a number of indexes that described the progression of the case and the interaction between clients and LESFU. In Chapter 7, we described an index of the mother's motivation to work with LESFU that had a Cronbach's alpha of .89. In Chapter 3, we described an index of the father's motivation as a LESFU client that had a Cronbach alpha of .91. Finally, in Chapter 9, we described our index of the first child's motivation as a LESFU client, an index whose Cronbach's alpha was .88. These indexes were reliable measures of the SWA's assessment at Debriefing II of the motivation of the members of the client family.

Debriefing II Index of Case Activity

Table 12.10 defines a three-item index that measured the current level of case activity. The internal reliability of the index as measured by Cronbach's alpha was .53, a value much lower than that of the other measures of case activity and responsiveness of the clients. There were no statistically significant differences on the average of this measure for the various family types ($p > .10$) or for the four ethnic groups ($p > .25$).

As shown in Table 12.11, the SWAs regarded 46% of their cases as active and 20% as hardly active or not at all active. These percentages were more in line with Briar's (1966) report. On an historical note, we observe that in the two decades following World War II there was a strong tendency to view problems of dysfunctional clients as requiring long-term treatment effort. The influence of Freudian psychoanalytic treatment theory and experience was highly influential in establishing treatment perspectives (Hollis 1964). A series of studies beginning in the 1960s, however, appeared to establish quite conclusively that planned short-term treatment could be as efficacious as open-ended, extended treatment for certain kinds of problems (Reid and Shyne 1969).

As shown in Table 12.12, there was an overall lessening of contact between the Debriefing I and Debriefing II interviews, with 33% of the cases having less frequent contact compared to 15% with more contact and 52% with the same level of contact.

As shown in Table 12.13, in 51% of the 45 cases in which the contact with the client had decreased, the SWA reported that the client's problems had been solved, stabilized, reduced, or temporarily abated. In the remaining cases, the reason for the decrease was client resistance or dissatisfaction with LESFU's services. In three cases, the client moved out of the LESFU catchment area. In the 18 cases in which client contact increased, the SWAs thought that in 78% of these cases greater client problems and greater client motivation were the causes of the increase. In 22% of the cases with an increase, the cause of the increase was an action on the part of the SWA.

Debriefing II Index of Case Progress

Table 12.14 defines the items in an index of the SWA's evaluation of the progress in the case that had an internal reliability of .71 as measured by Cronbach's alpha. There were six items in the index with item-criterion correlations as shown in the table, and each dealt with an aspect of case progress. The four types of family structure had essentially the same observed average on this index ($p >$ .25); the four ethnic groups had essentially the same observed average ($p > .50$).

As shown in Table 12.15, the SWAs reported that 65% of the clients still being seen had improved conditions and that only 7% had situations that had become worse. As suggested by the index, there were no major differences in whether the situation had improved among the four ethnic groups.

The SWAs also reported the specific improvements they had seen, and we summarized these improvements by whether they reflected better material circumstances, improved family relations, or improved parent-child relations. Table 12.16 is the tabulation by ethnic group of the areas of improvement that the SWAs reported. Of the 135 families who were the subjects in the Debriefing II interview results, 33% had improved material circumstances since the Debriefing I interview, 22% had improved adult adjustment and family relations, and 16% had improved parent-child relations. There were no significant variations among the four ethnic groups.

The SWAs were optimistic about the prospects for those cases that were still open at Debriefing II. They regarded the prospects as "good" for 47% of the cases and as poor for only 6% of the cases as shown in Table 12.17.

Debriefing II Index of Involvement of Other Family Members

The final index from items in the Debriefing II interview that had relevance for the description of a case's progress is a two-item index that measured the involvement of other family members in the case. The items in this index are shown in Table 12.18, and the index had an internal reliability of .63 as measured by Cronbach's alpha. A family in which the mother was out of the home had other family members more extensively involved in the case compared to a family with the mother alone or mother and father together ($p < .0001$). This difference reflected the definition of the index and was almost tautological. The four ethnic groups had essentially the same average with respect to this index ($p > .10$).

The SWAs' Work Program at Debriefing II

The SWAs reported a considerable amount of information about the involvement of external agencies and their plans for the case that were not summarizable in our index strategy. In this section, we present the major findings from these reports.

Table 12.19 is a tabulation by ethnic group of the problems that the SWA was dealing with at the time of the Debriefing II interview. The patterns were essentially the same for the four ethnic groups. The most common problem being worked on at this stage of the casework was a housing problem (in 36% of the 135 cases open at this time). Financial problems were being worked on in 30% of the cases. Child school problems and child behavioral problems were also commonly worked on. In 10% of the cases, an adult health service need was being worked on, and in 10% a child health need problem was being worked on.

The percentages of cases with a problem being worked on as reported by the SWAs differed considerably from the prevalence rates reported in Table 12.3. For example, the prevalence rate of child health problems was 56%, and the prevalence rate of adult health problems was 54%. These reports suggested that the SWAs had a strategy of focusing on housing and financial problems at the opening stages of the casework.

The SWAs reported that 61% of their clients had recognized all of the problems that they faced while 39% ($n = 53$) had one or more unrecognized problems. There were no significant differences among the four ethnic groups. The vast majority of unrecognized problems were adult problems. As might be expected, among the most commonly occurring unrecognized problems were lack of communication between spouses (seven cases), exhaustion and overwork (six cases), a family member's need for psychotherapy (five cases), and lack of cooperation with LESFU (three cases). The implications of criminal activity were surprisingly common among the unrecognized problems: the release of a spouse from prison was an unrecognized problem in four cases, drinking or drug usage was not recognized in three cases, and a relative placing the client at risk legally in two cases.

Unrecognized child-related problems were less common and less severe. There were five clients who did not recognize that they had poor parenting skills, three with unrecognized mother-child conflicts, one who did not recognize the child's need for summer camp, and one who did not recognize a child's emotional problems.

LESFU was the entry point for social services for 41% of the clients; these clients were not involved with any other agencies. Of the remaining 59%, the most common service being provided prior to LESFU's entry was income or financial. The next most common services were health care and housing as shown in Table 12.20.

In Table 12.21, we enumerate the agencies that the clients had sought out prior to contacting LESFU. Of the 135 clients, 30% had involved agencies that could provide public assistance. These were the New York City Department of Social Services Income Maintenance Program (35 cases) and the Supplemental Security Income Program (five cases). Agencies that provided medical services were involved in 27% of the cases. These were primarily city hospitals—Bellevue for 15 cases and Gouverneur for nine. A smaller number of clients sought out clinics, private hospitals, and private physicians. The educational system was involved in 15% of the cases, primarily the public school system. Only one client had sought out the Committee on the Handicapped for classifying the needs of school children, indicating a lack of awareness of this service among these clients. Six cases involved the Mobilization for Youth program whose legal services were sought, an unusually high utilization pattern. Only 9% of the clients had been involved with the New York City Housing Authority. A surprisingly large 9% of the clients had prior involvement with the justice system, primarily family court (eight cases) and the police (two cases). Four percent of the clients were involved with the foster care system, primarily with Special Services for Children (four cases). A fairly large number of clients were involved with a variety of social work service providers.

The SWAs reported that they had sought out one new agency on behalf of their clients in 26% of the 135 cases still open, two agencies in 29% of the cases, three agencies in 19% of the cases, and four agencies in 10% of the cases. The SWA made no additional contacts for the client in only 16% of the cases. The agencies that the SWAs involved in their cases are categorized in Table 12.22.

The range of additional agencies used shows the importance of the SWA's experience and knowledge of the available systems. The SWAs had sought out additional providers of funds in 41% of the 135 cases still open at the second debriefing. The SWAs were alert to using the food stamp program and Medicaid as sources of support for the clients. They did not report that the clients had used these programs on their own before coming to LESFU. The SWAs had linked 33% of their clients to medical providers. They used private hospitals and clinics for about a third of their referrals compared to the very minor usage that the clients made of the private hospitals on their own initiative. The SWAs referred 28% of their clients to providers of educational services. Many of these referrals were to the Board of Education's Committee on the Handicapped. The clients were aware and made use of the Mobilization for Youth program primarily for legal assistance and advocacy, and the SWAs found only one family that could potentially make use of the program. The SWAs referred 22% of their cases to housing providers. They were aware of the Plaza I Housing Services, an option unknown to the clients. Finally, the SWAs referred 4% of the clients to the foster care system, primarily Special Services for Children.

The SWAs specified their plans about seeking services from additional providers, and their responses are tabulated in Table 12.23. The SWAs had completed their referrals for 48% of the cases still open at the Debriefing II interview. Their future plans focused on therapy in 19% of the cases and on adult education and training in 10% of the cases. The SWAs' policy seems to have been to give priority treatment to child issues, housing, and income and to postpone adult issues until this stage in their casework.

One aspect of the case management approach was the use of a family worker to provide services. In a family emergency, the family worker could be sent into the home to keep the family going. The family workers gave the SWA an opportunity to monitor the performance of the parents in their transactions with their children and thus add to knowledge available for developing future plans for the case. They were also used to help introduce order into family life and provide models of better household management to dysfunctional parents. The time of the family workers also went into escorting clients to service providers, interpreting for them when they could not speak English, engaging in parent education, organizing the households to be better managed, and engaging in child care if the parents were absent from the home on a temporary basis.

Table 12.24 is the cross-tabulation of whether the family worker was involved in a case by the ethnicity of the case. Overall, 39% of the cases received the attention of a family worker. The percentage of black families that had a family worker was smaller, 22%, than the percentage for the other ethnic groups ($p < .05$).

DISCUSSION AND CONCLUSION

In the next chapter we will continue with our presentation of case flow information and focus on the information obtained from the clients in the interviews that took place about a year after the cases opened with 129 subjects.

NOTES

1. Our collaborator in this research effort, Paul Marsters, developed the multiple regression model to allocate the time reported by SWAs on their monthly case reports into the various problem groups. This work is presented in an earlier project report (Finch, S. J., P. Marsters, D. Fanshel, and H. C. Thode. 1986. "Allocation of Reported Time to Tasks Based on Reports Submitted in a Management Information System." Unpublished.).

2. Based upon field observations of a number of research personnel available to Fanshel, there was reason to believe that these staff were relatively demoralized and unmotivated in carrying out their service responsibilities.

Table 12.1
Estimated Distribution of Total SWA Time Investment by Problem Group

Problem Group	Percent
Child Educational and Vocational Training	19.0
Adult Income and Employment	17.7
Adult Family Relations	15.1
Child Health	14.1
Adult Health	10.2
Family Housing and Environment	9.4
Child Social Relations	6.7
Child Family Relations	4.6
Adult Social Relations	2.7
Child Life Skills	0.5
Total	100.0

Figure 12.1
Highest Level Case Reaches within Service Model; Frequency Count by Stage and Percentage Reaching Stage or Higher

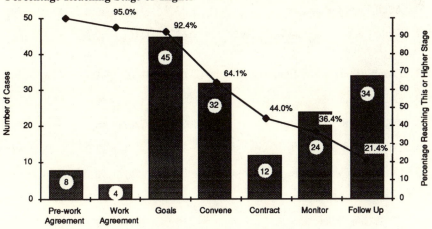

Note: N=159 cases; one case with data about model stage missing.

Table 12.2
Analysis of Variance Results: Reported Resolution Ratio by Highest Stage of LESFU Model Reached

	Stage Highest Level of Model	Mean Ratio	Std Dev Ratio	Number of Cases
1	Pre-Work Agreement	.28	.80	8
2	Work Agreement	.21	.30	4
3	Goals	.93	.75	45
4	Convene	.89	.74	32
5	Contract	1.28	.56	12
6	Monitor	1.04	.76	24
7	Follow-Up	1.10	.84	34
	Total	.95	.77	159

Analysis of Variance Table

Source	D.F.	Mean Square	F	Significance
Between Levels	6	1.367	2.374	.0320
Within Levels	152	.576		

Table 12.3
Prevalence, Resolution, and Referral Rates by Problem Group ($N = 160$)

	Problem Group	Prevalence Rate %	(N)	Res Rate	Referral %	(N)
2	Adult Income and Employment	74.3	(119)	56.7	65.5	(78)
0	Adult Family Relations	73.7	(118)	40.8	27.9	(33)
7	Child Educational and Vocational Training	68.7	(110)	49.2	61.8	(68)
3	Family Housing and Environment	68.7	(110)	36.6	41.8	(46)
9	Child Health	56.2	(90)	36.1	51.1	(46)
4	Adult Health	53.7	(86)	36.1	59.3	(51)
6	Child Social Relations	36.8	(59)	32.0	30.5	(18)
5	Child Family Relations	36.2	(58)	36.1	22.4	(13)
1	Adult Social Relations	31.2	(50)	25.0	14.0	(7)
8	Child Life Skills	16.8	(27)	30.3	11.1	(3)

Note: Numbers to the left of the specified problem groups are the codes used in the information system.

Table 12.4
Information at Case Closing: Nature of Closing, by Ethnicity

	Hispanic [96]	Chinese [29]	Black [23]	White, Other [12]	Total [160]
			(percent)		
Closing was planned or anticipated	49.5	62.1	47.8	41.7	50.9
Closing was unplanned	35.8	20.7	30.4	25.0	31.4
Closed by public agency	2.1	3.4	13.0	16.7	5.0
Closed, family no longer eligible for service*	8.4	6.9	8.7	16.7	8.8
Case still active	4.2	6.9	--	--	3.8

*Of the 14 cases closed where service was interrupted, there were eight where the family moved from the area served by the agency and thus were no longer eligible for service. There were three children where changes in custody resulted in the children not being considered at risk. One case involved movement from the area and change in custody. Two cases were considered no longer at risk because of changes in the circumstances facing the families.

Table 12.5
Source of Termination of Case, by Ethnicity*

	Hispanic [91]	Chinese [27]	Black [23]	White, Other [11]	Total [152]
			(percent)		
Mutual decision of client and worker	53.8	74.1	39.1	18.2	52.6
Client is source of termination	31.9	18.5	30.4	45.5	30.3
Other (client moved, etc.)	14.3	7.4	30.4	36.4	17.1

*Six active cases are not included in this table. Two cases are omitted because information is lacking.

Table 12.6
Status Information and Problems Identified at Case Closing, by Ethnicity

	Hispanic No.	%	Chinese No.	%	Black No.	%	White, Other No.	%	Total No.	%
Service completed	46	47.9	21	72.9	13	56.6	5	41.7	85	53.1
Client unwilling to continue	38	39.6	11	37.9	9	39.1	5	41.7	63	39.4
Client resistant	25	26.0	7	24.1	5	21.7	4	33.3	41	25.6
Attempt to induce client to continue	22	22.9	4	13.8	6	26.1	3	25.0	35	21.9
Closed because client moved	22	22.9	4	13.8	4	17.4	2	16.7	32	20.0
Total	96	100.0	29	100.0	23	100.0	12	100.0	160	100.0

Table 12.7
Debriefing I: Index of Agency Services Required by Clients

Item	Item-Total Correlation
A. Family requires services of a second agency? (no/yes)	.63
B. Family requires services of a third agency? (no/yes)	.52
C. Family requires services of a first external agency? (no/yes)	.35
Cronbach alpha coefficient = .67	

Table 12.8
Summary Information on Problems Clients Most Frequently Identified as Being of Concern at Case Opening ($N = 160$)

Problem	Frequency	Percent
Housing	74	46.3
Parental performance failure	43	26.9
Adult need for service	42	26.3
Child behavior and adjustment	41	25.6
Financial problems, concrete	41	25.6
Family relationship problems	40	25.0
Child school problem	28	17.5
Child care needs	26	16.3
Adult physical health problem	23	14.4
Adult behavior and adjustment	21	13.1
Child physical health problem	17	10.6

Table 12.9
What Did Client Expect LESFU to Do?

	Frequency	Percent
ADVOCACY FOR CLIENTS IN SPECIFIC AREAS	93	58.1
Public assistance	16	10.0
Housing	15	9.4
School, Commission on Handicap	10	6.3
Public assistance and housing	9	5.6
Public assistance, housing and other	6	3.8
Advocate among agencies	5	3.1
Legal	4	2.5
Housing, legal and emotional support	3	1.9
Public assist, housing and child care	2	1.3
Public assist, emotional support and homemaker	2	1.3
Public assistance and other	2	1.3
Public assist, housing and school	1	.6
Public assist, housing and parent training	1	.6
Public assist and school system	1	.6
Public assist and child care	1	.6
Public assistance and parental responsibility	1	.6
Housing, school and child behavior	1	.6
Medicaid	1	.6
Medicaid and entitlement benefits	1	.6
Medicaid, homemaker, child care	1	.6
Medicaid and education and training	1	.6
Medicaid and day care	1	.6
Employment, health and housing	1	.6
PA, housing, alcohol, school	1	.6
Child care and psychiatric treatment	1	.6
Housing, employment and training, child care	1	.6
PA, training, child return from foster care	1	.6
School and child care	1	.6
Housing and other	2	1.3

(Continued)

Table 12.9
(Continued)

	Frequency	Percent
HOMEMAKER AND CHILD CARE ASSISTANCE	16	10.0
Finding child care	8	5.0
Parenting responsibilities	5	3.1
Parenting responsibilities and homemaking	2	1.3
Parenting responsibilities and employment	1	.6
Provide homemaker	4	2.5
TRADITIONAL SOCIAL WORK FUNCTIONS OTHER THAN FOSTER CARE	15	9.4
Help change child's behavior	9	5.6
Coordinate family therapy	3	1.9
Help with consumer services	2	1.3
Help secure vocational training	1	.6
EMOTIONAL SUPPORT	12	7.5
Provide emotional support	6	3.8
Emotional support and employment	1	.6
Emotional support and legal advice	3	1.9
Emotional support and child support	1	.6
Emotional support and language/cultural	1	.6
FOSTER CARE SYSTEM	7	4.4
Secure foster care placement of child	5	3.1
Secure return of child from foster care	2	1.3
OTHER	8	5.0
Language interpretation, cultural understanding	5	3.1
Escort client to service provider	1	.6
Other	2	1.3
NONE	5	3.1
Total	160	100.0

Table 12.10
Debriefing II: Index of Current Level of Case Activity

Item	Item-Total Correlation
A. How active is the case? (active/somewhat/not at all)	.50
B. Has frequency of contact changed? (increased/stayed the same/decreased)	.36
C. Is LESFU family worker participating? (no/yes)	.27
Cronbach alpha coefficient = .53	

Table 12.11
Level of Activity of Case at Time of Debriefing II, by Ethnicity

	Hispanic No.	Hispanic %	Chinese No.	Chinese %	Black No.	Black %	White, Other No.	White, Other %	Total No.	Total %
Active	39	50.0	9	32.1	9	50.0	5	45.5	62	45.9
Somewhat active	23	29.5	15	53.6	5	27.8	3	27.3	46	34.1
Hardly active	16	20.5	2	7.1	4	16.7	2	18.2	24	17.8
Not at all active			2	7.1			1	9.1	3	2.2
Total	78	100.0	28	100.0	18	100.0	11	100.0	135	100.0

Table 12.12
Changes in Frequency of Contact, by Ethnicity

| | Hispanic | | Chinese | | Black | | White, Other | | Total | |
	No.	%	No.	%	No.	%	No.	%	No.	%
Increased	12	15.4	3	10.7	3	16.7	2	18.2	20	14.8
Stayed the same	44	56.4	13	46.4	7	38.9	6	54.5	70	51.9
Decreased	22	28.2	12	42.9	8	44.4	3	27.3	45	33.3
Total	78	100.0	28	100.0	18	100.0	11	100.0	135	100.0

Table 12.13
Debriefing II: Reasons for Changes in Frequency of Contact

	Frequency	Percent
Reasons for Decrease:		
Does not apply, no change	70	51.9
PROBLEM SOLVED OR PROGRESS MADE	20	14.8
Problems solved, goals have been met	11	8.1
Problems stabilized, being monitored only	4	3.0
Problems experienced as less intense	3	2.2
Child returned from foster care	1	.7
Client problems stabilized and child returned	1	.7
TEMPORARY ABATEMENT	3	2.2
School vacation, problem subsided	1	.7
Child in camp, problem subsided	1	.7
Client moved and school recess lessens problem	1	.7
CLIENT RESISTANCE, HOSTILITY, OR OPPOSITION	22	16.3
Client resists involvement	5	3.7
Parents not available (e.g., out of country)	2	1.5
Client sees LESFU's services as limited	2	1.5
Client lacks motivation	2	1.5
Client not satisfied with service	1	.7
Client working, not satisfied with service	1	.7
Client relocated out of catchment area	1	.7
Client resists involvement and now out of country	1	.7
Client language different from worker, fear	1	.7
Client prefers own solutions to problems	1	.7
Client more independent, can make it on own	1	.7
Client is busy working	1	.7
Parent at home, babysitting	1	.7
Some resolution but client moved from area	1	.7
Some goals met, client resists further work	1	.7
Reasons for Increase:		
GREATER CLIENT NEED OR MOTIVATION	14	10.4
Client's problems became more urgent	4	3.0
Client more motivated to see SWA for advice	4	3.0
Client trust leads to keeping appointments	2	1.5
Services from provider being arranged	1	.7
New problems emerged, more time required	1	.7
Client in need of increased advocacy effort	1	.7
More family members became involved	1	.7
GREATER LESFU COMMITMENT	4	3.0
More counseling time offered client	2	1.5
SWA has more time for the case	1	.7
More effort needed to overcome low motivation	1	.7
Other reasons	3	2.2

Table 12.14
Debriefing II: Index of Case Progress

Item	Item-Total Correlation
A. Number of problems solved? (five or more/none)	.66
B. Has the situation improved? (has improved/same/worse)	.49
C. Changes taken place since case opening? (yes/no)	.47
D. Improvement in material resources? (no change/better)	.47
E. Social service agency involved with client? (no/yes)	.34
F. Prospects for the case? (good/mixed/poor)	.28
Cronbach alpha coefficient = .71	

Table 12.15
Debriefing II: Estimate as to Whether Family Situation Has Improved, by Ethnicity

	Hispanic No.	%	Chinese No.	%	Black No.	%	White, Other No.	%	Total No.	%
Has improved	51	65.4	20	71.4	11	61.1	6	54.5	88	65.2
Essentially the same	21	26.9	6	21.4	7	38.9	4	36.4	38	28.1
Has become worse	6	7.7	2	7.1			1	9.1	9	6.7
Total	78	100.0	28	100.0	18	100.0	11	100.0	135	100.0

Table 12.16
Changes Reported in Family Situation, by Ethnicity

	Hispanic No.	Hispanic %	Chinese No.	Chinese %	Black No.	Black %	White, Other No.	White, Other %	Total No.	Total %
Better material circumstances	29	37.2	6	21.4	5	27.8	5	45.5	45	33.3
Improved adult adjustment and family relations	18	23.1	7	25.0	3	16.7	1	9.1	29	21.5
Improved parent and child relations	15	19.2	4	14.3	2	11.1	1	9.1	22	16.3

Note: Each row shows the proportion of clients where the social work associate identified the designated area as having improved.

Table 12.17
Debriefing II: Prospects for the Case, by Ethnicity*

	Hispanic No.	Hispanic %	Chinese No.	Chinese %	Black No.	Black %	White, Other No.	White, Other %	Total No.	Total %
Good prospects	35	44.9	17	60.7	8	44.4	4	36.4	64	47.4
Mixed prospects	39	50.0	9	32.1	9	50.0	6	54.5	63	46.7
Poor prospects	4	5.1	2	7.1	1	5.6	1	9.1	8	5.9
Total	78	100.0	28	100.0	18	100.0	11	100.0	135	100.0

*Question posed to the social work associate:
In your judgment, what are the prospects for helping this family resolve its major problems as you see the overall situation?

Table 12.18
Debriefing II: Index of Case Involvement of Other Family Members

Item	Item-Total Correlation
A. Other family members seen? (no/yes)	.46
B. Caretaker of children at Time II? (mother and father/ mother/other family member)	.46
Cronbach alpha coefficient = .63	

Table 12.19
Problems Occupying Attention of Social Work Associate at Debriefing II, by Ethnicity

	Hispanic No.	%	Chinese No.	%	Black No.	%	White, Other No.	%	Total No.	%
Housing problem	29	37.2	5	17.9	9	50.0	5	45.5	48	35.6
Financial problem	26	33.3	7	25.0	4	22.2	3	27.3	40	29.6
Child school problem	23	29.5	6	21.4	3	16.7	3	27.3	35	25.9
Child behavior problem	16	20.5	2	7.1	5	27.8	1	9.1	24	17.8
Adult service need	15	19.2	3	10.7			4	36.4	22	16.3
Adult adjust- ment problem	12	15.4	2	7.1	3	16.7	2	18.2	19	14.1
Family relation problem	10	12.8	3	10.7	5	27.8			18	13.3
Parenting problem	10	12.8	3	10.7	3	16.7	1	9.1	17	12.6
Adult health service need	8	10.3	1	3.6			4	36.4	13	9.6
Child health service	3	3.8	7	25.0	1	5.6	2	18.2	13	9.6

Table 12.20
Services Provided by Providers Not Brought in by LESFU

	Frequency	Percent
Not applicable	54	40.8
Income, financial aid	41	30.4
Health care	24	17.8
Housing	16	11.9
Child care	10	7.4
Meet child's educational needs	7	5.2
Pre- and postnatal health care	7	5.2
Therapy, counseling for adults	5	3.7
Legal assistance	5	3.7
Placement of child	5	3.7
Family therapy	4	3.0
Therapy, counseling for children	4	3.0
Law enforcement	2	1.5
Medical evaluation	2	1.5
Psychiatric evaluation	2	1.5
Instruction in English	1	.7
Employment	1	.7
Home attendant	1	.7
Adult educational need	1	.7
Other	12	8.9

Note: Multiple responses cause percentages to total more than 100%.

Table 12.21
Service Providers Not Brought in by LESFU*

	Frequency	Percent
Not applicable	54	40.8
PROVIDERS TO GET ACCESS TO PUBLIC FUNDS	41	30.4
NYC Income Maintenance Program	35	25.9
Supplemental Security Income (SSI)	5	3.7
Veterans Administration	1	.7
MEDICAL PROVIDERS	37	27.4
Bellevue Hospital	15	11.1
Gouverneur Hospital	9	6.7
Other hospital	5	3.7
Nina Clinic	3	2.2
Beth Israel Hospital	2	1.5
Private physician	2	1.5
St. Vincent's Hospital	1	.7
SCHOOLING AND EDUCATION	20	14.8
Public school	10	7.4
Mobilization for Youth	6	4.4
Educational Alliance	3	2.2
Board of Education, Committee on the Handicapped	1	.7
HOUSING PROVIDERS	12	8.9
NYC Housing Authority	12	8.9
JUSTICE SYSTEM	12	8.9
Family Court	8	5.9
NYC Police Department	2	1.5
U.S. Department of Probation	1	.7
Private lawyer	1	.7
FOSTER CARE SYSTEM	5	3.7
NYC Special Services for Children	4	3.0
New York Foundling Hospital	1	.7
OTHERS		
University Settlement House	2	1.5
Other governmental agency	2	1.5
Day care center	2	1.5
Grand Street Settlement House	1	.7
Its Time	1	.7
Boys Club of New York	1	.7
Employees Union	1	.7
General social services	1	.7
Chinatown Planning Council	1	.7
University Family Counseling	1	.7
Not specified	2	1.5
Other	9	6.7

*Question posed to the social work associates:
Are there service providers in the picture other than those sought out by LESFU?

Table 12.22
Service Providers Sought Out by LESFU and Currently Involved with Family

	Frequency	Percent
Does not apply, no provider cited	22	16.3
PROVIDERS TO GET ACCESS TO PUBLIC FUNDS	55	40.7
NYC Income Maintenance Program	37	27.4
Food Stamp Program	6	4.4
Medicaid	5	3.7
Supplemental Security Income (SSI)	5	3.7
Tap Center	2	1.5
MEDICAL PROVIDERS	44	32.6
Bellevue Hospital	18	13.3
Beth Israel Hospital	11	8.1
Gouverneur Hospital	6	4.4
Other hospital	2	1.5
Physician (private practice)	2	1.5
St. Vincent's Hospital	2	1.5
Dunlap Psychiatric Clinic	1	.7
Health clinic, public	1	.7
Nina Clinic	1	.7
SCHOOLING AND EDUCATION	38	28.1
Neighborhood public school	20	14.8
Board of Education, Committee on the Handicapped	15	11.1
Educational Alliance	3	2.2
Mobilization for Youth	1	.7
HOUSING PROVIDERS	29	21.5
NYC Housing Authority	24	17.8
Plaza I Housing Services	5	3.7
JUSTICE SYSTEM	7	5.2
Family Court	6	4.4
Legal Aid Society	1	.7
FOSTER CARE SYSTEM	6	4.4
NYC Special Services for Children	4	3.0
Euphrasian House	1	.7
New York Foundling Hospital	1	.7

(continued)

Table 12.22

(Continued)

	Frequency	Percent
OTHERS		
Day care center	10	7.4
University Settlement House	6	4.4
Other governmental agency	5	3.7
Action for Progress	2	1.5
Employment, vocational agency	2	1.5
General social services	2	1.5
Hamilton-Madison House	2	1.5
Its Time	2	1.5
Pueblo Nuevo	2	1.5
Save Summer Youth Program	2	1.5
Ackerman Family Institute	1	.7
Chinatown Planning Council	1	.7
Concilio P.R.	1	.7
Grand Street Settlement House	1	.7
Henry Street Settlement House	1	.7
Immigrant social service agency	1	.7
Kennedy Child Study Center	1	.7
Lower East Side Service Center	1	.7
Planned Parenthood	1	.7
Solidarida Humana	1	.7
Other	17	12.6

Note: Based on 135 cases. Multiple responses cause percentages to total more than 100%.

Table 12.23
Services to Be Sought from Other Service Providers in the Future*

	Frequency	Percent
Not applicable	65	48.1
Family therapy	14	10.4
Adult education, vocational training	14	10.4
Therapy, counseling for parents	12	8.9
Child care	10	7.4
Housing	9	6.7
Employment	6	4.4
Meet child's educational needs	6	4.4
Placement of child	5	3.7
Home attendant	4	3.8
Therapy, counseling for children	4	3.0
Psychiatric evaluation	3	2.2
Training in parenting skills	3	2.2
English instruction	2	1.5
Financial aid	2	1.5
Health care	2	1.5
Legal assistance	1	.7
Uncertain	1	.7
Other	9	6.7

*Question posed to social work associate:
Do you expect to seek the involvement of other providers in the foreseeable future? For what services?

Table 12.24
Participation of LESFU Family Worker, by Ethnicity

	Hispanic		Chinese		Black		White, Other		Total	
	No.	%	No.	%	No.	%	No.	%	No.	%
Not participating	44	56.4	19	67.9	14	77.8	5	45.5	82	60.7
Yes, participating	34	43.6	9	32.1	4	22.2	6	54.5	53	39.3
Total	78	100.0	28	100.0	18	100.0	11	100.0	135	100.0

The LESFU Model and Case Flow Patterns: Client Interview and Factor Analysis Results

The client interview and factor analysis results of the LESFU model and the progression of work on cases are the subject of this chapter. The client interview results are especially important because the information came from the most involved actor in the service encounter. Because the interviews with the clients were held about a year after the cases were opened at LESFU, the information secured represented a more solid portrayal of the culmination of the service effort, especially as related to the results achieved in solving the client family's problems. This contrasted with the two debriefing interviews with the SWAs which covered the early developments in the cases.

CLIENT INTERVIEW RESULTS (C)

Overall, 64% of the clients said that their approach to LESFU for assistance represented a time of major crisis in their lives. Another 23% said that it was a moderately troubled time, while only 12% said that it was a time of usual troubles. There were no differences among the four ethnic groups with respect to the reported extent of troubles.

There was a positive reaction to the agency: 65% of those interviewed had very positive things to say, 26% were somewhat positive, and 8% were not at all positive. The overwhelming majority of clients reported that their expectations for service had been met: 59% said very much, 25% some, and 13% not at all. There was only a small fraction of clients interviewed who had negative opinions to express about LESFU: 5% of the clients were very negative, 15% somewhat negative, and 77% not at all negative.

Index of the Client's Evaluation of LESFU

Based upon the factor analysis of all the items from the client interview, we extracted an index measuring the client's evaluation of LESFU that was based on the 16 items shown in Table 13.1. The internal reliability of this index as measured by Cronbach's alpha was .88. The index was a measure of client satisfaction because it was focused on the overall image of the agency developed by the client as opposed to exclusively a case outcome measure. The four types of family structures had the same level of client satisfaction with LESFU as measured by this index ($p > .25$). Chinese and Hispanic families were somewhat more satisfied with LESFU than black and mixed families ($.05 < p < .10$).

Families that were at high risk of placement of their children in foster care, as identified in the Debriefing I interview, tended to be positive in their evaluation of LESFU ($p < .05$). Cases with a greater degree of case activity and with SWAs in greater contact with each other, as measured by a Debriefing II index, tended to involve clients who felt more positively about the agency ($p < .05$). There were indications in various areas of the client interview of correlates of a more positive evaluation of LESFU. For example, clients who had more extensive contacts with other staff members at LESFU were more positive in their view of the agency ($p < .05$). Clients who saw the risk of placement of their children gave more positive evaluations ($p < .05$). Clients who received the services of a LESFU family worker coming into their homes and participating in a variety of home-based services were more positive in evaluating the agency ($p < .01$).

Cases that remained open for longer periods with LESFU, as reported in the monthly reports of staff submitted to the agency's management information system, received more positive evaluations ($p < .05$). Cases in which the closing of cases was based upon service goals being accomplished, coded as service completed, involved clients who felt more positive about the agency ($p < .01$). Clients who were coded in the case closing research review as being unwilling to continue working with the agency were negatively oriented in their agency evaluations ($p < .05$).

There were two associations found in a multiple regression analysis of this measure of client satisfaction with LESFU using the Debriefing I and Debriefing II variables as predictors. Together these two associations explained 14% of the variance of this index of client satisfaction ($p < .001$). A case in which the SWA reported adult adjustment problems as an area being worked on at the Debriefing II interview had a higher evaluation of LESFU on average ($p < .01$). A case in which the SWA indicated at the Debriefing I interview an intention of involving other agencies in the case was one that had a better evaluation of LESFU on average ($p < .01$).

The clients reported considerable improvement in their problems, and many credited LESFU. In earlier chapters we have documented clients' reports of specific improvements in their lives in a variety of problem areas that were the focus of service activity. As a summary, Table 13.2 contains a tabulation of the clients' reports about whether their problems were better and whether the clients thought that LESFU had been a source of help by problem type. The most prevalent type of problem reported by the clients was an income problem. The prevalence and rate of reported improvement were roughly consistent with the statistics based upon the reports of the SWAs reported in Table 12.3. For income problems, 72% of the clients reported an improvement, and 65% of those with improved incomes credited LESFU as a source of help. The client reports on housing were consistent with the MIS reports as well.

The third most prevalent problem that the clients reported was in the area of a need for resources or other help in the parenting role. This problem area had a high rate of improvement, and 62% of the clients with improvements credited LESFU as a source of help. Child school problems and child behavioral problems were the next most prevalent. More than half of the clients regarded LESFU as a source of help in dealing with these problems. LESFU was equally effective in dealing with problems of family relations and adult behavioral problems. The clients were less likely to report positive changes relative to adult education and training needs; LESFU was regarded as a source of help in 31% of those who reported improvements.

The prevalence rate of health problems reported by the clients was much less than that reported in the MIS in Table 12.3. The rates of reported improvement were consistent with the rates of reported resolution.

Of the 129 clients interviewed, 58% ($n = 75$) reported that LESFU's help was a factor responsible for improvement in their condition, and 3% reported a deterioration in their situation with LESFU offering no help. It was of interest to find that two-thirds of the clients felt it important to have an agency serve them where they could speak their own language and find understanding of their culture. This was especially strong among the Chinese clients and quite strong for the Hispanic clients.

Index of the Client's Receiving Services from Other Agencies

Our index construction strategy extracted a three-item index defined in Table 13.3 that measured the extent to which a client family was receiving services from other agencies. The internal reliability of this index as measured by Cronbach's alpha was .87. There were no differences among the four family types with respect to the average of this index ($p > .50$). Chinese and mixed-race families received less service from other agencies than did Hispanic and black families ($p < .05$).

We used this index as an outcome measure—that is, a dependent variable—in a multiple regression analysis with the indexes constructed from the two debriefing interviews as independent variables. This analysis found four associations that together accounted for 36% of the variation in the index of use of other social services ($p < .0001$).

A case with family problems identified by the SWA in the Debriefing I interview was more extensively involved with other agencies as measured by this client interview–based index ($p < .0001$). The correlation coefficient between these two measures was .39, representing a strong association. A case with child health problems identified by the SWA at the Debriefing I interview was more extensively involved with other agencies ($p < .001$). A case in which the SWA reported a higher risk of placement of children had greater involvement with external agencies as measured by this index ($p < .001$). A case that the SWA reported as receiving services from health care providers at the Debriefing II interview was more extensively involved with external agencies ($p < .01$).

The associations of involvement with the external agency and the SWA's report of health problems were natural and expected associations. The strength of the association between the SWA's report of family problems in the Debriefing I interview and involvement with other agencies could be hypothesized as the result of a casework program to get external resources involved. Similarly, the association between the risk of placement as reported by the SWA and the involvement with external agencies could have been confirmation of the LESFU staff's being attentive to the mission of child welfare preventive services to exert maximum effort to prevent the placement of children in foster care.

The extent of involvement reported by the clients with other agencies was noteworthy. Of those interviewed, 61% had made at least one connection with a service provider on their own, and some reported two and even three such connections. Altogether, 128 such service connections were accounted for. By and large, these received positive evaluations: 47% of clients responded that these agencies were very helpful, 85% that they were helpful or better, and 89% that they were somewhat helpful or better. Only 6% categorized them negatively as unhelpful or inadequate.

Services being received included income maintenance, family therapy, health care, child care, and housing. Specifically, 32% reported being involved with the New York City Department of Social Services for income maintenance benefits, 18% reported ongoing involvements with hospitals or other health service providers, and 14% had relationships with ethnically oriented agencies such as the Chinatown Planning Council; Praca, an agency serving Puerto Rican families in the main; and settlement houses. Surprisingly, only 5% ($n = 7$) of the clients reported contact with the New York City Housing Authority. At the time of the client interview, 20% of the clients were involved with the same service providers as at case opening with LESFU, and 12% were still involved with a second provider.

A majority of the interviewees (51%) said that one or more referrals to external agencies had been made by the SWAs. For the 66 cases involving a referral, 38% were made on the initiative of the SWA, 26% were made on the initiative of the client, and 26% were based upon the mutual exploration of the client and the SWA. Three cases (5%) involved the suggestion of a family member and two cases (3%) involved the recommendation of another agency, with the SWA picking up on the suggestion for both types of initiative. Two cases (3%) involved a referral to an agency with which the client was familiar for a different kind of service.

In 74% of the cases, the client said that the SWA had made a call to the agency or program from which service was desired to obtain information and to help clear the way for the client to obtain service. In 44% of the referrals, a letter was sent on behalf of the client. In 33% of the referrals, the SWA arranged for the client to meet a representative of the agency; in 50% of the referrals, the SWA accompanied the client to the agency, sometimes with an appointment and sometimes without one. Some clients described assistance received in filling out applications or described the SWA helping with the application through language interpretation.

Services sought included therapy or counseling (23% of 66 referrals), financial aid (21%), child care (15%), housing (12%), health care (8%), psychiatric evaluation (8%), legal services (6%), and the placement of a child (5%). In 65% of the cases, the clients reported that they had received the services for which the referral had been made. In 11% of the cases, additional services were received as well. Some clients (8%) had filed applications and were still awaiting service. On the negative side, 15% had not followed through on the referral so that nothing happened; 12% of the clients did not receive the services hoped for; and 8% ($n = 5$) complained of being discouraged by the service provider.

Eight clients (6% of those interviewed) reported that they and the SWA had agreed that a service was needed, but the referral was not made. The clients felt that responsibility for this was about equally divided between the client's failure to follow through on a task and the SWA's lack of effort.

The clients were able to evaluate 55 of the service providers to which they were referred by LESFU. They were quite positive in their estimates of the responsiveness of the service organizations: 58% were seen as very responsive, 29% as somewhat responsive, 2% as somewhat unresponsive, and 11% as not at all responsive.

Table 13.4 is a tabulation of the clients' opinions of the worth of the services provided by agencies to which they had been referred by the SWA. Overall, 18% of the clients rated these services as excellent, and 52% rated them as good or better. Only 17% rated the services as not so good or worse.

Index of Frequency of Reported Contact with LESFU SWA

We extracted a three-item index that measured the frequency of reported contact of the client with the LESFU SWA. This index is defined in Table 13.5 and had an internal reliability of .59 as measured by Cronbach's alpha. The frequency of reported contact with LESFU staff was the same on average for the four types of families ($p > .05$) and for the four ethnic groups ($p > .50$).

We ran a multiple regression analysis with this index as the dependent variable and the indexes from the Debriefing I and Debriefing II interviews as the independent variables. This analysis found two significant associations that together explained 20% of the variation in the index of client contact ($p < .001$). A client with a greater extent of mother motivation as perceived by the SWA in the Debriefing I interview had more contact with the SWA as measured by this index ($p < .001$). A client whose housing problems were occupying the attention of the SWA at the Debriefing II interview spent more time with the SWA as measured by this index ($p < .001$). Our hypothesis is that families beset by housing problems had more formal service involvements with the agency.

Index of Involvement of the Spouse

An index that measured the involvement of the spouse is shown in Table 13.7. The index was based on eight items and had an internal reliability of .80 as measured by Cronbach's alpha. As would be expected, a family with both mother and father together had a much greater degree of spousal contact than a family missing one of the partners ($p < .0001$). Since Chinese families had both a father and mother more frequently than other ethnic groups, Chinese families had a greater extent of spousal involvement as measured by this index ($p < .0001$).

We ran a multiple regression analysis using the index of spousal involvement as the dependent variable and the indexes from the Debriefing I and Debriefing II interviews as independent variables. This analysis found five significant associations that together explained 61% of the variance of the client interview–based index of spousal involvement.

The first three associations verified the consistency of the client report of spousal involvement and the SWA's report in the Debriefing II interview. A family in which the SWA reported working with the father in the Debriefing II interview had more extensive spousal contact ($p < .0001$). The correlation between these two measures was .66 and was evidence of strong agreement between client and SWA on what had transpired in the service transactions in the area measured by the index. A family in which the SWA reported working with the mother in the Debriefing II interview had a more extensive level of spousal contact ($p < .0001$). That is, husbands and wives tended to be jointly involved in cases where spouses were seen. The third association was that a family in which the SWA reported a high degree of father motivation in the Debriefing II interview had a higher degree of spousal contact as derived from the client interview ($p < .0001$).

The last two associations had more substantive interest. A family that was in need of child care as reported by the SWA in the Debriefing I interview had less involvement of spouses as measured by this index ($p < .001$). We hypothesize that the causal direction is the reverse: the lack of involvement of the spouse causes a greater need for child care. A family with a lesser need of housing as measured by the index of housing need in the Debriefing II interview had greater involvement of the spouse ($p < .001$). Our hypothesized relation is that families with greater spousal involvement had greater financial resources on average, resulting in the ability to purchase better housing.

FACTOR ANALYSIS (FA)

We identified two of the factors in the 14-factor solution that largely dealt with case flow issues and will be discussed below.

Evaluation of LESFU

The fifth factor in the 14-factor solution is displayed in Table 13.7 and focused on whether LESFU's service was completed and on the client's evaluation of LESFU. The SWA's report in the case closing information that service was completed had the loading with highest magnitude (loading = 0.68), and the report that the case was closed because the client was unwilling to continue had the next highest loading (−0.62). The implied negative association between these two variables was virtually tautological. The latent variable implied by the variables with the two largest loadings was that of a client completing service on one end of the variable and a client unwilling to continue at the other end.

The variables with the next highest loadings were the indirectly standardized ratio of problems reported resolved from the MIS information (0.51) and the number of problems the SWA reported resolved in the MIS (0.51). There was a strong implied positive association between whether a case was closed because the work was complete and the MIS-derived index of case success. The implied positive association between whether a case was closed because the service was completed and the number of problems reported resolved was supporting documentation of the validity of the two measures.

The next variable by order of magnitude of loading was the index of the client's evaluation of LESFU (−0.49). This index was defined so that a lower score indicated a more positive evaluation of LESFU. The loadings in the factor implied a strong association between whether the case was closed because service was completed and whether the client had a positive evaluation of LESFU. There was also an implied positive association between whether the client had a positive view of LESFU and the extent to which the SWA reported more problems resolved than were expected based on the experience of the agency. These positive associations supported the view that the client's evaluation of LESFU reflected the worth of the LESFU services to the client, that the SWA's report on the reasons for the case's closing were correlated with the client's evaluation of the services and the SWA's ongoing report of case progress made in the MIS forms, and that the indirectly standardized ratio of the problems reported resolved had validity as a measure of case success. Consequently, the client's evaluation of LESFU, the indirectly standardized ratio of the number of problems reported resolved, and the SWA's report that the case was closed because service was completed were measures of the success of the case work.

There were two variables from the Debriefing I interview whose loadings were next largest. The SWA's report that the client required services from other social agencies (.48) was positively associated with the three measures of case success. Similarly, there was a positive association between the SWA's report in the

Debriefing I interview that the client had child care needs (.45) and these measures of casework success. These two sets of associations were consistent with the SWA's being effective at serving clients who needed coordination of social services and who had child care problems.

As shown by their smaller loadings, there were less strong positive associations between the length of time that a case was opened (.38), the SWA's report of case progress in the Debriefing II interview (−.31), the SWA's report of the amount of time spent on the case (.27), and the index of the client's contact with the SWA (−.26). These smaller associations suggested that simply increasing the amount of time devoted to a case had a relatively small positive association with the three measures of case success.

Finally, there were relatively small associations between the three measures of case success and the SWA's report in the Debriefing II interview of a focus on child health needs (−.38), the client's report that the SWA saw the children in the family (−.26), and the SWA's Debriefing I report that other agencies were involved (.25).

Despite the reputation of the service arena as being chaotic and unknowable, these results had a clear and easily interpretable theme across the five data sets and the participants in the service process. The report of the client in a special interview was consistent with the reports of the SWA made in two interviews, in the ongoing MIS reporting, and in the case closing report. The consistency of these findings suggested that it would be possible to track the clients of child welfare agencies offering preventive services.

Client Searching for Solutions

The second factor is displayed in Table 13.8 and was the 11th factor in the 14-factor solution. The general theme of the factor was that a case with long-standing problems tended to be characterized by the more difficult problems. The variables with the two largest loadings were the client's report of trying to work with another agency (−.69) and the client's report of trying to solve the problem before (.68). The conflicting signs suggest a latent variable measuring the extent to which a client had extensive problems and would not seek help when the problems proved hard to solve. The next largest loading (.42) was on whether another agency was in the picture.

Such a client had a child with a lower risk of placement as reported by the SWA at Debriefing I (−.38), was less satisfied with life based on the index of the client's responses (−.38), and had a child with more extensive behavioral problems (−.37). Such a client had fewer problems reported resolved (−.27).

SUMMARY COMMENTS FOR CHAPTERS 12 AND 13

The overall client evaluation of LESFU was quite positive: 65% of those interviewed had positive comments about LESFU, and 59% said that their expectations had been met. The clients also confirmed the improvements reported by the SWAs.

Only about half of the cases (51%) had planned closings suggesting that many clients could not sustain an extended contact with this kind of service. Some of the case closings were due to the fact that clients resolved their housing problems and moved out of the area or their cases were closed because the public child welfare agency decided the client families were not eligible for preventive child welfare services. The proportions of continuers and noncontinuers reflected statistics going back several decades from the experience of clients of family service agencies: many simply did not sign up "for the duration" but rather sought immediate surcease to problems that had arisen. One in four clients in our study was characterized by their SWAs as being resistant to ongoing involvement in service. It was an achievement that service was successfully completed in 53% of the cases.

Many clients (61%)were involved with service providers before making contact with LESFU, and there was considerable referral activity engaged in by LESFU staff. The numbers and kinds of service providers involved in the cases covered many types of needs. The LESFU SWAs reported high rates of referral and ongoing involvement of their clients with the agencies referred to.

By and large, there was marked agreement between what the SWAs reported in the debriefing interviews and the self-reports of the clients in research interviews. All of this bodes well for future research in this field and for using research to make knowledge available for social policy analysts and those concerned with direct practice. The challenges inherent in the use of survey procedures to secure information from a client population with limited education is well recognized.[1] The emergence in this study of a strong evaluative measure with obvious coherence of content raises hope that, in research with clients living in poverty and in stressful urban areas such as the Lower East Side, client feedback can be elicited in a manner that facilitates the task of evaluating service programs designed to serve such clients. Client input is at the heart of the evaluative effort.

NOTE

1. For a review of the survey literature on the topic of response sets introducing bias into survey results, see DeMaio (1984).

Table 13.1
Client Interview Index: Evaluation of Lower East Side Family Union

Item	Item-Total Correlation
A. Client had negative things to say about agency? (no/yes)	.81
B. Client had positive things to say about agency? (yes/no)	.73
C. Client expressed positive feeling for agency staff? (yes/no)	.72
D. Client felt agency had met expectation of service? (yes/no)	.70
E. How service provided influenced change? (specified/ not specified)	.70
F. Did you see social worker as often as you wanted? (yes/no)	.61
G. Did you feel you and the social worker understood each other? (yes/no)	.58
H. Were there things that displeased you in way received? (yes/no)	.58
I. Did LESFU efforts lead to positive change? (yes/no)	.56
J. Did social worker want to see you often enough? (yes/no)	.48
K. Did social worker feel you were being seen often enough? (yes/no)	.46
L. Like the way you were received at LESFU? (yes/no)	.44
M. Can you suggest way in which LESFU can improve work? (yes/no)	.39
N. When did you last see the social worker? (recently/ not recently)	.34
O. Consideration in seeking help: wanted agency where people could speak own language? (important/not important)	.32
P. Was social worker helpful in any way? (yes/no)	.32
Cronbach alpha coefficient = .88	

Table 13.2
Problems for Which Client Sought Help from LESFU, Whether Problem Got Better, and Whether LESFU Helped*

Type of Problem	No. of Clients with Problem	% Better	LESFU as Source of Help(%)**
Income	76	72.4	64.5
Housing	62	56.5	35.5
Need for resources or other help in parenting role	39	76.9	61.5
Child behavior or mental health problem	32	62.5	50.0
Child school problem	32	75.0	62.5
Family relationships	21	57.1	52.4
Adult behavior or mental health problem	19	73.7	68.4
Adult education and training needs	13	46.2	30.8
Seeking return of child from foster care placement	9	77.8	55.6
Adult physical health	8	57.5	62.5
Child physical health	8	62.5	37.5
Meeting need of child for foster care	4	25.0	25.0
Parent-child relations	3	66.7	66.7
Threat of foster care placement	3	100.0	100.0
Other problems	21	85.7	85.7

*Based upon client interview sample of 129. For five possible problem designations by clients, the question posed was:
For the first problem INTERVIEWER MENTIONS PROBLEM BY NAME, e.g.,"your housing problem," would you say the problem is now better, the same, or worse? If "better": was LESFU staff helpful in bringing about this change?
**Percent of respondents who described the problem as "better" and indicated that agency was helpful in bringing about change.

Table 13.3
Client Interview: Index of Family Receiving Service from Other Agencies

Item	Item-Total Correlation
A. How helpful were the services? (high/low)	.83
B. Family receiving services from other agencies? (yes/no)	.78
C. Is service still being provided? (yes/no)	.67
Cronbach alpha coefficient = .87	

Table 13.4
Client Ratings of Service-Providing Agencies Whose Services Were Secured through LESFU Referral

Rating	Number	Percent of Responses
Service was excellent	16	18.0
Service was good	30	33.6
Service was fair	17	19.1
Service was not so good	4	4.5
Service was poor	11	12.4
Unknown	7	7.9
Other	4	4.5
Total	89	100.0

Table 13.5
Client Interview: Index of Frequency of Contact with Social Worker

Item	Item-Total Correlation
A. How often did you tend to meet SWA? (infrequent/frequent)	.47
B. How often was there telephone contact with the social worker? (infrequent/frequent)	.38
C. How often did the social worker want to see you? (infrequent/frequent)	.37
Cronbach alpha coefficient = .59	

Table 13.6
Client Interview: Index of Involvement of Spouse

Item	Item-Total Correlation
A. Identified as married respondent, common law, or shared living arrangement? (yes/no)	.75
B. If yes, did he go with R to agency? (regularly/never)	.68
C. Was he seen when SWA made home visits? (yes/no)	.68
D. Does R object to questions about father/mother of child? (no/yes)	.54
E. R satisfied with involvement of spouse? (yes/no)	.47
F. Attitude of spouse to first approach to LESFU (favorable/unfavorable)	.42
G. How much contact children had with father/mother (much/none or little)	.35
H. Was father/mother of the child seen by SWA or otherwise involved with agency? (yes/no)	.34
Cronbach alpha coefficient = .80	

Table 13.7
Evaluation of LESFU's Service to the Family*

Variable		Loading

Debriefing I
5. AOTHAGDN	Other agencies involved with family	.25
11. ACHCARE	Child care need identified	.45
18. ASOCSVCR	Service required from social agency	.48

Debriefing II
| 22. BCHANGE | Treatment progress | (-) | .31 |
| 33. BCHELTHN | Focus of work on child's health needs | (-) | .38 |

Client Interview
44. CEVALAGY	Client evaluation of LESFU	(-)	.49
47. CFREQSRV	Frequency of contact with SWA	(-)	.26
62. CQD06	Were children ever seen?	(-)	.26

LESFU MIS Data
91. MNPRESEN	Number of problems reported resolved	.51
92. MSUMTIME	Sum of all time spent on case	.27
94. MNUMOFMO	Number of months case remained open	.38
95. MENRATIO	Ratio of no. problems solved/expected	.51

Case Closing Information
| 96. XSERCOMP | Service completed | .68 |
| 97. XCLUNWIL | Family unwilling to continue with LESFU | (-) | .62 |

*This table is Factor 5 from the factor analysis varimax rotation (14-factor solution).

Table 13.8
Client Searching for Solutions to Problems*

Variable			Loading
Debriefing I			
3. AMOTIVAT	Client's motivation		.30
16. ARISKPLC	Risk of placement of children	(-)	.38
Client Interview			
46. COTHRAGY	Other agency in the picture		.42
54. CSATISFY	Satisfaction with life	(-)	.38
56. CVOLORGS	Participation in voluntary organizations		.31
58. CQA03	How long had the problem been going on?	(-)	.34
60. CQB02	Had client tried to solve problem before?		.68
63. CANYCHPR	Any child in family with problem	(-)	.33
81. CPRBSOLV	Tried to work with other agency	(-)	.69
87. CCFSEXM	Gender of child with most problems	(-)	.40
89. CHPROBM	Index of child behavioral adjustment	(-)	.37
Management Information System			
91. MNPRESEN	Number of problems reported resolved	(-)	.27

*This table is Factor 11 from the factor analysis varimax rotation (14-factor solution).

Chapter 14

The Study's Conclusions

INTRODUCTION

The strategy of the United States, developed under the Adoption Assistance and Child Welfare Act of 1980 (Public Law 96-272), gave priority in federal funding to programs designed to prevent dismemberment of families and the placement of children in foster care. All of the states adopted this preventive strategy, and New York State allocated over one hundred million dollars annually to support such services. Despite the almost universal concurrence with the intention of this landmark legislation, legislators and public officials have been concerned about whether such services were effective in carrying out their purposes. The results of our analyses confirmed that LESFU's work was valuable and that its model should be replicated.

MAJOR FINDINGS

The Risk and the Reality of Foster Care Placement of Children

There were 12 cases (7.5%) in which a child was in care when the case opened at LESFU; seven cases (4.4%) in which a child was placed while the case was open; and two cases (1.2%) in which a child was in care when the case opened, returned home, and reentered foster care placement. There were 21 families (13.1%) that had experienced the foster care placement of one or more of their children by the time the case had closed. Wells and Biegel (1990) reviewed research dealing with the results of family preservation services and reported placement rates that varied from 12% to 16% within varying lengths of service contacts up to a year. The LESFU placement rate of an incremental 6% of client families having a child enter foster care was clearly in line with, and may have been better than, other professional experience.

The time-ordered data sets used in the study revealed a coherent theme of LESFU concern with placement risks. At the Debriefing I interview, the SWAs identified the risk of foster care placement of the family's children in 53% of the cases with small numbers of additional children at risk of institutional care or remaining in foster care if already in placement. The SWA reported spending more time on a case that the SWA had identified as at risk of placement at the Debriefing I interview. Cases that were regarded as at risk of placement remained open for a longer time than cases regarded as not at risk. Cases regarded as at risk had more problems reported and had more problems reported resolved.

Families regarded as at risk of placement reported in the client interview that they had experienced a relatively higher number of stressful events during the past year in the form of death in the family, sickness of a family member, and breakup of adult paired relationships. Clients with prior family separation experiences were more likely to have children in foster care placement at the time of approaching LESFU and were also more likely to have children in placement at the time of case closing. Prior family separation from children was thus an important indicator of a child's being at risk of foster care placement. Although almost half of the families in the study had past histories of separation of parents and children, the majority of these separations did not involve foster care.

Of those who had experienced separation, more than half the children had been away from their parents for one year or more. The reasons for the separations varied. Most often mentioned were family separations due to immigration, death of a parent, ill health of a parent and hospitalization, marital discord and separation disputes, and transfer of children among family members as economic and housing emergencies required improvisation in living arrangements.

The interviews with the parents yielded an important perspective about the phenomenon of "parents at risk." On the whole, parents were quite antagonistic to the idea of their children ever being placed in a foster home. They found much fault with the foster care system and saw the system as having many oppressive features.

LESFU's Services Showed Good Results

Our research showed that LESFU achieved an encouraging degree of success in helping to resolve problems besetting its client families. Income problems were the most prevalent problem type. Of 76 clients who came to the agency with financial need as a problem, almost three-fourths reported their condition better, and two-thirds of the improved cases viewed LESFU as the source of help. There was improvement in over 70% of clients with income problems with a need for resources or other help in parenting (primarily day care), with child school problems, with adult behavior or mental health problems, and with the return of a child from foster care placement. The large majority of cases with problems in these types credited LESFU as helpful. The problem types with less than 50% reporting improvement were adult education and training needs and assisting the client to place a child in foster care.

The clients reported effective work by LESFU on areas directly related to its mission of preventing foster care placement. Over 50% of improved cases regarded LESFU as a source of help in improving finances, in finding day care (finding resources or other help in the parenting role), in child behavioral or mental health problems, in child school problems, in family relationships, in adult behavioral or mental health problems, in the return of a child from foster care placement, in adult physical health problems, and in parent-child relations.

There was strong agreement between the SWAs and their clients about the problems and results of the work, and a consistent picture of improvement in the lives of the client families due to the LESFU efforts emerged from the five data sets. For example, our analysis of the data from the agency's management information system found that of the 1,309 problems reported among the 160 cases studied, 455 were reported resolved at the end of the case. The overall rate—for example, the crude rate of reported resolution—was 35%.

Children of the Poor and How They Fared

Child behavioral problems and child school problems were identified in the interviews with the SWAs and the clients as important reasons for families seeking help. In the client interview, half of the respondents said that they often had reason to worry about how their oldest child was doing. About a third of the families worried about their younger children as well. The SWAs and the parents cited risks of delinquency, school failure, and a variety of child behavioral problems.

We constructed a 13-item Child Behavioral Adjustment Index based upon the parent's responses to specific questions about the child's behaviors such as moodiness, school attendance problems, rejection of parental values, low motivation to learn, and problems with the police. This index had a high internal reliability (Cronbach's alpha was .84). The most common behavioral problems were the child's moodiness and refusal to accept parental guidance. About 10% of the client families had to deal with a child who ran away from home. There was a considerable involvement with drugs for the older children: 15% of children 11 or over were drug abusers.

There was an undeniable association between the problematic behavior of both the most troubled child and the oldest child with the extent of psychological pressure on the parent interviewed. The psychological pressure on the parent was measured by a seven-item index that combined measures of the concern about how the children were faring. Those parents measured as under considerable psychological pressure agreed with statements indicating they were feeling upset and depressed when they approached LESFU, were fed up with life, were afraid their children would be sent away, and wanted advice on how to handle their children. A parent whose family had experienced more stressful events in the past year had, on average, a most troubled child who showed a greater extent of problematic behavior. A parent whose morale was lower had more problematic behaviors in the most troubled child.

There were other associations that were not as significant statistically (that is, the *p*-value of the association was between .01 and .05) and did not appear consistently in the three sets. For both the oldest and second-oldest child, a parent who was more isolated had a child with more problematic behaviors. A client who reported more financial problems had an oldest child who showed a greater extent of behavioral problems. There was a weaker association between a client who reported more dissatisfaction with housing and an oldest child with a greater extent of problematic behavior. A family regarded as more afflicted with family violence and dysfunction at the first debriefing had an oldest child with more troubled behavior.

Key Role of Mothers in Single-Parent Households

The mother was absent from her children for 15% of the children in this study population. A child whose mother was out of the home was twice as likely to be in the foster child care system or in an unsatisfactory living arrangement (such as undomiciled, runaway, or whereabouts unknown). When the mother was absent, the presence of the child's grandmother, usually the maternal grandmother, greatly reduced the risk of placement.

The majority of the mothers showed an ability to struggle under conditions of social handicap to help their families remain together and to help their children to survive with some intactness of personality. Most were not embittered and did not regret having had children. In fact, many felt great satisfaction in being a parent. Many of the subjects apparently responded well to the support and counseling offered by the SWAs and showed a resiliency that permitted them to overcome crises even when these came in groups.

Clients were overwhelmingly confronted with agencies in authority such as schools, income maintenance centers, and legal authorities against whom they felt powerless. Eighty percent of the clients reported that a reason for coming to LESFU was to secure help in dealing with an agency. An SWA at their side apparently enabled them to meet better the challenges of dealing with bureaucratic systems. Our data suggested that advocacy worked for many of them.

Saliency of Housing Need

Housing was an important reason for seeking help from LESFU for 56% of the clients interviewed. They were quite specific in describing the many ways in which the lack of housing, or other adverse conditions related to housing, impacted upon them as parents and upon their children. In view of the housing shortages in Manhattan, there was a surprising improvement in housing conditions reported by the clients. Of 62 cases where problems were identified, improvement was reported in 56% of them, and LESFU was credited with being the source of the gains in about a third of the improved cases. This indication of agency success, albeit relatively modest, was consistent with the data reported by the SWAs.

The approach of the SWAs to serving clients in need of housing was often to help file applications for housing in publicly owned projects with the New York City Housing Authority. These applications were frequently followed by telephone calls and letters. Beyond this, the SWAs did what well-functioning families in need of housing would do in similar circumstances. They went hand and hand with the clients through the streets of the Lower East Side inquiring of superintendents of buildings about empty apartments. They also reviewed newspaper advertisements and engaged in networking among clients and others to garner information about available housing. This kind of personal attention won considerable praise in the client interviews and was much appreciated.

ANSWERS TO QUESTIONS

In Chapter 1, we raised a number of questions that we are now prepared to answer. Rapoport reported our preliminary questions, and we will address them first.

1. The cases were not as intractable as we feared. The participation rate in the interviews was 81% and showed the extent of the subjects' cooperation. The majority of clients were very concerned about their children and were motivated to work to solve their problems. One picture of the clients that emerged from the interviewers' reports was that of families in poor economic condition who were hit by serious health problems that swamped them. Several of the case studies illustrated this exogenous sequence. The death of Mrs. IVA's husband was the start of her problems. Mrs. IVB's surgery was coincident with her husband's abandonment of her and the family. Mrs. VIII was a grandmother who was custodial parent of her grandchildren and was swamped by the death of her husband. The illness of one of Family XI's younger children and the consequent stresses were contributors to the problems that the family had with the daughter.

   Another picture that emerged was that of a family trying to manage with a member, often a parent, who was addicted. Mrs. VIII's daughter was a drug addict whose children were under their grandmother's care. Mrs. VI reported that her husband was an alcoholic, and Mrs. VII said that her husband was a drug user. The oldest son of Mrs. IVA was on drugs, and Ms. IXA's daughter, who had been returned from foster care, was addicted and in deep trouble. Although the prognosis for an individual addict might be poor, there were considerable strengths in the other family members.

   Of course, we did not get interviews from cases that were truly intractable, and so we have no insights into their problems. The case histories reflected the majority of families in the study. There were strengths that could be built on in each.

2. The definition of a reasonable expectation for a case required understanding of the problems present in a case and the success rate for solving each case. The indirectly

standardized ratio of the problems reported resolved was a measure of the performance of LESFU on a case that was highly correlated with the client's report of satisfaction with LESFU and with the SWA's report of the nature of the case closing. To answer whether allotting funds to a preventive service organization like LESFU was the best use of public money required comparing the value of LESFU's solution of a client's problems with alternate uses of the funds. Our exploratory study of LESFU was unable to resolve this question definitively but did offer insights into the nature of the problem. The definition and evaluation of preventive services should include a broader criterion than simply the prevention of placement of children in foster care. The mandate of these services should be expanded to include the prevention of drug abuse, criminality, and dependence among teenagers. Their mandate should be expanded to include work with children of nine or ten years of age who show signs of the depression that appeared to be a precursor of drug usage and teenage criminality.

3. The LESFU service model had some positive impacts on the clients studied. The SWAs had a tendency to transform client problems of family relations and need for social work services to problems dealing with housing and finance. They were arguably effective at dealing with these problems. The positive side of these efforts was that the simpler of the client's problems were solved and that this positive outcome was the basis of a deeper attack on the more fundamental problems in the case. Case studies IVA, IVB, VI, and IXA were examples in which the SWAs dealt effectively with a relatively simple problem and went to work on a larger agenda. The formalism of the model apparently did not well serve the process of working with extensive family problems. The SWAs apparently followed a more traditional social work model. On balance, the model was helpful in that it reminded the staff of the need to have visible accomplishments for the client. In a larger sense, however, the work at LESFU was essentially the same as the work at any effective social work agency in that attention to the client's needs and establishing a basis of trust and optimism were fundamental to the solution of the client's problems and reducing the factors placing the client at risk. There was a potential for the LESFU effort to focus on specific material tasks to the exclusion of the larger problems facing the client. There was no evidence that this was a serious problem in the efforts made for these clients.

4. Our evaluation strategy was to ask the clients directly about the service encounter, to ask the SWAs directly about the nature of the cases, and to analyze all of the case reporting documents, especially the MIS forms and the case closing documents. Each component of this strategy contributed unique insights into our evaluation of the organization. The client interviews provided key information about their points of view, their motivations, and the facts of the case. The interviewer's summary reports were vital to understanding the relation between the quantitative analysis and the mechanisms that affected the clients' lives. The SWAs' reports provided key insights into the mechanisms of their casework and their strategies for dealing with problems. The MIS and case closing documents provided the context by which the success of each case could be assessed approximately. The indirectly standardized ratio of the number of problems reported resolved was a statistic that had clear value as a measure of case success. The time allocation based on the MIS reports provided a reasonably accurate measure of how the staff invested its time resources.

If we were to replicate this study, we would surely include these research instruments. In addition, we would supplement the debriefing interviews of the SWAs with the Child Well-Being Scales measuring parenting (Magura and Moses, 1986). These scales were not available at the time of our data collection effort, but they would have provided important information about the extent to which the children were at risk of abuse, neglect, and placement in foster care.

Research about preventive services needs to yield better understanding of the exogenous variables that are the ultimate causes of the client's problems. Our examination of the case reports found medical crises and drug addiction or alcoholism as root causes of some of the problems in these families. The presence of the mother, the strength of the family, and the extent of prior separation of the children from their parents were other variables that were important in understanding the outcome of the case. We would revise our instruments to explore these and other potential areas more carefully.

5. There were clear benefits to aspects of the LESFU structure, and some of these benefits would most probably apply in many other settings. The emphasis on bottom line accountability implicit in the model and the reports in the MIS would probably enhance productivity in a wide range of preventive service agencies and would certainly be the basis of a data base that could be used to estimate key parameters of the agency's work, such as the rates of reported resolution for various problems and the indirectly standardized ratio of the number of cases reported resolved. Of course, if such a data base were used for evaluation rather than research, auditing procedures would have to be implemented as well.

The training of residents in the area to be SWAs and using them to work on the more routine problems of a client were other parts of the LESFU structure that had many advantages. The work of the SWAs was quite solid and meritorious. Their rates of reported resolution of problems seemed to be quite comparable to rates of workers with more training. The training of SWAs from the community should be a promising way of developing them into community leaders and social service professionals. Additionally, the structure had the effect of increasing the fraction of the agency's budget that was spent as wages paid to members of the community so that the funds allocated to LESFU provided double benefits to the community.

6. There were differences among the four ethnic groups. The most essential difference was that the Chinese families were more likely to be intact and the black families least likely to be intact. The black families in this study were more likely to have had children separated from the parents and were not as well integrated into the economy as the Chinese and Hispanic families. The ordering of case success followed that of the ordering of family intactness. Cases involving Chinese families were more likely to close by mutual agreement of worker and client or because the goals of the effort had been accomplished. Black cases were more likely to be closed because of ineligibility. There was an overall pattern for cases involving Chinese clients to be more orderly in their progression.

Chapter 1 contains a list of questions that evolved as we analyzed the data. We have answered some of these questions in related discussions in this chapter and apologize to the reader for our obsessiveness in answering the list of questions in order:

• The incremental rate of foster placement was comparable to that of other preventive service programs reported in the literature.

- We believe that the mandate of preventive service should be expanded to include the prevention of delinquency and the restoration of mental health to children in the age range of nine to 12.
- The indirectly standardized ratio of the number of problems reported resolved had a number of strengths as a measure of the success of LESFU's efforts.
- The exogenous variables that appeared to have the greatest impact on these families were the strength of the family, the extent to which they were victims of medical crises, the existence of prior separations of children from parents, and the number of family members who were victims of drug addiction or alcoholism.
- LESFU appeared to be quite effective, and its focus on bottom line results and use of residents in the area as SWAs appeared to help it accomplish its mandate better.
- Clients valued the services, and the approach of tending to specific problems appeared to work quite well.

DISCUSSION

Expanded Support for Preventive Services Is Warranted

These findings should encourage those concerned with child welfare policy that money being spent on child welfare prevention services is being used to good purposes. While the absence of an experimental design and the limited number of cases in this project precluded us from finding airtight results about the benefits derived from service, there was considerable evidence that serious preventive work was going on with indication of good results.

The core axiom of the present national policy is that the integrity of the family as a unit and the prevention of placement of children in foster care are essential to child welfare. Our results replicated two key aspects of this axiom: that the absence of the mother from the home and the prior separation of a family's children from the parents were important factors putting the children at risk of placement. The underlying concept of the work at LESFU was validated in that the placement rate of its families at high risk was equal to and may have been better than that of other preventive agencies.

The goals of preventive service efforts should not be too ambitious. The solution of a client's problem may require far more resources than those needed to improve the client's life. The value of the improvements in the clients' lives just reported must not be underestimated. One perspective appropriate for a clientele that was as beleaguered and beset with problems as many of these subjects were is that of the "straw that broke the camel's back." A common pattern of problems for a client was that of a family living under adverse housing conditions, facing tight financial circumstances, and having a family member suffering from a major physical illness or serious emotional difficulty, such as case study XI. For a family like this, the loss of a child care arrangement or some other adversity, such as dealing with a teenage daughter realizing the extent of her potential independence, might have consequences far greater than would occur in less troubled times. Relief of this source of stress, the "last straw," would not be a magic and powerful solution for all problems facing the family and would not put an end to its overall vulnerability. It might, however, contribute to the continuity and effectiveness of parental functioning.

The findings offer encouragement that the national policy of putting an emphasis upon child welfare preventive services in dealing with the problems related to foster care of children and other vicissitudes of childhood—a product of the struggles of child welfare policy advocates over several decades—is essentially a sound perspective that can help to create a solid foundation for ongoing social service program development.

Supporting Families with Children in Drug-Infested Environments Is Wiser Than Sending the Children to a Foster Care Placement

The major emphasis of national policy should be to support families living under adverse conditions in areas of urban poverty. In the war on drugs, the parents of the children at risk of developing drug abuse are the key players, and policies leading to such a major social expenditure as paying for the foster care placement of a child would more profitably start with sustaining families who are in high-risk neighborhoods.

The mothers living alone with their children were particularly vulnerable to the vagaries of this drug-infested environment. Clearly, they occupied the lower rungs of the economic ladder, the teenage mothers grown older, and they resided in the middle of a drug-infested neighborhood. These mothers tended to the needs of their children in one of the most hazardous areas in New York City. We saw them overcoming the fear the environment engendered and wending their baby carriages through the drug pushers and addicts who crowded the streets.

The extent of drug involvement, 15% of children 11 or over, and the extent of involvement with the policy and court systems, 23% of children 11 or over, were proofs of the importance of helping these families deal with their children's risk of developing a drug problem. The prevalence of symptoms of depression in children between six and ten was quite high, 32%. Attention to symptoms of predelinquency such as depression and other antisocial behaviors deserves a higher priority in the agenda of the war against drugs and delinquency.

It is important to note that our data about the degree of problematic behavior reported for the older children are based upon a one-time data-gathering occasion. With the passage of time, it is quite likely that the number of children showing difficulty will increase. If not helped, these older children can become more immersed in an antisocial life adaptation. Further, younger children in the families are in danger of emulating their older siblings by going on the same path.

Addressing Housing Issues and the Problems of Living in
Crowded Quarters Deserves the Highest Priority

Public housing projects are a major source of housing for the poor. There should be a review undertaken by legislative groups that examines the procedures for allocation of apartment space through public housing authorities with a view to determining whether special measures can be taken to secure housing for families at risk of losing their ability to take care of their own children. While housing allowances for families on public assistance who are at risk of dismemberment have been made more flexible in recent years, the amount of the allowances should be reviewed to verify its adequacy.

Gentrification of areas like the Lower East Side continuously threatens to deprive the poor of the private housing available to them. The policies of urban planning commissions require review to insure that a high priority is assigned to retaining the housing resources of the poor, upgrading them through renovation, and insuring the allocation of housing space for the poor in any new building initiatives in the community. The stability of cash flow to these families is important if they are to live outside of public housing. A system for reducing the discontinuities in their reception of public benefits should be a high priority in a program to integrate these families into the private housing market and out of public housing.

Additionally, programs that help families make better use of the space in their present housing or that offer community space should be expanded. Board of Education, library, church, settlement house, and storefront community programs provide important outlets during the day and evening for families living in conditions of severe crowding. Financial support for these programs should be considered investments in family stability and the mental health of adults and children. Community groups should be encouraged to inventory the recreational resources of communities such as the Lower East Side and do needs assessment studies to insure that suitable recreational space is available to children and adults in crowded housing. LESFU's effort of having an after-school homework assistance program for children is an example of a promising escape valve for children and parents that could yield great dividends.

In addition to assisting clients in securing new housing, it would be useful for theoreticians of social work practice to develop interventions designed to make more tolerable the effects of crowding, doubling up of families, and deteriorated housing. Intervention strategies could include the use of behavioral techniques to train individuals to handle better adult-adult, adult-child, and child-child interactions that lead to emotional blowups under stressful physical conditions. Additionally, they could develop counseling approaches that strengthen client abilities to enhance the physical attractiveness of their housing environments and to use space in a more versatile manner so that there is enhanced capacity to create private space and some sense of order in the midst of physical chaos.

RESEARCH PERSPECTIVES

The Epidemiology of Childhood Behavioral Disorders

The findings about the nature of the relationship between the psychological and social contexts in which parents in the study were living and the pressures that impacted upon parental performance and the behavioral adjustment of the children opened up important perspectives for future investigation. It came as no surprise that parents who revealed a high degree of personal emotional distress as a strong motivating force in seeking help from the agency had children who were showing poor adjustment and engaged in problematic behaviors. We also expected that family crisis events (e.g., death of a family member, serious illness, and breakup of a relationship), low morale of the parent, and social isolation of the parent would be strongly linked to the behavioral adjustment problems in children. It was somewhat less obvious that parents who were financially pressed and living in housing that was particularly oppressive and dehumanizing also had children showing more problematic child behavioral symptoms. Social workers see this phenomena played out in their everyday practice encounters. What was quite surprising was that each of these contextual factors contributed a significant piece of explained variance in a measure of child behavioral adjustment. We expected that the conditions would be so strongly intercorrelated that the analysis would find only one or two of these variables as associated with the child behavioral adjustment index. These results were exceptionally promising for the understanding of a key component of this problem.

The findings suggested that the profession of social work has a special contribution to make to the knowledge base of the mental health professions in the area of research dealing with the mental health of children. A challenge to the profession was made by Lewis L. Judd, director of the National Institute of Mental Health, in establishing the National Task Force in Social Work Research in 1988: "One of the obligations of being a major profession is to contribute to the common knowledge base of society" (quoted from David Austin, chairperson of the Task Force). This research on the LESFU strongly suggests that the social conditions of life affecting clients of social agencies serving the poor were contributory to parental dysfunction which in turn had serious negative consequences for the mental health of children. One can study children with behavioral disorders in service systems that have a specific mental health treatment mission. However, another advantageous site for research on the onset of emotional problems of children is the child welfare preventive service agency. In the context of family eviction from housing, dismissal from the public assistance rolls, the death of a family member, the breakup of parental relationships, or the expulsion of children from schools, we can see the exogenous factors that presage the collapse of parental performance and the onset of serious emotional problems in children.

The Rationale for the Child Welfare Preventive Service Agency

The substantial data provided about the nature of services offered by LESFU and the responses of clients to these efforts can facilitate the task of defining the child welfare preventive service agency with respect to its mission and its place in the spectrum of types of service agencies dealing with the problems of families and children. Based upon this research experience, we view child welfare preventive service agencies as having the mission of serving clients who voluntarily seek services, or who are persuaded to seek help through agency outreach efforts, at points of crisis when the integrity of the family is threatened and when parents are carrying on under siege. The sources of stress are highly varied but often reflect the vicissitudes experienced by families who suffer disadvantaged social status and reside in areas of extreme urban blight. It is primarily a service focused upon the urban poor, although rural populations and families residing in suburban areas might benefit from such services.

The agency should not impose a fixed set of goals upon its clients; the clients should be active participants in determining the working agenda with the agency. The clients often choose not to work on problems that the agency worker sees as pressing. Sometimes the problems are fairly simple, such as an immigrant family overcoming language difficulty in order to secure financial entitlements from a none-too-friendly public assistance office. Sometimes the problems involve complicated family relationship difficulties in which major service investments are required.

The general approach requires problem solving, linkage to service providers, emotional support, advocacy to secure benefits, and improvisational troubleshooting to overcome crisis periods in a family's life. These ingredients are fairly commonplace among agencies serving the urban poor despite variations in service formats, staffing, and subcomponents of the program. The training of residents from the area to provide services under the provision of a trained leader is a structure that worked to great advantage for LESFU.

The relief of the psychological stress that beleaguered parents experience, which makes them emotionally labile and vulnerable to engaging in destructive interactions with their children, should be addressed in child welfare preventive service programs as a case focus that has its own validity. Such work should not be dismissed as "Band-Aids" because the human anguish involved is considerable and the consequences for the children may be most serious.

It makes sense to think of the preventive child welfare service agency as fairly distinct from the child welfare protective service agency, although a portion of clients served might be the same and approaches to helping them meet their problems may reflect some common orientations. Obviously, parents who have physically abused or neglected their children are often acting under the stress of adverse social conditions and personal circumstances. Many of the needs they manifest are similar to those of the population served by LESFU. The thrust of the preventive service agency, however, is to attract clients before gross neglect and abuse have taken place and where the more authoritative and potentially coercive stance of the legal system is not brought into play. A caseload in a preventive service agency ideally involves a client population where there has not been a major erosion in the client's parental functioning capacity.

The preventive child welfare service agency can be seen as the successor to the system whereby the income maintenance worker also ministers to the nonfinancial social service needs of the family. With the separation of income maintenance and social services in New York City several decades ago and the loss of direct service to families by such large voluntary agencies as the Community Service Society of New York, the urban poor of New York City were deprived of vital social services. The policy now carried out by the Human Resources Administration provides for funding of a network of voluntary child welfare preventive service agencies throughout the city. Community-based and responsive to local conditions, these agencies have promise of being the major frontline resource of the City of New York in meeting the needs of large population groups located in impoverished areas throughout the city.

While misgivings have been expressed by social service leaders about the decision to separate income maintenance and social service, it is clear that the new arrangement has advantages. Flexibility and innovation can be encouraged. Instead of having one large bureaucracy carrying out services under a uniform design as part of a huge civil service system, small agencies such as LESFU in working style can take place so that various forms of service delivery are available for scrutiny. In this context, it is likely that "small is better." The government obviously has major areas of responsibility for hands-on work with the poor, and its mission is enormously critical. The collaborative mix of public and voluntary organization service responsibility makes great sense in this period in which major social problems loom large in national, state, and local concerns.

Complementary Approaches to Prevention

The Homebuilders program is an alternative model for providing preventive services that uses intensive caseworker support for a family in imminent danger of having a child placed in foster care (Kinney, Haapala, and Booth 1991). This program has a different design objective, and programs such as LESFU should be considered as a complement to Homebuilders rather than as an alternative. Certainly, the concept of investing resources in families at the brink of placement makes the probability of seeing the results of the investment large and is one part of a preventive approach. It does not have the wisdom of the "stitch in time that saved nine" approach that is the strength of a preventive strategy based on early intervention. The resources devoted to a case handled early, such as case study XI, may be far less and more effective than resources invested at the point of near family breakdown, such as case study IXA in which investment was made after the major surgery on the mother for the purpose of getting her out of hospital care. More important, the prevention of gross suffering that these families have endured is an important objective in its own right. There should be no need for a family to be on the verge of disaster before help is offered.

Finally, the early intervention programs can potentially impact on other problems that are equal in importance to foster care placement. These programs are also ideally suited to deal with drug problems and juvenile delinquency. Broadening their mandate might well improve their cost-effectiveness. An alternative expression of the same point is that the evaluation of the effectiveness of early intervention programs must include an examination of all the areas in which the program produces benefits, rather than focusing exclusively on its core mandate.

The Debriefing I Schedule for Interviewing Social Work Associates

This is an interview with the social work associate at LESFU designed to take place within a week of the signing of the New York State Department of Social Services Form 2560 developed for preventive service agencies. This takes place some 20 days after the client's first contact with the agency and represents a kind of contractual agreement between agency and client to work together. The interview will usually take place on an in-person basis and is expected to last about one-half hour. It may be occasionally required to conduct the interview by telephone. All interviews will be conducted on a prearranged appointment basis. Interviews will follow the topics as set forth in the schedule. The interviewer will state the questions as worded but will be free to probe creatively for information that is especially relevant to the purposes of the study. Interviews will be tape recorded to permit extraction of qualitative materials useful in the final report. Recordings will also permit quality control in the conduct of the research such as providing for reliability checks on the codification of open-ended questions.

The content of the interview will be wide ranging. The purpose is to provide information about how case goals are formulated in the early stages of engagement with the clients. A baseline of information about the nature of the client's problems, expectations of the agency, and the nature of service orientation will be developed. It is recognized that some areas of work will not be sufficiently developed in this early phase to permit full responses to questions. The aim is to permit the social work associates to share their early impressions of the tasks facing the agency.

NAME OF CLIENT:_____

(case name)

Head of Household:_____

Research Number:_____

Team Number:_____

Social Work Associate:_____

Date of Research Interview:_____ Time Began_____

* *

A. FIRST FORMULATION OF PROBLEMS

1. Was there a particular precipitating event associated with the opening of this case? (Or,
   what triggered LESFU's intervention in this
   case?)

   ☐ Yes   ☐ No   __   (15-16)

   Please describe the circumstances:_____

   _____

   _____

   _____

2. Was the client coming on own initiative or at
   the urging of others?

   ☐ Own initiative   __   (17-18)

   ☐ Urging of others

   ☐ A mixture of both

   ☐ Other

   Please explain:_____

   _____

   _____

3. How did the client verbalize the problems being faced by the family when they were first seen at LESFU?_____   __   (19-20)

_____

_____

4. What other problems did the client(s) mention as a source of concern?

a._____   __   (21-22)

_____

b._____   __   (23-24)

_____

c._____   __   (25-26)

_____

5. What problem do you feel the client is seeking to alleviate most? (Or, put another way, what do you feel is the most pressing problem faced by this client?)_____   __   (27-28)

_____

_____

_____

Why is that?_____   __   (29-30)

_____

6. How urgent does client feel about resolving the problem (cited in 5 above)? Would you say:

☐ Extremely urgent   _   (31)

☐ Urgent

☐ Somewhat urgent

☐ Hardly urgent

☐ Other (_____)

7. How long has the problem been going on?_____

              _   (32)

8. From your perspective, how stressful is the problem facing the client? Would you say:

   ☐ Very stressful   _   (33)

   ☐ Stressful

   ☐ Somewhat stressful

   ☐ Hardly stressful (or not at all)

9. What is likely to happen if the problem is not solved? What are the risks?_____   __   (34-35)

10. What did the client(s) expect LESFU to do on their behalf when first seen?_____   __   (36-37)

   Has the client's expectations changed since then?

   ☐ Yes   ☐ No   __   (38)

   In what way?_____

B. CLIENT ATTITUDES ABOUT PROBLEMS

11. How motivated was the client to work with
    LESFU on his/her problems at the time the
    case opened? Now?

Motivation	At Opening	Now
High motivation	☐	☐
Moderate motivation	☐	☐
Low motivation	☐	☐
Other (_____)		

_   (41)

_   (42)

12. What is your sense of the client's attitude
    toward the possibility of solving his/her
    problem?

    ☐ Optimism

    ☐ Resignation

    ☐ Defeat

    ☐ Other (_____)

_   (43)

13. a. Did the client show any resistance to
       ongoing involvement with LESFU?

       ☐ Yes   ☐ No

       In what way?_____

       _____

       _____

_   (44)

    b. Is there a secure hold on this client? (Is
       client committed to working with the agency?)

       _____

       _____

       _____

__   (47-48)

c. What would it take to hold this client in
a working relationship with the agency?

_____   __   (49-50)

_____

14. a. Who signed the DSS Form 2560?_____   _   (51)

b. What was the client's reaction to the idea of
signing the 2560 when you first raised the
matter? Would you say he/she was:

☐ Very receptive   ☐ Other (_____   _   (52)

☐ Somewhat receptive   _____

☐ Cautious or suspicious   _____)

☐ Negative

> What do you think was the basis for this
feeling?_____   __   (53-54)

_____

_____

c. What was the reaction of other significant
family members to signing the form?_____   __   (55-56)

_____

C. TARGETS OF CHANGE

15. What would it take to make a positive impact
upon the client's problems from the service
point of view?_____ ._____   __   (57-58)

_____

_____

_____

a. Is there a change in the material resources available to this family (e.g., food, clothing, shelter, amenities of life, etc.) required in order to meet the problems being presented?

☐ Yes   ☐ No   ☐ Other (_____

_____)

_   (59)

Please describe what is needed:_____

_____

_____

__   (60-61)

Is this change:

☐ Very important

☐ Important

☐ Somewhat important

☐ Slightly important

_   (62)

b. Is there a change required in the behavior of the client(s)?

☐ Yes   ☐ No   ☐ Other (_____

_____)

_   (63)

Please describe what is needed:_____

_____

_____

__   (64-65)

Is this change:

☐ Very important

☐ Important

☐ Somewhat important

☐ Slightly important

__   (66)

c. Changes in behavior or attitudes of significant others (e.g., relatives, in-laws,
friends, neighbors, teachers, boyfriends,
etc.)?

   ☐ Yes   ☐ No   ☐ Other (_____   _   (67)
                                               _____)

→ Please describe what is needed:_____   __   (68-69)

   _____
   _____
   _____

→ Is this change:

☐ Very important   _   (70)

☐ Important

☐ Somewhat important

☐ Slightly important

d. How about changes required in community conditions (e.g., deteriorated housing, gangs,
school system, services, etc.)?

   ☐ Yes   ☐ No   ☐ Other (_____   _   (71)
                                               _____)

→ Please describe what is needed:_____   __   (72-73)

   _____
   _____
   _____

→ Is this change:

☐ Very important   _   (74)

☐ Important

☐ Somewhat important

☐ Slightly important

239

D. PARENTAL FUNCTIONING

Considering what you know about the functioning of
the parents in this case, how would you respond to
the following questions?

About the Mother

16. a. How responsible is she in carrying out her
       parental obligations? Would you say:

   ☐ Very responsible   _   (75)

   ☐ Somewhat responsible

   ☐ Somewhat irresponsible

   ☐ Very irresponsible

   ☐ Other (_____)

   In what way is she irresponsible?_____   __   (76-77)
   _____
   _____

   b. How motivated does the mother appear to be to
      keep her family intact, that is, keep her
      children at home? Would you say she is:

   ☐ Strongly motivated   _   (78)

   ☐ Moderately motivated

   ☐ Hardly motivated

   ☐ Other (_____)

   Please explain why she is less than fully   __   (79-80)
   motivated:_____
   _____
   _____
   _____

240

c. What are the mother's strengths as a
   parent as you see it?

1._____

<u>0 2</u> (1-2)

_____

__ (3-4)

2._____

__ (5-6)

3._____

__ (7-8)

_____

d. What are her weaknesses?

1._____

_____

__ (9-10)

2._____

_____

__ (11-12)

3._____

_____

__ (13-14)

About the father

17. Tell me about the father's role in the family.
    First, is there more than one father represented
    among the child? (if none, state so.)_____

_ (15)

_____

_____

a. For the most recently involved father, does he
   live with the family?_____

_ (16)

_____

_____

b. What responsibility does he assume in the
   family?_____

__ (17-18)

_____

_____

c. How motivated is he to keep the family
   together?_____

_ (19)

_____

_____

241

d. What are the father's strengths as a parent as you see it?

1._____   __   (20-21)

  _____

2._____   __   (22-23)

  _____

3._____   __   (24-25)

  _____

e. What are his weaknesses?

1._____   __   (26-27)

  _____

2._____   __   (28-29)

  _____

3._____   __   (30-31)

  _____

E. FAMILY'S LIVING CONDITIONS

18. Please describe the family's current housing situation:_____   __   (32-33)

  _____

  _____

  _____

a. How adequate is the family's housing? Would you say:

☐ Very adequate   _   (34)

☐ Adequate

☐ Inadequate

☐ Very inadequate

☐ Other (_____)

☐ Unknown

242

b. As far as you know, has the family been faced with housing problems of the following kind in this current period? (Check all that apply.)

☐ Overcrowding of living quarters   —   (35)

☐ Seriously deteriorated housing   —   (36)

☐ Threat of loss of housing   —   (37)

☐ Lack of its own housing (living with relatives or friends)   —   (38)

☐ Recent burnout of housing   —   (39)

☐ Other (_____)   —   (40)

c. Does this family require new housing (that is, replacement of current housing)?

☐ No   —   (41)

☐ Yes

☐ Unknown

☐ Other (_____)

19. From your knowledge, how adequate is the family's income?_____   — —   (42-43)

_____

_____

_____

_____

a. What are the sources of income?

☐ Public assistance (full coverage)   —   (44)

☐ Public assistance (supplementation)

☐ Wages (_____)

☐ Other (_____)

b. From the standpoint of managing the use of their income, how well is this family managing to meet their basic needs? Would you say they are:

☐ Managing fairly well   _   (45)

☐ Managing adequately

☐ Barely managing

☐ Not managing at all

Please describe this. Is any of the problem due to mismanagement of funds? Are problems simply related to the fact of low income?_____

_____   __   (46-47)

_____

_____

_____

20. In the following areas, please indicate if the family has evidenced any problems or behavior otherwise defined as a cause of concern.

a. Physical health of family members?_____   __   (48-49)

_____

_____

_____

b. Mental health of family members?_____   __   (50-51)

_____

_____

_____

c. Family violence?_____   _   (52)

_____

_____

_____

d. Criminal behavior in the family (members
engaged in crime or delinquency)? _____   _   (53)

_____

_____

_____

e. Illiteracy in the family?_____   _   (54)

_____

_____

_____

f. Chronic unemployment in the family?_____   _   (55)

_____

_____

_____

g. Other significant problems?_____   _   (56)

_____

_____

_____

F. THE FAMILY AND OTHER AGENCIES

21. Were there other service providers who were
already involved with this family at the time
of their first contact with LESFU?

☐ Yes   _   (57)

☐ No

☐ Unknown

Please specify:

a._____   __   (58-59)

_____

b._____

_____

c._____

_____

245

22. Do you think this family needs the service of another agency or organization to deal with its problems? (Note: In addition to those already involved.)

☐ Yes   —   (60)

☐ No

AGENCY #1

a. What is the name of the agency you have in mind (or have already sought out)?_____   __   (61-62)

_____

b. What service do you want this agency to render?_____   __   (63-64)

_____

c. Have you had any indications whether the client would accept the service?_____   —   (65)

_____

_____

_____

d. Is the client clearly eligible for the agency service?_____   —   (66)

_____

e. What are the chances that the client will indeed get the service? (Are there waiting lists?)_____   —   (67)

_____

Why is this so?_____   __   (68-69)

_____

_____

(Instruction: Information to be repeated for all service providers.)

AGENCY #2:

a. What is the name of the agency you have in mind (or have already sought out)?_____

_   (70)

__   (71-72)

b. What service do you want this agency to render?_____

__   (73-74)

c. Have you had any indications whether the client would accept the service?_____

_   (75)

d. Is the client clearly eligible for the agency service?_____

_   (76)

e. What are the chances that the client will indeed get the service? (Are there waiting lists?)_____

_   (77)

AGENCY #3:

a. What is the name of the agency you have in mind (or have already sought out)?_____

_   (78)

__   (79-80)

CARD NUMBER 3

b. What service do you want this agency to render?_____

0 3   (1-2)

__   (3-4)

c. Have you had any indications whether the client would accept the service?_____

_   (5)

d. Is the client clearly eligible for the agency service?_____

_   (6)

e. What are the chances that the client will indeed get the service? (Are there waiting lists?)_____

G. ETHNIC FACTORS

23. a. Has the client's ethnicity required you to
handle this case in any special way?

☐ Yes   _   (8)

☐ No

Please describe:_____   __   (9-10)
_____
_____
_____

23. b. (For workers with the same ethnicity as
client) Has the fact that you are of the
same ethnic background as the client played
a role in how this case has progressed?

☐ Yes   ☐ Not applicable   _   (11)

☐ No   ➔(Go to Question 23c)

Please describe:_____   __   (12-13)
_____
_____

23. c. (For workers with different ethnicity from
clients) Has the fact that you are of different ethnicity from the client(s) played a
role in how this case has progressed?

☐ Yes   _   (14)

☐ No

In what way?_____   __   (15-16)
_____
_____

248

H. RISK FACTORS

24. A final question: Please summarize the factors that you feel place this family at <u>risk</u>.

a._____   __   (17-18)
_____
_____
_____

b._____   __   (19-20)
_____
_____
_____

c._____   __   (21-22)
_____
_____
_____

d._____   __   (23-24)
_____
_____
_____

e._____   __   (25-26)
_____
_____
_____

25. Any other comments on aspects of the case that seem important to you that were not covered in the interview?

                                                    _   (27)

Interviewed by: Time interview ended:

_____   _____   __   (28-29)

The Debriefing II Schedule for Interviewing Social Work Associates

This is a follow-up telephone interview with the social work associate. The interview should be scheduled to take place approximately eight weeks after the first debriefing interview. It is intended to last about 15 to 20 minutes. The aim is to provide an update on what has been taking place in the case since the first debriefing. An effort will be made to carry out the interview at a time convenient for the social work associate.

NAME OF CLIENT:_____   Coding   Columns
                    (case name)   _____
                                                      CARD NUMBER
Head of Household:_____   04_   (1-2)

Research Number:_____   _ _ _   (3-5)

Team Number:_____   _   (6)

Social Work Associate:_____   _ _   (7-8)

Date of Research Interview:_____ Time Began:_____   _ _ _ _ _ _ (9-14)

* *

A. CURRENT STATUS OF THE CASE

    1a. Is the case still open?

        ☐ Yes   ☐ No (If No, do not complete this   _   (15)
                            form. Complete the "Closing
                            Information" form instead.)

    1b. How active is the case? Would you say: _   (16)

        ☐ Active

        ☐ Somewhat active

    ┌───☐ Hardly active

    │ ┌─☐ Not at all active

    │ │ ☐ Other:_____

    │ │
    └→│1c. Why is the case not fully active?
    └→│
      │ _____   _ _   (17-18)
      │
      │ _____
      │
      │ _____
      └──

2. In order of the client's priorities, what problems of this family and its members occupy your attention at this time (i.e., problems where you are attempting to provide service)?

   a._____   _ _   (19-20)

   _____

   b._____   _ _   (21-22)

   _____

   c._____   _ _   (23-24)

   _____

   d._____   _ _   (25-26)

   _____

3. Are there any problems in the family which concern you but which the client does not recognize and/or does not want the agency to get involved in?

   ☐ Yes   ☐ No   _   (27)

   Please describe:

   a._____   _ _   (28-29)

   _____

   b._____   _ _   (30-31)

   _____

254

4. Have any of the following changes taken place in the problems identified by the family since they first came to LESFU? *(Check all that apply.)*

☐ a. No changes have taken place.   _   (32)

☐ b. Some problems have been solved and are no longer at issue. *(Describe:_____*   _   (33)
_____ *)*

☐ c. The client's priorities have changed.   _   (34)

   (Describe:_____
_____ *)*

☐ d. New problems have emerged.   _   (35)

   (Describe:_____
_____ *)*

☐ e. The focus of attention has either shifted to another family member or has been expanded to include that member.   _   (36)

   (Describe:_____
_____ *)*

B. CASE ACTIVITY

5. Have you seen the mother since the opening of the case? If so, what has been the overall frequency of contact? Where? What would you say is her (his) present level of motivation? Now, about the father... *(Repeat for others shown below. Check all that apply.)*

	a. If seen, what has been the overall frequency? (1) Hardly or Not At All; (2) Occasionally; (3) Somewhat Often; (4) Often?					b. Where seen?					c. What is client's present level of motivation in working with LESFU on his/her problems?			Coding Columns
	NA**	(1) e.g., no contact, almost never	(2) e.g., once a month or less	(3) e.g., 2 or 3 times a month	(4) e.g., once a week or more	In office	At home	Tel. contact	Other	High	Moderate	Low	
Mother													__ __ __ (37-39)
Father (most recently involved)													__ __ __ (40-42)
Child* (1st name & age:)													__ __ __ (43-45)
Child* (1st name & age:)													__ __ __ (46-48)
Other (Who?)													__ __ __ (49-51)

*Indicate "seen" if for purposes of direct involvement (e.g., counseling), advocacy, or diagnostic observation and/or evaluation.

**Specify why Not Applicable: i.e., institutionalized, deceased, whereabouts unknown, paternity not acknowledged, etc.

256

6. Has the frequency of client contact changed
    since the opening of the case? (for the
    whole family)

    ☐ Increased   _   (52)

    ☐ Stayed the same

    ☐ Decreased

    ☐ Other (_____)

    a. Explain any changes:_____   _ _   (53-54)

    _____

    _____

257

C. WORKING WITH THE FAMILY

7. Have any of the following problems been evidenced in attempting to work with any members of this family who you think should be involved with LESFU?

	a. Resists seeing Social Work Associate?			b. Fails to keep appointments?			c. Is late for appointments?			d. Is unable to discuss personal problems?			Coding Columns
	YES		NO	YES		NO	YES		NO	YES		NO	
	Very Much	Some-what		Very Much	Some-what		Very Much	Some-what		Very Much	Some-what		
Mother													_ _ _ (55-58)
Father (most recently involved)													_ _ _ (59-62)
Child(1st name & age: ____)													_ _ _ (63-66)
Child(1st name & age: ____)													_ _ _ (67-70)
Other (Who: ____)													_ _ _ (71-74)

Note: If family member not available or if question is otherwise not applicable, indicate "NA."

258

8. How would you characterize the quality of the working relationship between the family and LEFSU (the Social Work Associate) as it has manifested itself since the case opened? For example, let us take the mother -- has it been good, fairly good, mixed or average, fairly poor, or very poor? *(Repeat for others shown below.)*

	NA	Good	Fairly Good	Mixed or Average	Fairly Poor	Very Poor		
Mother							_	(75)
Father							_	(76)
Child (1st name & age:_____)							_	(77)
Child (1st name & age:_____)							_	(78)
Other (Who: _____)							_	(79)

9. Given all the problems facing this family, would you say that overall the family situation has improved, stayed essentially the same, or has gotten worse since the case has been open with LESFU?

- ☐ a. Situation has improved _ (80)
- ☐ b. Situation is essentially the same CARD NUMBER
- ☐ c. Situation has gotten worse 05_ (1-2)
- ☐ d. Other (Explain:_____
  _____)

- e. In what way:_____
  _____ _ _ (3-4)
  _____

10. Are there family members who ought to be
    involved with the efforts of LESFU, but are not?

    ☐ No   _   (5)

    ☐ Yes

    ☐ Other: (Explain:_____

    _____)

    a. Who are these other persons?

    _____   _   (6)

    _____

    b. Why are they not involved?

    _____   _ _   (7-8)

    _____

    c. Are you still trying to involve them?

    _____   _   (9)

    _____

D. INVOLVEMENT OF SERVICE PROVIDERS

11. What service providers sought out by LESFU
    are involved with this family at this time?

    a._____   __ __   (10-11)

    b._____   __ __   (12-13)

    c._____   __ __   (14-15)

    d._____   __ __   (16-17)

12. Do you expect to seek the involvement of other
    providers in the foreseeable future?

    ☐ No

    ☐ Yes   __   (18)

        For what services?

        a._____   __ __   (19-20)

        b._____   __ __   (21-22)

        c._____   __ __   (23-24)

13. Are there service providers in the picture other
    than those sought out by LESFU?

    ☐ No

    ☐ Yes   __   (25)

        a. Name of Agency:_____   __ __   (26-27)

        Service being provided:_____   __ __   (28-29)

        b. Name of Agency:_____   __ __   (30-31)

        Service being provided:_____   __ __   (32-33)

        c. Name of Agency:_____   __ __   (34-35)

        Service being provided:_____   __ __   (36-37)

E. OTHER CONCERNS

14. In your judgment, what are the prospects for
    helping this family resolve its major problems
    as you see the overall situation now?

    ☐ Good

    ☐ Mixed

    ☐ Poor

    ☐ Other (_____)

    _   (38)

15. What are the factors that put this family at
    risk now?

    a._____   _ _   (39-40)

    b._____   _ _   (41-42)

    c._____   _ _   (43-44)

    d._____   _ _   (45-46)

    e._____   _ _   (47-48)

16. Is there a LESFU Family Worker participating with
    you in this case?

    ☐ No

    ☐ Yes   _   (49)

    In what way?_____

    _____   _ _   (50-51)

    _____

    _____

262

17. Are there any additional comments you would like
    to add that have not been covered in the interview?

    ☐ No   _   (52)

    ☐ Yes

    Comments:_____

    _____

    _____

Interviewer:_____ Time Ended:_____   _ _   (53-54)

The Client Interviewing Schedule

1. To be conducted with clients who have been assigned a research number and where Debriefing I and Debriefing II interviews with social work associates have been completed. Clients who discontinued shortly after the Debriefing I interview and where a Debriefing II interview was not appropriate will also be included.

2. To be conducted only after consultation with social work associate or team leader at LESFU and conditions for interview have been reviewed and go-ahead agreed upon.

3. To be conducted only after client has been informed of purposes of the interview, assured confidentiality, and told of right to refuse to participate with no negative consequence associated with such refusal.

Research Number _____

A study carried out under contract between the Lower East Side Family Union, 91 Canal Street, New York, N.Y. and the Columbia University School of Social Work under a joint grant from the Eleanor Sterling Clark Foundation and the William T. Grant Foundation.
The LESFU research staff is located on the premises occupied by Team I at 630 East 6th Street, New York, N.Y. 10009.

Designation by research staff of family member(s) whose participation as an interviewee will be sought. Double-check (✓✓)
indicates an essential interviewee; single-check (✓) indicates
an optional interviewee.

       ___ Mother

       ___ Father

       ___ Maternal grandmother

       ___ Other relative (identification: _____)

       ___ Child (Name: _____)

RECORD OF ATTEMPTS TO CONTACT CLIENT(S)

Calls or Letters	Date and Time of Each Call (or date of letter)	What Happened?
1		
2		
3		
4		

STATEMENT TO INTERVIEWEE(S)

We wish to talk to you about your experience in seeking help from the
Lower East Side Family Union (which is also called "LESFU"). We represent
Columbia University which has been given a contract by the Union to study
the quality of the service given people like yourself. The Union wants to
do everything it can to better serve families raising their children and
meeting problems of living on the Lower East Side. You are in a position
to be of assistance in this evaluation because you have experienced the
Union's services directly and only you know what was helpful and what was
not helpful, what you may have liked and what you may not have liked about
the way your situation was handled. LESFU will of course be glad to hear
reports that its efforts have been found helpful and that users have liked
what was done for them. However, it is also important to know when
problems were not solved, when service was not helpful, and if you were
displeased with any aspect of the way you were treated. Your positive and
negative comments will be welcome because they can help to improve the way
LESFU carries out its work.

What you say will be held strictly confidential. Responses from individual
families will not be reported back to staff. We will be interviewing 150
families who have used the services of LESFU, and we will summarize what
everyone tells us so that LESFU will receive an overall report. Sugges-
tions for change in service will be reported to the staff but not in a way
that individual families can be identified.

We will be paying you twenty-five dollars for your time and effort in
participating in this interview. We want to be able to cover any expenses
associated with participation, such as paying for a baby sitter. We are
also offering payment because your cooperation is important to our study
and, in this instance, you are being asked to give a service to the agency
which can be very valuable.

You should feel free to ask questions before making up your mind about
whether you wish to be interviewed. You should feel free to refuse to be
interviewed if you experience discomfort about participation or object to
such an interview for other reasons. Your relationship to LESFU staff
will in no way be influenced by your decision and every effort will be
made to serve you now and/or in the future in your efforts to seek help
from the Union.

Date:_____

I have explained the purposes of the research to the
interviewee, emphasized the voluntary nature of participation,
and elicited the following response to the question, "Do you
consent to being interviewed?"

_____ Client agrees to being interviewed

_____ Client refuses to be interviewed*

*Reason stated:

_____

_____

_____
Interviewer

HOUSEHOLD COMPOSITION

Name or Identification	Sex	Age	Relation To Interviewee
1.			
2.			
3.			
4.			
5.			
6.			
7.			
8.			
9.			
10.			

TO BE FILLED OUT BY RESEARCH STAFF USING NYS DSS FORM 2560 PRIOR
TO INTERVIEW. INFORMATION IS TO BE CONFIRMED WITH RESPONDENT.

Client Interview

```
                                                        |Code| Col.
                                                        | No.|  No.
NAME OF FAMILY_____           |    |
                                                        |    |
NAME OF FAMILY HEAD_____           |    |
                                      RESEARCH NO. ____  |____| 1-3
                                                        |    |
IDENTIFICATION OF INTERVIEWEE(S)                        |    |
                                                        |    |
     ___ Mother      ___ Child        CARD NO. _06_     | 06 | 4-5
                                                        |    |
     ___ Father      ___ Other relative  TEAM NO. ____  |____|  6
                                                        |    |
     ___ Grandmother ___ Other        INTERVIEWEE(S)    |____|  7
                                                        |    |
DATE OF RESEARCH INTERVIEW _____  TIME BEGAN _____  |____| 8-13
```

****

A. BASIS FOR CONTACT WITH THE AGENCY
   In order to better understand how you became a client of
   the Lower East Side Family Union, please think back to the
   time when you first came to the agency. Please tell me how
   you happened to have contact with the agency. (OPEN-ENDED)

   |____| 14-15

   |____| 16-17

   |____| 18-19

     (PROBE IF APPROPRIATE) Was there a particular incident
     or event that made you turn to LESFU for help? Please
     describe this.

   |____| 20-21

272

A.1.   Whose idea was it to come to the agency?

       |‾| Came on own initiative |___| 22

       |‾| Came on urging of others (specify_____)

       |‾| Referred by other service organization

       |‾| Other (specify) _____

      _____

      _____

a)   How did you happen to know about LESFU (the
    agency)? _____ |___|23-24

    _____

    _____

b)   What organization (agency) was it and how did
    they come to suggest LESFU to you? _____ |___|25-26

    _____ |___|27-28

    _____

A.2.   What would you say was the <u>main</u> problem that brought you to
the agency?

    _____ |___|29-30

    _____

    _____

A.3.   About how long had the problem been going on?
Would you say

       |‾| Less than a month? |___|31

       |‾| At least a month or two?

       |‾| Three to six months?

       |‾| Over six months to a year?

       |‾| More than a year?

       |‾| Other (specify) _____

    _____

A.4. Did you have other problems you wanted LESFU to help you with
(in addition to the one already mentioned)?

|‾| No   (Go to question A.5.) |___|32

┌─|‾| Yes
│
│ |‾| Other (specify) _____
│
│   _____
│
│   _____
│
│ ┌──┐
└─→│ What were these?   │
   │   │
   │ 1. _____   │ |___|33-34
   │   │
   │ 2. _____   │ |___|35-36
   │   │
   │ 3. _____   │ |___|37-38
   └──┘

A.5. What were you hoping the agency might do for you when you
first came? (PROBE, IF NECESSARY: Did you expect the agency
to help in some way?) |___|39-40

a) Besides what you have just told me, did you expect
anything else from the agency in the way of dealing
with your problem(s)? |___|41

┌─|‾| Yes
│
│ |‾| No   (Go to question A.6.)
│
│ ┌──┐
└─→│ What was your expectation? _____│ |___|42-43
   │   │
   │ _____│
   │   │
   │ _____│
   └──┘

A.6.   In your own words, please tell me what your understanding
was of the purposes of the Lower East Side Family Union?
(PROBE, IF NECESSARY: What kind of problems was the agency
established to deal with?)

|____|44-45

|____|46-47

|____|48-49

A.7.   Has your impression of the purposes of the agency changed
since the time you first came? (PROBE, IF NECESSARY: What
kinds of people, with what kinds of problems, is the agency
set up to serve?)

|____|50-51

|____|52-53

|____|54-55

A.8.   When you came to the agency, did you expect your social work
associate to keep private family matters confidential
(i.e., kept private)?

     |_| Yes

     |_| No |____|56

     |_| Other (Specify: _____)   blank57-58

  a.   Do you think the agency has a policy about keeping
client information confidential?

        _____

        _____ |____|59-60

  b.   How important to you was it that what you said would be
kept private? Would you say... |____|61

     |_| Important?

     |_| Somewhat important?

     |_| Not at all important?

     |_| Other (Specify:_____)

A.9. Again, thinking back to when you first came to the Lower East Side Family Union, how important were the following considerations in seeking help? Would you say _important_, _somewhat important_, or _not at all important_ as a reason for coming to the agency?

		Import- ant	Some- what	Not at All	NA		
a)	Wanted help with your housing situation.	|_|	|_|	|_|	|_|	|___	62
b)	Wanted help with your lack of money.	|_|	|_|	|_|	|_|	|___	63
c)	Wanted advice on how to handle your children; get them to behave in a different way.	|_|	|_|	|_|	|_|	|___	64
d)	Was feeling upset or de- pressed; wanted somebody to listen to you with sympathy.	|_|	|_|	|_|	|_|	|___	65
e)	Came because people in authority urged or insisted that you do this.	|_|	|_|	|_|	|_|	|___	66
f)	Came because you were fed up with how life was going; wanted help in getting more out of life.	|_|	|_|	|_|	|_|	|___	67
g)	Came because you were afraid your children would be sent away if you did not come.	|_|	|_|	|_|	|_|	|___	68
h)	You wanted an agency where people could speak your own language or understand your cultural background.	|_|	|_|	|_|	|_|	|___	69
i)	You wanted to understand your- self better and figure out out what you were doing wrong	|_|	|_|	|_|	|_|	|___	70
j)	You were afraid your child(ren) weren't doing well; doing things wrong in school or the neighborhood.	|_|	|_|	|_|	|_|	|___	71
k)	Wanted help in dealing with an agency (e.g. public assistance, school).	|_|	|_|	|_|	|_|	|___	72

A.10. Considering how you felt when you came to LESFU, how
       upsetting were the problems you were facing?
       Would you say...

                                                          |73

       |‾| Very upsetting?

       |‾| Somewhat upsetting?

       |‾| Slightly upsetting?

       |‾| Not especially upsetting?

       |‾| Other (specify)_____

       _____

A.10.1. What did you think was likely to happen if the problems were
        not solved in some way? (OPEN-ENDED)
                                                          |74-75

                                                          |76-77

        PROBE (if necessary) Why do you say that? |78-79

A.10.2. When you consider the problems you were facing when you
        came to the agency, would you say this was (1) a very
        troubled time in the life of your family--a crisis, or |80
        (2) troubled but not a crisis, or (3) was it an average
        time?

        |‾| Troubled time/major crisis

        |‾| Troubled time/moderate crisis

        |‾| Average time - usual troubles/not a crisis

        |‾| Other (specify)_____

        _____

277

B.   THE EARLY EXPERIENCE AT LESFU

RESEARCH NO. _____ |____| 1-3

CARD NO. _07_ | 07 | 4-5

B.1   In considering the problems that brought you to LESFU, what
      do you think was the cause (or causes) of the problem(s).
      Please tell me in your own words.... how had these problems
      come about?

                                               |____| 6-7

                                               |____| 8-9

                                               |____|10-11

B.2.   Had you tried to solve the problem(s) in any way before
       coming to LESFU? |____|12

       |‾| Yes

       |‾| No

       |‾| Other (specify)_____

       a)   In what way? |____|13-14

                                                 |____|15-16

       b)   Did this approach help in any way?

            |‾| Yes |____|17

            |‾| No

            |‾| Other (specify) _____

278

B.3.　When you first came to the Lower East Side Family Union, were there things about the way you were received and dealt with that you liked or appealed to you?

|‾| Yes

|‾| No

|‾| Other (specify) _____

PROBE: What were these?

|___| 18

|___|19-20

|___|21-22

|___|23-24

B.4.　Remember I said in the beginning that as much as we want to know what you liked, we also want to know what you didn't like. Now we want to know if there was anything you did not like or that displeased you in the way you were dealt with? (PROBE: Or were there problems created for you by the way the agency did things?)

|___| 25

|‾| Yes

|‾| No　(GO TO B.5.)

|‾| Other (specify)_____

a)　Please tell me about this. What bothered you specifically?

|___|26-27

|___|28-29

|___|30-31

b)　How much did this bother you? Would you say...

|___| 32

|‾| Very much?

|‾| Somewhat?

|‾| Not much?

|‾| Other (specify) _____

Continued...

c) Did this interfere with your ability to use the
    agency to help solve your problems? |___| 33

    |‾| Yes (specify) _____

    _____

    |‾| No

    |‾| Other (specify) _____

    _____

B.5. Again, thinking back to your first contact with the agency,
      what did the social work associate tell you he/she could do |___|34-35
      to help with the problems you were faced with?

      _____ |___|36-37

      _____

      _____ |___|38-39

B.6. What did you and the social work associate agree to work
      on when you first came to LESFU? (OPEN-ENDED)

                                                                        |blank 40

      _____

      _____

      _____ |___|41-42

                                                                        |___|43-44

B.7.   Did the social work associate tell you about anything <u>you</u>
       would have to do to help solve the problems you were
       presenting?

            |‾| Yes |____| 45

            |‾| No

            |‾| Other (Specify: _____

            _____

       a.   What was expected of you?
            _____ |____|46-47

            _____ |____|48-49

            _____ |____|50-51

B.8.   How often did the worker want to see you? Would you say...

            |‾| At least several times a week? |____| 52

            |‾| Once a week?

            |‾| Several times a month?

            |‾| Other: _____

            _____

       a.   From your point of view did the worker want to see you
            often enough or not often enough?

                 |‾| No problem - it was as often as I wanted |____| 53

                 |‾| Somewhat of a problem

                 |‾| A problem, difficult to see worker this often

                 |‾| Other: _____

            _____

       b.   Why was it a problem to have regular contact with the
            worker? |____|54-55

            _____ |____|56-57

            _____

B.9. Did you feel that you and _____ (social work associate)
      understood each other? Would you say there was....

    |‾| Good understanding between you? |____| 58

    |‾| Fairly good understanding?

    |‾| Only a little understanding?

    |‾| None at all?

    |‾| Other (specify: _____

               _____)

B.9.a) What was it like talking to the social work associate -
        how did it make you feel?

                        |____|59-60

    _____

    _____

    _____

B.10. Can you suggest any way in which LESFU can improve its work
       in the way it deals with people when they first come to the
       agency?

    |‾| Yes |____| 61

    |‾| No

    |‾| Other (specify) _____

    a) Please tell me about this. |____|62-63

    b) Do you have any other suggestions for improvement? |____| 64-65

C.   ON-GOING EXPERIENCE WITH AGENCY |Code|Col.
                                                                        | No.| No.

We have been talking about your initial experience with LESFU.
I would now like to focus our discussion on your reactions to
your _later_, on-going contacts with the agency. Say after a
month or so had passed until now (or until your last contact
with the agency).

C.1. How often did you tend to meet with Mr./Ms. _____ (the
      worker)? Would you say....

            |⁻| One or more times a week?   . |____| 66

            |⁻| About every other week?

            |⁻| One or two times a month?

            |⁻| Once a month?

            |⁻| Every once in a while?

            |⁻| Hardly ever?

            |⁻| Other (specify) _____

      a) How often did you have telephone contact with the social
          work associate? |____| 67
          _____

C.2. From your point of view, did you see Mr./Ms. _____ as
      often as you wanted to?

            |⁻| Yes, as often as wanted |____| 68

            |⁻| No, less often than wanted

            |⁻| No, more often than wanted

            |⁻| Other (specify: _____ |____| 69

                _____)

      | Why do you say this? Please elaborate. |____|70-71
      | _____
      | _____
      | _____
      | _____

283

C.3. Do you think the social work associate felt you were seeing
or talking to each other as often as he/she thought necessary
to deal with the problems you had?

|_| Yes, as often as needed | | 72

|_| No, less often than needed

|_| No, more often than needed

|_| Other (specify: _____

_____)

> Why did he/she feel this way?

_____

_____ | | 73

_____

C.4. When did you last see the worker? (INTERVIEWER TO CLARIFY:
Other than for research interview arrangements.)

|_| Within past week | | 74

|_| Within past month

|_| 2 or 3 months ago

|_| 4 to 6 months ago

|_| More than 6 months ago

|_| Other (specify: _____

_____)

(PROBE, IF APPROPRIATE)
C.5. Why have you not seen the worker in this recent period? | | 75

_____

_____

C.6. Did you have contact with any other staff member of LESFU,
e.g. family worker (OTHER THAN RECEPTIONIST AND SECRETARIES
OR CLERKS)?

|_| Yes | | 76

|_| No

|_| Other (specify) _____

a) Who was this person? | | 77

_____

_____

b) What did he/she do?

_____ |78-79

_____

(PROBE, IF NECESSARY)
c) Was he/she helpful to you in any way? | | 80

_____

_____

I would now like to ask you about members of your
family and how they felt (feel) about LESFU.

285

D. CONTACT WITH OTHER FAMILY MEMBERS

|Code|Col.
| No.| No.

RESEARCH NO. ____ |____| 1-3

CARD NO. _08_ | 08 | 4-5

FOR MARRIED RESPONDENTS AND THOSE IN COMMON LAW OR
OTHER SHARED LIVING ARRANGEMENTS

|‾| Check here if section not appropriate and GO TO p. 17. |____| 6

D.1. Did your spouse (husband or wife, girl/boyfriend...) know you
were going to the agency for help?
(Specify relation: _____)

|‾| Yes |____| 7

|‾| No

|‾| Other (specify) _____

```
If NO, why not?_____
                                                         |____| 8
_____

_____
```

a. If YES, did he/she go with you to the agency?

|‾| Never |____| 9

|‾| Just the first time

|‾| Occasionally or once later

|‾| Regularly or fairly regularly

|‾| Other (specify: _____

_____)

```
PROBE, IF APPROPRIATE
Why didn't he/she come (or come more often) to the agency?
                                                         |____| 10
_____

_____

_____
```

b. Was he/she seen when social work associate made home
visits? |____| 11

_____

286

|Code|Col.
| No.| No.

D.2. Are you satisfied with the degree of involvement of your
spouse (friend....) with LESFU?

|‾| Yes   12

|‾| No

|‾| Other (specify) _____

PROBE, IF APPROPRIATE
Why do you say this?   13-14

_____

_____

_____

D.3. What do you think was the attitude of your spouse (friend....)
about LESFU when you first came to the agency?

_____   15-16

_____   17-18

_____

a. Has his/her attitude changed since you first came?   19

_____

_____

287

D.4   Would you have any objection to our asking you questions
      about the father(s)/mother(s) of the children?

          |‾| Yes (GO TO NEXT PAGE, QUESTION D.6.)   20

          |‾| No

          |‾| Other (specify) _____

D.5. Was the father/mother* of your children ever seen by the LESFU
      social work associate or otherwise involved with the agency?

          |‾| Yes   21

          |‾| No

          |‾| Other (specify) _____

      IF NOT,
      a) Why was he/she not involved?   22

          _____

          a.1) Did you wish he/she were involved?   23

      b) In what way was he/she involved?   24

          _____
          _____
          _____
          _____

      c) How did he/she feel about LESFU?   25

          _____
          _____
          _____
          _____

* Use plural if appropriate. Use extra page(s) for more than
                              one father.

FOR ALL RESPONDENTS

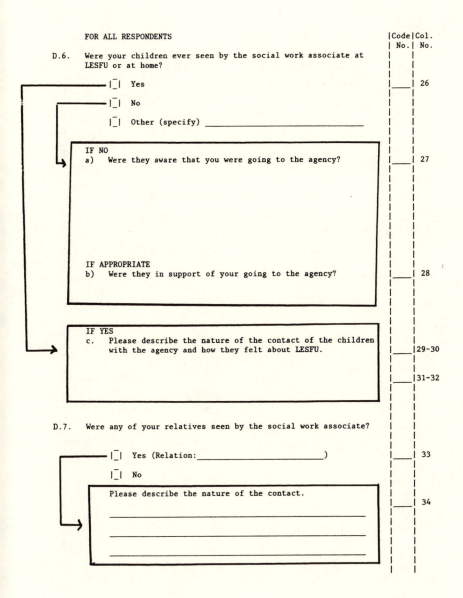

|Code|Col.
| No.| No.

D.6. Were your children ever seen by the social work associate at LESFU or at home?

|‾| Yes |____| 26

|‾| No

|‾| Other (specify) _____

IF NO
a) Were they aware that you were going to the agency? |____| 27

IF APPROPRIATE
b) Were they in support of your going to the agency? |____| 28

IF YES
c. Please describe the nature of the contact of the children with the agency and how they felt about LESFU. |____|29-30

|____|31-32

D.7. Were any of your relatives seen by the social work associate?

|‾| Yes (Relation:_____) |____| 33

|‾| No

Please describe the nature of the contact. |____| 34

_____

_____

_____

E. CLIENT EVALUATION OF HELPFULNESS OF SERVICE |Code|Col.
| No.| No.

I would now like you to consider what help you may have gotten
from the agency. First let us again review the problems that
were bothering you when you came and those for which you are
seeking help. What are these problems? (INTERVIEWER TO
PROBE AS NEEDED, e.g., were there any other problems facing
your family at that time?)

E.1.   Problem mentioned first: |____|35-36

_____

E.2.   Problem mentioned second: |____|37-38

_____

E.3.   Problem mentioned third: |____|39-40

_____

E.4.   Problem mentioned fourth: |____|41-42

_____

E.5.   Problem mentioned fifth: |____|43-44

_____

E.6. For the first problem (INTERVIEWER MENTION PROBLEM BY NAME,
      e.g. "your housing problem"), would you say the problem is now
      <u>better</u>, <u>the same</u>, or <u>worse</u>

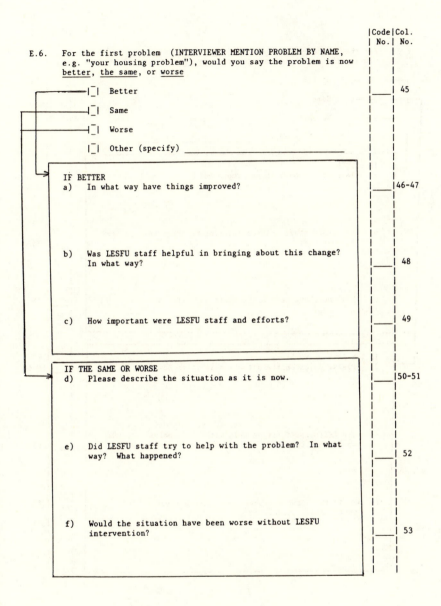

|‾| Better | 45

|‾| Same

|‾| Worse

|‾| Other (specify) _____

IF BETTER
a) In what way have things improved? |___|46-47

b) Was LESFU staff helpful in bringing about this change? |___| 48
    In what way?

c) How important were LESFU staff and efforts? |___| 49

IF THE SAME OR WORSE
d) Please describe the situation as it is now. |___|50-51

e) Did LESFU staff try to help with the problem? In what |___| 52
    way? What happened?

f) Would the situation have been worse without LESFU |___| 53
    intervention?

E.7.   For the second problem mentioned _____ , would
       you say the problem is now <u>better</u>, <u>the same</u>, or <u>worse</u>?

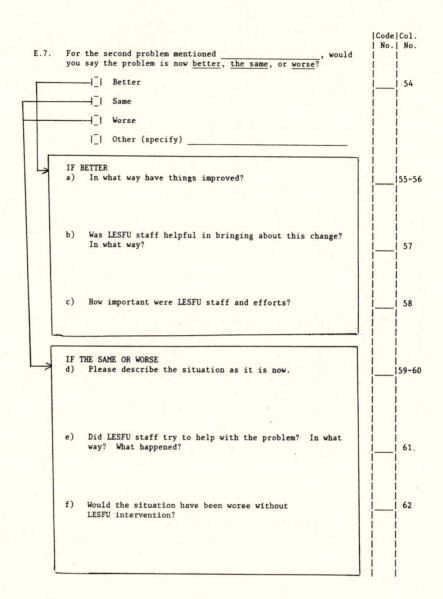

|‾| Better | | 54

|‾| Same

|‾| Worse

|‾| Other (specify) _____

IF BETTER
a)   In what way have things improved? | |55-56

b)   Was LESFU staff helpful in bringing about this change? | | 57
     In what way?

c)   How important were LESFU staff and efforts? | | 58

IF THE SAME OR WORSE
d)   Please describe the situation as it is now. | |59-60

e)   Did LESFU staff try to help with the problem? In what | | 61.
     way? What happened?

f)   Would the situation have been worse without | | 62
     LESFU intervention?

292

E.8. For the third problem (INTERVIEWER MENTION PROBLEM BY NAME,
      e.g. "your housing problem"), would you say the problem is now
      <u>better</u>, <u>the same</u>, or <u>worse</u>

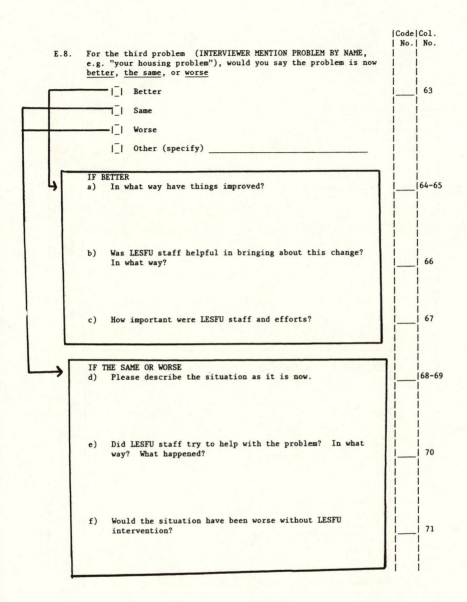

            |‾| Better |___| 63

            |‾| Same

            |‾| Worse

            |‾| Other (specify) _____

      IF BETTER
      a) In what way have things improved? |___|64-65

      b) Was LESFU staff helpful in bringing about this change? |___| 66
          In what way?

      c) How important were LESFU staff and efforts? |___| 67

      IF THE SAME OR WORSE
      d) Please describe the situation as it is now. |___|68-69

      e) Did LESFU staff try to help with the problem? In what |___| 70
          way? What happened?

      f) Would the situation have been worse without LESFU |___| 71
          intervention?

293

E.9.   For the fourth problem   (INTERVIEWER MENTION PROBLEM BY NAME,
       e.g. "your housing problem"), would you say the problem is now
       better, the same, or worse

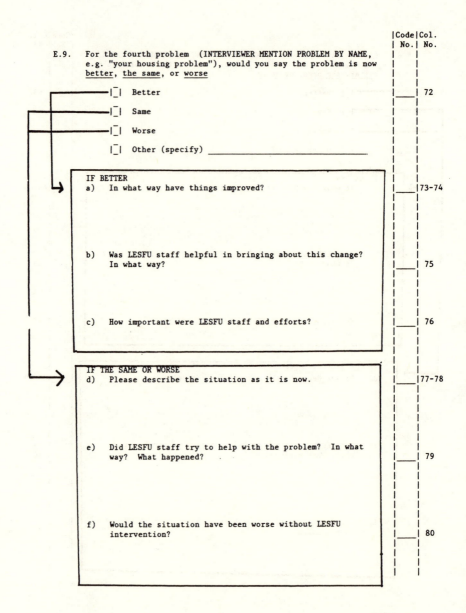

                    |‾| Better |___| 72

                    |‾| Same

                    |‾| Worse

                    |‾| Other (specify) _____

        IF BETTER
        a)   In what way have things improved? |___|73-74

        b)   Was LESFU staff helpful in bringing about this change?
             In what way? |___| 75

        c)   How important were LESFU staff and efforts? |___| 76

        IF THE SAME OR WORSE
        d)   Please describe the situation as it is now. |___|77-78

        e)   Did LESFU staff try to help with the problem? In what
             way? What happened? |___| 79

        f)   Would the situation have been worse without LESFU
             intervention? |___| 80

294

RESEARCH NO. ____ |____| 1-3

CARD NO. _09_ | 09 | 4-5

E.10. For the fifth problem mentioned _____, would
       you say the problem is now <u>better</u>, <u>the same</u>, or <u>worse</u>?

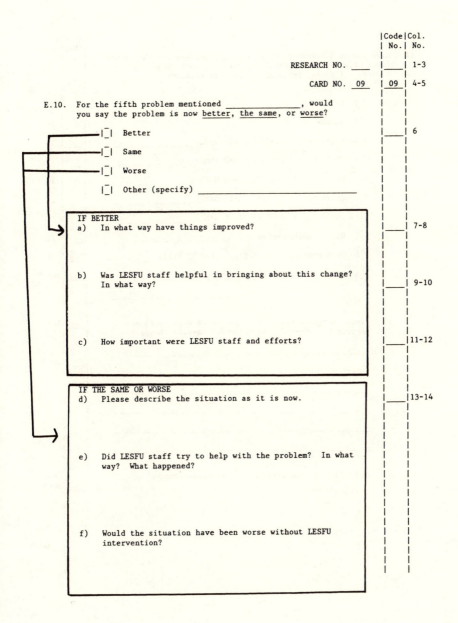

|‾| Better |____| 6

|‾| Same

|‾| Worse

|‾| Other (specify) _____

IF BETTER
a)   In what way have things improved? |____| 7-8

b)   Was LESFU staff helpful in bringing about this change? |____| 9-10
     In what way?

c)   How important were LESFU staff and efforts? |____|11-12

IF THE SAME OR WORSE
d)   Please describe the situation as it is now. |____|13-14

e)   Did LESFU staff try to help with the problem? In what
     way? What happened?

f)   Would the situation have been worse without LESFU
     intervention?

E.11. Have you or any members of your family changed for the <u>better</u>
(even slightly) since you first came to LESFU (e.g., in behavior, attitudes, feelings, or ability to handle problems)?
(CHECK IF "YES")

|‾| Self |___| 15

|‾| Spouse |___| 16

|‾| Child No. 1 SPECIFY FIRST NAME: _____ |___| 17

|‾| Child No. 2 SPECIFY FIRST NAME: _____ |___| 18

|‾| Child No. 3 SPECIFY FIRST NAME: _____ |___| 19

|‾| Child No. 4 SPECIFY FIRST NAME: _____ |___| 20

|‾| Child No. 5 SPECIFY FIRST NAME: _____ |___| 21

|‾| Other family member: _____ |___| 22

|‾| No one changed for better   [GO TO E.12] |___| 23

|‾| Other (Specify: _____ |___|24-25

_____)

a) Please describe the changes you think were (are) most |___|26-27
    important. (Specify family member showing change.)

    _____
                                                                |___|28-29
    _____

    _____

    _____

    _____

    _____

b) Did LESFU efforts lead to some of these changes?
                                                                |___|30-31
    |‾| Yes

    |‾| No

    |‾| Other (specify) _____

E.12. Have you or any members of your family changed for the <u>worse</u>
      since you first came to LESFU (e.g, in behavior, attitudes,
      feelings, or ability to handle problems)? (CHECK IF "YES")

     |‾| Self |____| 32

     |‾| Spouse |____| 33

     |‾| Child No. 1   Specify First Name: _____ |____| 34

     |‾| Child No. 2   Specify First Name: _____ |____| 35

     |‾| Child No. 3   Specify First Name: _____ |____| 36

     |‾| Child No. 4   Specify First Name: _____ |____| 37

     |‾| Child No. 5   Specify First Name: _____ |____| 38

     |‾| Other family member: _____ |____| 39

     |‾| No one changed for worse [GO TO SECTION F, p.28] |____| 40

     |‾| Other (Specify: _____ |____|41-42

                _____)

   a)   Please describe some of the changes you think were (are)
       most important. (Specify family member showing change.) |____|43-44

       _____

       _____ |____|45-46

       _____

   b)   Would the situation have been worse without LESFU? |____|47-48

     |‾| Yes

     |‾| No

     |‾| Other (specify) _____

E.13. If you feel there have been any changes in any members of your
      family or in any problem situations since you first went to the
      agency, what do you think was the <u>main</u> <u>reason</u> for the changes
      you reported?

                                               |____|49-50

                                             |____|51-52

                                             |____|53-54

E.14. How do you feel the <u>service provided by the agency</u> influenced the changes you have reported? Would you say....

|‾| Helped to make things better? |___| 55

|‾| Made no difference?

|‾| Made things worse?

|‾| Other (specify: _____

_____)

PROBE (IF APPROPRIATE)

a) Why do you say this?

|___|56-57

|___|58-59

|___|60-61

E.15. Did anything <u>not related</u> to the agency influence the changes you have reported?

|‾| Yes |___| 62

|‾| No

|‾| Other (specify) _____

IF YES
What was this? (Did it make things better or worse?)

|___|63-64

|___|65-66

|___|67-68

We would now like to talk with you about how you and your family are getting along. What life is like for you these days.

298

F.   ABOUT YOUR CHILDREN

F.1.   We are interested in how well you feel your children are
        getting along. For each child, please tell me whether during
        the past year you have had reason to worry about how your child
        is doing. Say for _____ (CHILD NO. 1),
        would you say you <u>often</u>, <u>sometimes</u>, <u>hardly ever</u>, or <u>never</u>
        have had reason to worry about him (or her)?

		Often	Some-times	Hardly ever	Never	NA		
INSERT	Child No. 1 (_____)	(4)	(3)	(2)	(1)	(9)	|___|	69
FIRST NAMES	Child No. 2 (_____)	(4)	(3)	(2)	(1)	(9)	|___|	70
PRIOR TO	Child No. 3 (_____)	(4)	(3)	(2)	(1)	(9)	|___|	71
INTERVIEW	Child No. 4 (_____)	(4)	(3)	(2)	(1)	(9)	|___|	72
	Child No. 5 (_____)	(4)	(3)	(2)	(1)	(9)	|___|	73
	Child No. 6 (_____)	(4)	(3)	(2)	(1)	(9)	|___|	74
	Child No. 7 (_____)	(4)	(3)	(2)	(1)	(9)	|___|	75
	Child No. 8 (_____)	(4)	(3)	(2)	(1)	(9)	|___|	76

RESEARCH NO. ____ |___| | 1-3

F.2.   What was the basis for your worrying about him or her?
                                                   CARD NO.   10 | 10 | 4-5

FOR THOSE WHO RESPONDED "OFTEN" FOR ANY CHILD	Child Number	Basis for worry		
	_____	_____	|___|	6-7
	_____	_____	|___|	8-9
	_____	_____	|___|	10-11
	_____	_____	|___|	12-13
	_____	_____	|___|	14-15
	_____	_____	|___|	16-17
	_____	_____	|___|	18-19
	_____	_____	|___|	20-21

F.3.   During this past year have you had concern about any of
       your children because of the following kinds of problems?

CHECK ALL
IDENTIFIED
PROBLEMS   Children Showing Problems

                                      Child Number:

___ Moodiness-child often   1 2 3 4 5 6 7 8 |___| 22
    not happy   CIRCLE
                                                           FOR
___ School attendance   1 2 3 4 5 6 7 8   EACH |___| 23
    problems, truancy   CHILD
                                                           WHERE
___ Rejection of parents or   1 2 3 4 5 6 7 8   CONCERN |___| 24
    parental values   IS
                                                           INDICATED|
___ Low motivation to   1 2 3 4 5 6 7 8 |___| 25
    learn

___ Failure to do homework   1 2 3 4 5 6 7 8 |___| 26

___ Problems with   1 2 3 4 5 6 7 8 |___| 27
    police or courts

___ Alcohol problem   1 2 3 4 5 6 7 8 |___| 28

___ Drug abuse problem   1 2 3 4 5 6 7 8 |___| 29

___ Refusal to accept   1 2 3 4 5 6 7 8 |___| 30
    your guidance or
    discipline

___ Staying out overnight   1 2 3 4 5 6 7 8 |___| 31

___ Girl friend/boy   1 2 3 4 5 6 7 8 |___| 32
    friend problems

___ Other problems?

    (1)_____   1 2 3 4 5 6 7 8 |___| 33

    (2)_____   1 2 3 4 5 6 7 8 |___| 34

300

F.4.1. We know that raising children is not always a matter of
having problems. Parents often feel positive things about
their children -- their talents, their personal qualities
ability to work, and so forth. For each of your children,
please tell me whether you have had such feelings and what
they are. Say for _____(CHILD NO. 1), how often
do you feel good about how he/she is doing? Would you say...

|‾| Often? -------------->   ____ ____ Please |___| 35
                          give me an example of what
|‾| Sometimes? ----------> you mean. _____

|‾| Hardly ever or never? _____

|‾| Other (specify)   _____

_____   _____

F.4.2. How about _____(CHILD NO. 2) Would you say...

|‾| Often? -------------->   ____ ____ Please |___| 36
                          give me an example of what
|‾| Sometimes? ----------> you mean. _____

|‾| Hardly ever or never? _____

|‾| Other (specify)   _____

_____   _____

F.4.3. How about _____ (CHILD NO. 3) How often do you
feel good about how he/she is doing?

|‾| Often? ------------->   ____ Please |___| 37
                          give me an example of what
|‾| Sometimes? ---------> you mean. _____

|‾| Hardly ever or never? _____

|‾| Other (specify)   _____

_____   _____

IF MORE THAN THREE CHILDREN, PROVIDE
INFORMATION ON OTHER SIDE OF THIS PAGE.

F.4.4. Have there been any times since your oldest child was born
when you were separated from him/her for a month or longer
- either because you were away or because he/she was away
from home?

|‾| Yes

|‾| No   38

|‾| Other (specify) _____

a) How long were you and your child separated from
each other? (THE FIRST TIME IF MORE THAN ONE
SEPARATION)   39

b) How old was your child when this separation took
place?   40-41

c) What was the reason for the separation?   42-43

d) Were there other occasions when he/she was separated
from you for more than a month? (PROBE, IF NECESSARY
FOR NUMBER OF SEPARATIONS, LENGTH, AND CIRCUMSTANCES)   44-45

                                                              46-47

                                                              48-49

F.4.5. Were you separated from any of your <u>other</u> children for a
month or longer?

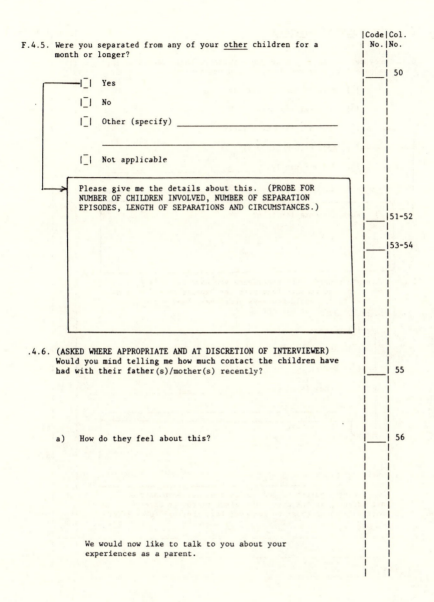

|‾| Yes

|‾| No

|‾| Other (specify) _____

_____

|‾| Not applicable

Please give me the details about this. (PROBE FOR
NUMBER OF CHILDREN INVOLVED, NUMBER OF SEPARATION
EPISODES, LENGTH OF SEPARATIONS AND CIRCUMSTANCES.)

50

|51-52

|53-54

.4.6. (ASKED WHERE APPROPRIATE AND AT DISCRETION OF INTERVIEWER)
Would you mind telling me how much contact the children have
had with their father(s)/mother(s) recently?

55

a) How do they feel about this?

56

We would now like to talk to you about your
experiences as a parent.

G.   THE PARENTING EXPERIENCE

G.1.   How much satisfaction do you experience these days in being
       a parent to your children? Would you say...

              |‾| A great deal of satisfaction? |___| 57

              |‾| Some satisfaction?

              |‾| Just a little satisfaction?

              |‾| None or almost none?

              |‾| Other (specify) _____

              _____

        a)   What accounts for this? |___|58-59

G.2.   When you consider the experience you have had raising your
       children, and compare them with the experiences of friends
       and relatives, would you says yours have been _easier_,
       about the same, or _harder_?

              |‾| Easier |___| 60

              |‾| About the same

              |‾| Harder

              |‾| Other (specify) _____

              _____

              Why is that? |___|61-62

                                                                  |___|63-64

G.3.   When being a parent to your child(ren) has been hard or
       discouraging in the past, what kinds of things have you found
       most helpful in order to get over this feeling? (OPEN-ENDED) |___|65-66

       _____ |___|67-68

       _____ |___|69-70

       _____

304

G.4. What do you find the hardest thing about being a parent these days?

|____|71-72

|____|73-74

|____|75-76

a) Why is that?

|____|77-78

G.5. (1) Do you have any feelings, positive or negative, about the age at which you first became a parent. For instance do you think that you became a parent at too young an age, or too old, or just right?

|‾| Too young

|‾| Too old

|‾| Just right

|‾| Other (specify) _____

|____| 79

_____

a) What has made you feel this way?

|____| 80

RESEARCH NO. ____

|____| 1-3

CARD NO. 11

| 11 | 4-5

G.5. (2) Do you have any feelings, positive or negative, about the number of children you have had?

|‾| Yes, positive

|‾| Yes, negative

|‾| No

|‾| Other (specify) _____

|____| 6

_____

a) How has the number of children you had affected you?

|____| 7-8

|____| 9-10

305

H.   CONDITIONS OF LIFE FOR FAMILY

We would like to have some sense of the conditions your
family faced when you came to the agency and what your
circumstances are now. For example, concerning your housing...

H.1. When you first came to the agency how satisfied were you with
your housing arrangements? In general, would you say... |____| 11

        |‾| Very satisfied? (GO TO P.38)

        |‾| Fairly satisfied? (GO TO P.38)

        |‾| Neither?   (GO TO P.38)

     ┌──────|‾| Fairly dissatisfied?

     ├─────|‾| Very dissatisfied?

     │ |‾| Other (specify) _____

     │ ┌───┐
     └─→│ a) Why were you dissatisfied? (PROBE: What conditions |____|12-13
        │   did you object to?)
        │   _____ |____|14-15
        │   _____
        │   _____
        │
        │ b) Has the situation changed? |____| 16
        │ ┌──────|‾| Yes
        │ │ |‾| No
        │ │ |‾| Other (specify) _____
        │ │ ┌──┐
        │ └─→│ In what way has it changed?   │ |____|17-18
        │   │ _____   │
        │   │ _____   │
        │   └──┘
        │
        │ c) Have you made any effort to improve the situation? |____| 19
        │   (PROBE: Have you looked for new housing in the past
        │   year?)
        │ |‾| No
        │   ┌──|‾| Yes
        │   └─→Please tell me what you did? |____|20-21
        │   _____
        │   _____
        └───┘

306

H.2.   Has LESFU staff tried to help you with your housing problems?

      |⁻| Yes |___| 22

      |⁻| No

      |⁻| Other (specify) _____

a)   In what way? |___|23-24

                                                    |___|25-26

b)   How do you evaluate the agency's effort to help? |___| 27
      Would you say...

      |⁻| It helped accomplish a change in housing?

      |⁻| There has been no change in housing but effort
           is still going on?

      |⁻| There has been no change in housing and change
           does not seem likely?

      |⁻| Other (specify) _____

b.1) Please describe the change in your housing. |___| 28

b.2) Do you feel that LESFU did as much as it could
     to try to help you get your housing changed?

      |⁻| Yes |___| 29

      |⁻| No (Specify what should have been done
             further to change housing)

c)   Why was this? (PROBE, IF NECESSARY: Did you ask
      LESFU staff to help you? If <u>yes</u>, why was help not
      offered?) |___|30-31

      _____

      _____

      _____

H.3.   Since you have said you are dissatisfied with your housing,
       we are interested in knowing how you think this problem
       influences you and your children.

   a)   How does it affect you in carrying out your
        responsibilities as a parent? |____|32-33

                                                               |____|34-35

   b)   How does it affect the way in which family members
        get along with each other? |____|36-37

                                                               |____|38-39

   c)   In the adjustment of the children? |____|40-41

                                                               |____|42-43

   d)   Does your housing situation affect you in any other way? |____|44-45

                                                               |____|46-47

I.   CONCERNING THIS <u>NEIGHBORHOOD</u>...

I.1.   How do you feel about this neighborhood as a place in which
       to raise your family? Would you say it is...

                                                                        | 48

                 |‾| A very good place?

                 |‾| A fairly good place?

                 |‾| Average/a mixture of good and bad?

                 |‾| A pretty bad place?

)‾| A very bad place?

                 |‾| Other (specify) _____

         a)   Why do you feel this way? |____|49-50

                                                                        |____|51-52

         b)   How has living in this neighborhood influenced how
               you live? |____|53-54

                                                                        |____|55-56

         c)   How do you see the conditions of this neighborhood
               influencing your children? |____|57-58

                                                                        |____|59-60

309

J.   INCOME AND FINANCIAL MATTERS |Code|Col.
                                                                      | No.| No.

      We are interested in knowing something about the role of
      income and financial matters in your family's living
      situation.

J.1. What are the sources of income in your home?
      (CHECK ALL THAT APPLY)

      |‾| Public Assistance (full support) |___| 61

      |‾| Public Assistance (partial support) |___| 62

      |‾| Wages |___| 63

      |‾| Social security |___| 64

      |‾| Other (specify) _____ |___| 65

      _____

      |‾| No income of own (lives with relatives) |___| 66

      |‾| No income at all at this time |___| 67

J.2. How long have you been receiving public assistance? |___|68

      _____ Years   _____ Months |___|69

J.3. How long have you been receiving Social Security benefits? |___|70-71

      _____ Years   _____ Months |___|72-73

J.4. a) Who is employed in your family? |___| 74

      b) Please describe the occupation (s) _____ |___| 75

      _____ |___| 76

310

J.5. Do you have income from any other source?

       |⁻| Yes |___| 77

       |⁻| No

    a)   What is this source? |___| 78

    b)   What portion of family's total income does this
         source account for? |___|79-80

                                RESEARCH NO. ___ |___| 1-3

                             CARD NO. _12_ | 12 | 4-5

J.6. Do you regard your income as providing you with an adequate
      amount of money to raise your family decently? |___| 6

       |⁻| Income is adequate

       |⁻| Income is somewhat adequate

       |⁻| Income is inadequate

       |⁻| Other (specify) _____

               _____

J.7. During the past few months have you had to worry about money
      matters? Would you say... |___| 7

       |⁻| Very often?

       |⁻| Often?

       |⁻| Sometimes?

       |⁻| Hardly ever?

       |⁻| Never

       |⁻| Other (specify) _____

J.8. Do you ever run short of money or food stamps so that you
do not have the ability to buy food? Would you say this
happens...

|‾| Often?

|‾| Sometimes?

|‾| Never?

|‾| Other (specify) _____

_____

a)   Why do you think this happens?

b)   What do you usually do when this happens?
(PROBE: How do you get food for your family?)

J.9. Some people are able to budget their income very carefully
and "stretch a dollar" to make ends meet -- others find this
hard to do. Would you say that you find managing your income...

|‾| Easy or fairly easy to do?

|‾| Somewhat hard to do?

|‾| Hard or very hard to do?

|‾| Other (specify) _____

_____

a)   Why is this the case?

_____

_____

8

9-10

11-12

13-14

15-16

17

18-19

20-21

K.   WORK HISTORY |Code|Col.
                                                                         | No.| No.

K.1. Are you employed in either a full-time or part-time
      capacity? | |
                                                                         |____| 22
              ____|‾| Yes | |
             | | |
             | |‾| No (Go to Question K.2.) | |
             | | |
             | |‾| Other (specify) _____ | |
             | ┌──┐ | |
             └───→| Please describe your employment. | | |23-24
                  | | | |
                  | _____ | | |25-26
                  | | | |
                  | _____ | | |
                  | | | |
                  | (Go to Question K.4.) | | |
                  └──┘ | |

K.2. Do you think you will seek employment in the future? | |
                                                                         |____| 27
              ____|‾| Yes | |
             | | |
             | |‾| No (Go to Question K.3.) | |
             | | |
             | |‾| Other | |
             | ┌──┐ | |
             └───→| a) What kind of work do you think you might seek? |____| 28
                  | │ | |
                  | | | |
                  | (Go to Question K.3.) | |____| 29
                  └──┘ | |

K.3. Have you ever worked in paid employment of some kind? | |
                                                                         |____| 30
              ___|‾| Yes (Go to Question K.4.) | |
             | | |
             | |‾| No (Go to Question K.5.) | |
             | | |
             | |‾| Other (specify) _____ | |
             | ┌──┐ | |
             └→|K.4. What kind of work have you ever done for the longest | |
               | period? For how long? _____ | |31-32
               | (years) | |
               | | |
               | a) Please describe this employment (type of occupation,| |
               | employer, and work tasks). | |33-34
               | | |
               | _____ | |35-36
               | | |
               | _____ | |
               | | |
               | b) When was the last time you worked? | |37-38
               | | |
               └──┘ | |

                                    313

K.5. Have you ever felt that you would like to get more
      education for yourself?

      |‾| Yes |___| 39

      |‾| No

      |‾| Other (specify) _____

                           _____

a) Please describe what you would like in the way of
    further education? |___|40-41

                                            |___|42-43

b) What are the chances that you will actually get
    this education? |___|44-45

K.6. Have you ever thought of getting job training for yourself?

                                                        |___| 46

      |‾| Yes

      |‾| No

      |‾| Other (specify) _____

                           _____

a) Please describe what kind of training you would
    like? |___|47-48

                                            |___|49-50

L.   CLIENT MORALE AND OUTLOOK |Code|Col.
                                                                 | No.| No.

L.1.   On the whole, would you say that you are generally a pretty
        cheerful person in your outlook on life these days, not so
        cheerful, or somewhere in the middle? | 51

              |‾| Generally pretty cheerful

              |‾| Somewhere in the middle

        ──────|‾| Generally not so cheerful

              |‾| Other (specify) _____

        ┌──┐
        │ a)   What seems to get you down? (OPEN-ENDED) │ |52-53
        │   │ |54-55
        │   │
        │ b)   How bad do these feelings get? (PROBE: Would you
        │   say that you are often depressed?)   │ |56-57
        │   │
        └──┘

L.2.   Do you find yourself feeling bitter about the way things
        have turned out for you? Would you say...
                                                                         | 58
        ──────|‾| Yes, very often?

        ──────|‾| Yes, sometimes?

              |‾| No, hardly ever or never?

              |‾| Other (specify) _____

        ┌──┐
        │ a)   What generally causes you to feel this way?│ |59-60
        │   │ |61-62
        │   │
        └──┘

315

L.3. As far as your home life goes, has anything happened to change your routine in the past year or so? For example...

a) Has there been a death in your close family during the past year?

|_| No   63

|_| Yes (How did this affect you? _____   64-65

_____)

b) Any serious sickness within your close family?

|_| No   66

|_| Yes (How did this affect you? _____   67-68

_____)

c) A baby born?

|_| No   69

|_| Yes (How did this affect you? _____   70-71

_____)

d) Lost your job or had your public assistance terminated?

|_| No   72

|_| Yes (How did this affect you? _____   73-74

_____)

e) Breakup with husband/wife or boy friend/girl friend?

|_| No   75

|_| Yes (How did this affect you? _____   76-77

_____)

f) Anyone in trouble with police or other authority?

|_| No   78

|_| Yes (How did this affect you? _____   79-80

_____)

RESEARCH NO. ____ |____| 1-3

CARD NO. _13_ | 13 | 4-5

L.3. g) Child running away from home?

|‾| No |____| 6

|‾| Yes (How did this affect you? _____ |____| 7-8

_____)

h) Any other problems? |____| 9

|‾| No

|‾| Yes (How did this affect you? _____ |____| 10

_____)

i) Has anything positive happened in the last year to
change your routine? |____| 11

|‾| Yes (How did this affect you?

_____) |____| 12

|‾| No

|‾| Other (specify: _____

_____)

317

M. SOCIAL HEALTH BATTERY

We are interested in the social activities you and members of of your family are able to participate in.

M.1. About how many families in your neighborhood do you know well enough that you visit each other in your homes?

|_| None

|_| One or more (number:_____)

|_| Other (specify _____

_____)

|___| 13

M.2. About how many close friends do you have - people you feel at ease with and can talk with about what is on your mind? (You may include relatives.)

|_| None

|_| One or more (number:_____)

|_| Other (specify _____

_____)

|____|14-15

M.3. Over a year's time, about how often do you get together with friends or relatives, like going out together or visiting in each other's homes? Would you say....

|_| Every day?

|_| Several days a week?

|_| 2 or 3 times a month?

|_| About once a month?

|_| 5 to 10 times a year?

|_| 1 to 5 times a year?

|_| Never or almost never?

|_| Other (specify: _____

_____)

|____|16-17

| | Code | Col. |
| | No. | No. |

M.4. During the <u>past month</u>, about how often have you had friends over to your home? (Do <u>not</u> count relatives.) Would you say.... |____|18-19

    |_| Every day?

    |_| Several days a week?

    |_| About once a week?

    |_| 2 to 3 times in past month?

    |_| Once in past month?

    |_| Not at all in past month?

    |_| Other (specify: _____

    _____)

M.5. About how often have you visited with friends at <u>their</u> homes during the <u>past month</u>? (Do not count relatives.) Would you say.... |____|20-21

    |_| Every day?

    |_| Several days a week?

    |_| About once a week?

    |_| 2 to 3 times in past month?

    |_| Once in past month?

    |_| Not at all in past month?

    |_| Other (specify: _____

    _____)

M.6. About how often were you on the telephone with close friends or relatives during the <u>past month</u>? Would you say.... |____|22-23

    |_| Every day?

    |_| Several times a week?

    |_| About once a week?

    |_| 2 or 3 times?

    |_| Once?

    |_| Not at all?

    |_| Other (specify: _____

    _____)

M.7. About how often did you write a letter to a friend or relative
during the <u>past month</u>? Would you say....

|‾| Every day?

|‾| Several times a week?

|‾| About once a week?

|‾| 2 or 3 times in past month?

|‾| Once in past month?

|‾| Not at all in past month?

|‾| Other (specify: _____

_____)

M.8. In general, how well are you getting along with other people
these days - would you say better than usual, about the same,
or not as well as usual?

|‾| Better than usual?

|‾| About the same?

|‾| Not as well as usual?

|‾| Other (specify: _____

_____)

M.9. How often have you attended a religious service during the
<u>past month</u>?

|‾| Every day?

|‾| More than once a week?

|‾| Once a week?

|‾| 2 or 3 times in past month?

|‾| Once in past month?

|‾| Not at all in past month?

|‾| Other (specify: _____

_____)

320

M.10. About how many voluntary groups or organizations do you belong
       to - like church groups, clubs, parent groups, etc.
       ("Voluntary" means because you want to)

      |‾| None   (Check last item in M.11. below)

      |‾| One or more (specific number:_____)

      |‾] Other (specify _____

              _____)

M.11. How active are you in the affairs of these groups or clubs you
       belong to? Would you say....

      |‾| Very active, attend most meetings?

      |‾| Fairly active, attend fairly often?

      |‾| Not active, but hardly ever go?

      |‾| Do not belong to any groups or clubs?

Code column markers: |____|30-31 (for M.10) and |____|32-33 (for M.11)

N.   VIEWS ON SUBSTITUTE CARE

N.1.   In recent years, have you ever had the idea that you would
        like to totally stop taking care of your children by having
        someone else do this?

                                                                        34

                |_| No

        ┌──────|_| yes

        │   a) About how often have you felt this way?   35-36
        │
        │   b) Did you ever try to have someone else care for your
        └   children? (IF YES, INQUIRE ABOUT CIRCUMSTANCES)   37-38

N.2.   Can you think of any circumstances in the future in which you
        would stop taking care of your children?

                                                                        39

        ┌──────|_| Yes

            |_| No

            |_| Other (specify) _____

                _____

        │   a) Under what circumstances? Please tell me what
        └──▶   you had in mind?   40-41

                                                                       42-43

N.3.   What if a parent like yourself cannot take care of his/her
        children, say, because of physical illness. What would be
        the best arrangement a parent could secure for the care of
        his/her children? (PROBE FOR REASONS FOR SELECTING
        ARRANGEMENTS)   44-45

                                                                       46-47

        a) In your case, would such an arrangement be possible?

                                                                       48-49

        b) What would be the next-best arrangement?

                                                                       50-51

322

N.4. How do you feel about foster care -- where an agency places
      children with a family not related to the children? If, for
      example, you had a health problem and could not take care of
      your children. How would you feel about placing them in
      foster care?

|52-53

      |‾| Positive - <u>for</u> such a plan?

      |‾| Somewhat positive?

      |‾| Neutral?

      |‾| Somewhat negative?

      |‾| Negative - <u>against</u> such a plan?

      |‾| Other (specify) _____

      _____

N.5. What are the positive things that foster care might offer
      when parents are incapacitated?

|54-55

|56-57

N.6. What are the negative things that might be associated with
      foster care?

|58-59

|60-61

N.7. Do you have any relatives, friends, or neighbors who have
      had their children placed in foster care?

| 62

      |‾| No

      |‾| Yes

   a) What was it like? (PROBE, IF NECESSARY: How did
       things turn out?)

|63-64

O.   OTHER SERVICE PROVIDERS AT THE TIME OF CASE OPENING

|Code|Col.
| No.| No.

O.1. Before you came to LESFU were you or any members of your
      family receiving service from other agencies or service
      providers? | | 65

      |_| Yes

      |_| No

      |_| Other (specify) _____

      _____

      a) What agencies were these? | |66-67

                                                                      |____|68-69

                                                                      |____|70-71

      b) What services were being provided? |____|72-73

                                                                      |____|74-75

                                                                      |____|76-77

      c) How helpful were the services you were getting? |____| 78

                                                                      |____| 79

                                                                      |____| 80

                                          RESEARCH NO. _____ |____| 1-3

                                          CARD NO. 14 | 14 | 4-5

      d) Is service still being provided from this source? | | 6-7

                                                                      |____| 8-9

                                                                      |____|10-11

324

P   REFERRALS BY LESFU TO OTHER SERVICE AGENCIES |Code|Col.
                                                                        | No.| No.

P.1.   Did the LESFU social worker (Mr./Ms. _____) refer
        you to some other agency or service organization to get
        help that you or a member of your family needed?

            |‾| No

            |‾| Yes (PROCEED TO P.3.) |____| 12

            |‾| Other (specify) _____

            _____

P.2.   Was there a referral for service of some kind that you felt
        you or some member of your family needed but was not made on
        your behalf? |____| 13

            |‾| No (GO TO PAGE 58)

            |‾| Yes

            |‾| Other (specify) _____

            _____

        a) Why was the referral not made? |____|14-15

                                                                        |____|16-17
                                    (GO TO PAGE 58)
P.3.   What is the name of the agency you were referred to? |____|

        _____ |____|18-19

        _____ |____|20-21

        a) What was the reason the referral was made? (PROBE: What |____|22-23
            service were you supposed to receive from this agency?)
                                                                        |____|24-25

        b) Whose idea was it that you be referred to this agency? |____| 26

            |‾| Social worker suggested referral

            |‾| Referral was mutual idea of client and social worker

            |‾| Client suggested referral

            |‾| Other (specify) _____

            _____

325

P.3.   c) Did any of the following procedures take place as a way of
            getting you connected with this agency?

            Social worker telephoned the other agency to talk
            about your situation. |___| 27

                    |_| Yes

                    |_| No

                    |_| Other (specify) _____

        d) Social worker wrote referral letter to the other
            agency. |___| 28

                    |_| Yes

                    |_| No

                    |_| Other (specify) _____

        e) Social worker arranged for meeting at LESFU with
            representative of the other agency. |___| 29

                    |_| Yes

                    |_| No

                    |_| Other (specify) _____

        f) Social worker accompanied you to the other agency. |___| 30

                    |_| Yes

                    |_| No

                    |_| Other (specify) _____

        g) Other action: _____ |___|31-32

        h) Please describe your experience with _____ (agency)
            What services have they provided to you? |___|33-34

                                                                           |___|35-36

                                                                           |___|37-38

|Code|Col.
| No.| No.

P.3. i) Are you still in contact with _____ (agency)?

                                                          |____|39-40

        ─┤‾| Yes

         |‾| No

         |‾| Other (specify) _____

         _____

IF YES
j) How long do you think you will continue to have contact |____|41-42
    with the agency?

k) What is the nature of the service being provided you now? |____|43-44

                                                                 |____|45-46

                                                                 |____|47-48

l) What do you feel you have gained from your contact with |____|49-50
    _____(agency)?
         (FILL IN NAME OF AGENCY) |____|51-52

                                                                 |____|53-54

m) How responsive to your needs would you say this agency |____| 55
    was? Would you say...
                                                                 |____|56-57
    |‾| Very responsive - tried to help with the problem

    |‾| Somewhat responsive

   ─┤‾| Hardly responsive

   ─┤‾| Not at all responsive - did not try to help with
         the problem

    |‾| Other (specify) _____

    _____

    m.1) Why do you think they did not respond to your need? |____|58-59

                                                                 |____|60-61

327

P.3.   n)   Overall, how would you rate the service provided by
            _____ agency? Would you say... |___| 62

            |_| Excellent?

            |_| Good?

            |_| Fair?

            |_| Not so good?

            |_| Poor?

            |_| Other (specify) _____

            _____

            What reasons cause you to see the agency in this
            way? (OPEN-ENDED) |___|63-64

                                                                       |___|65-66

                                                                       |___|67-68

P.4.   Did the LESFU social worker refer you to a second agency?

            |_| Yes |___| 69

            |_| No

            |_| Other (specify _____

            _____)

       IF LESFU REFERRED CLIENT TO MORE THAN ONE AGENCY USE
       SUPPLEMENTAL FORMS

Q.1.   As far as you know, did the social worker at LESFU
        (Ms./Mr._____) intervene on your behalf with another
        organization to help you obtain something you were entitled
        to but were not getting?
        (IF CLIENT DOES NOT COMPREHEND OR OTHERWISE NEEDS HELP WITH
        THIS QUESTION: For example, did the social worker contact the
        public assistance agency (i.e. "Welfare") to help you get
        financial assistance you were entitled to? Or, the Housing
        Authority to support an application you had made for an
        apartment?)

                                                                        70
            |‾| No

            |‾| Yes

            |‾| Other (specify) _____

            _____

        a) Please tell me about it. What did Ms./Mr._____
            try to do for you?   71-72

        b) Would you say this effort was successful, helped
            you in some way?   73-74

                |‾| No, effort failed

                |‾| Effort still under way, but not hopeful

                |‾| Effort still under way, but hopeful

                |‾| Yes

                |‾| Other (specify) _____

                _____

            We are interested in whether you have any particular
            feeling about LESFU based upon how this effort turned
            out. For example...
        c. Do you feel LESFU did as much as it could for
            you in connection with this problem?   75

                |‾| Yes

                |‾| No

                |‾| Other (specify) _____

                _____

            What more would you have liked done?   76-77

Continued...

.... Continued

|Code|Col.
| No.| No.

Q.1.

d) How influential do you feel LESFU can be with other agencies of this type? Would you say it can have...

|‾| A great deal of influence?

|‾| Some influence?

|‾| Little influence?

|‾| No influence?

|‾| Other (specify) _____

_____

Why do you say this?

78

79-80

RESEARCH NO. _____ |____| 1-3

CARD NO. _15_ | 15 | 4-5

R. OTHER SERVICE PROVIDERS CONTACTED BY CLIENT ON OWN INITIATIVE

R.1. Are you or any members of your family now receiving service
from an agency or service provider that you made contact with
on your own or through the recommendation or referral from
a person or organization other than LESFU (OTHER THAN THOSE
ON PAGE 53)?

|____| 6

|‾| No

|‾| Yes

|‾| Other (specify) _____

_____

a) What agency is this? |____| 7-8

|____| 9-10

b) What services are being received from this source? |____|11-12

|____|13-14

|____|15-16

c) Have you (or your family) found the services helpful? |____|17-18
In what way?

|____|19-20

S.   CLOSING QUESTIONS

      Now finally,

S.1   Would you recommend LESFU to friends if they faced the same
      kind of difficulty you did? Would you say....

            |‾| Yes, I would take them there myself?

            |‾| Yes, I would suggest they go?

            |‾| No, would not recommend LESFU?

            |‾| Other (Specify: _____

            _____)

      a)   Why do you say this?

S.2. Is there anything that you think is important that I
      have not mentioned?

S.3. Is there anything else that you wanted to talk about?

S.4. How do you feel about this interview generally?

S.5. PROBE (IF NECESSARY): Did you get anything out of it?
                             Did it help you in any way?

      a)   Did it give you any problems?

FINALLY, THANK THE RESPONDENT FOR THE HELP AND COOPERATION GIVEN

Code	Col.
No.	No.
	21
	22-23
	24-25
	26-27
	28
	29-30
	31-32
	33-34

T.   INTERVIEWER REPORT

T.1.   RESPONDENT'S RACE OR ETHNICITY |___| 35

          |‾| White

          |‾| Black

          |‾| Puerto Rican

          |‾| Chinese

          |‾| Other (specify) _____

T.2.   INTERVIEW WAS CONDUCTED: |___| 36

          |‾| Entirely in English

          |‾| Entirely in Spanish

          |‾| Entirely in Chinese

          |‾| Mostly in English but partly in _____
                                                   (specify)
          |‾| Mostly in _____ but partly in English
                            (specify)

T.3.   WHO ELSE WAS PRESENT DURING THE INTERVIEW? (If household
       members, record first names.) |___| 37

                                                                       |___| 38

                                                                       |___| 39

T.4.   HOW GOOD WERE THE CONDITIONS FOR THE INTERVIEW? |___|40-41

CHECK ALL
THAT APPLY |‾| Noise interfering with audibility

          |‾| Distractions (Source: _____)

          |‾| Interruptions (Source: _____)

          |‾| Lack of privacy

          |‾| Other (specify) _____

333

T.5.   WERE ANY OF THE FOLLOWING BEHAVIORS MANIFESTED BY THE
       RESPONDENT DURING THE INTERVIEW?

	Very much	Some- what	Not at all		
a. Suspicious or guarded	|_|	|_|	|_|	|___|	42
b. Anxious or uncertain	|_|	|_|	|_|	|___|	43
c. Inappropriate in responses	|_|	|_|	|_|	|___|	44
d. Interested	|_|	|_|	|_|	|___|	45
e. Long-winded responses	|_|	|_|	|_|	|___|	46
f. Friendly	|_|	|_|	|_|	|___|	47
g. Found interview too long	|_|	|_|	|_|	|___|	48
h. Difficulty in understanding questions?	|_|	|_|	|_|	|___|	49
i. Other (specify) _____	|_|	|_|		|___|	50

T.6.   WHAT WAS THE RESPONDENT'S OVERALL ATTITUDE TOWARD THE
       LOWER EAST SIDE FAMILY UNION?

	Very much	Some- what	Not at all	NA/ Other		
a. Had difficulty remembering agency	|_|	|_|	|_|	|_|	|___|	51
b. Had positive things to say about agency	|_|	|_|	|_|	|_|	|___|	52
c. Had negative things to say about agency	|_|	|_|	|_|	|_|	|___|	53
d. Seemed clear about agency's program	|_|	|_|	|_|	|_|	|___|	54
e. Appeared to have positive feeling for agency staff	|_|	|_|	|_|	|_|	|___|	55
f. Felt agency had met ex- pectations for service	|_|	|_|	|_|	|_|	|___|	56
g. Seemed to understand agency's model of service	|_|	|_|	|_|	|_|	|___|	57
h. Other (specify) _____					|___|	58-59

Time Interview Ended: |___| 60-61
                      |___| 62-63

_____

334

Would you like to do another interview like this for another $25?

    ___Yes

    ___Maybe

    ___No

If YES, tell the client that someone will contact them regarding the scheduling of such an interview.

If MAYBE, ask the client when someone can contact them to discuss the possibility further:

_____

INTERVIEW SUMMARY

Scale Creation Strategy

This appendix contains a description of our index creation strategy. This strategy has been implemented in programs written by John Grundy. These programs are modifications of standard statistical programs that perform factor analysis. These strategies are the distillation of Grundy's experiences in many social science research applications. We have used them to advantage in our Casey research (Fanshel et al., 1990). Through simulation studies of factor analysis with data structured according to models that we hypothesize to hold in our research, we have found that the varimax rotation of the principal components produces satisfactory results, and we used this rotation here.[1]

Many of our variables are Likert scales, so we start our work by transforming the scales so that each has the same range. That is, each transformed scale has the same minimum value, m, and the same maximum value, M. A key concept is that of a "variable belonging to a factor." A variable belongs to a factor when the absolute value of the rotated coefficient of the variable in the factor, its loading, is greater than .35. The principal objective of our index construction strategy was to find sets of variables such that each set had high item-criterion correlations and did not share variables with other sets. Our strategy is to define indexes as the sum of variables that belong to a factor, as defined by an eight step process:

1. Inclusion of Relevant Variables: First, run the largest possible factor analysis, including as many variables as were germane to any one data gathering occasion. For example, one factor analysis considered variables from the first debriefing interview. Variables that described other data gathering efforts were not included in this factor analysis.

2. Choice of Number of Factors Extracted: For each factor analysis, it is necessary to determine the number of factors in the solution used. The initial number of factors extracted is the number of eigenvalues of the correlation matrix that were greater than one. We compute the varimax rotation of the solution with this number of factors. We then go through an iterative process to reduce the number of factors used. If no more than two variables belong to the last factor extracted, we reduce the number of factors

in the solution by one and recompute the rotated factors. We again examine the last factor extracted. If no more than two variables belong to it, we reduce the number of factors by one again and recompute again. This procedure continues until we find the largest integer such that the last factor in the rotated solution with one more factor has only one or two variables belonging to it.

3. Measuring Internal Consistency of Index: Each factor has a corresponding set of variables that includes each variable that belongs to the factor. Variables that appear in two or more sets generally are ambiguous or broader in concept than a simple component of a variable. We use Cronbach's alpha (Cronbach 1951) to measure the internal consistency of our indexes, especially those derived from factors with less than 10 or 12 variables. We calculate Cronbach's alpha for each set. Based on our past experience, we regard a Cronbach's alpha of .60 as a reasonable cutoff.

   We challenge any set of variables with ten or fewer items that has Cronbach's alpha less than .60. If such an index makes "sense" and represents a potentially important latent variable, we keep it. Otherwise, we discard the index.

4. Reversing Scale When the Coefficient is Negative: When a variable has a negative loading in the factor to which it belongs, then the index uses the reexpressed variable X' equal to the sum of the maximum and minimum possible values minus the value of the variable; that is;

   $$X' = m + M - X.$$

   At this point we can begin to form the indexes by examining the pattern of variables belonging to a factor.

5. Single Variable Factors: A factor with just one variable belonging to it does not require an index. If the variable has substantive importance, we exclude it from the index construction process and use it in our subsequent analyses directly, without attempting further reduction of variables.

6. Inclusion of Items in an Index: We next considered each factor in turn. The simplest situation is a factor containing variables that belong only to this one factor. The index uses only the variables belonging to the factor, and is the mean of the non-missing values of these variables. The next simplest situation is that there is a set of variables that belongs only to Factor A, another set that belongs only to Factor B, and a third set that belongs to both Factor A and Factor B, but to no other factors. Then, we create three indexes. The first uses only the variables that belong to Factor A, the second uses only the variables that belong to Factor B, and the third uses the variables common to Factor A and Factor B.

7. Dealing with Remaining Variables: If there are variables remaining that have not been included in an index, we run a factor analysis including just these variables and repeat the analysis procedure of steps one through six. In general, few indexes result from this step. The variables that remain are often very skewed (for example, status variables for a rare condition) or are measured with a great deal of error.

8. Assessing the reliability of an index: We calculate three measures of reliability: Cronbach's alpha, item-criterion correlations (the correlation of the item with the index minus the item), and the correlation of each item with indexes other than the one containing the item. If other measures, such as intraclass correlations are available, we use them as well.

We regard the item-criterion correlations as the most important evaluative statistics. Each correlation should, at a minimum, be statistically significant. Ideally, each should be high and essentially equal to the others. In this study, the item-criterion correlations ranged from .4 to .7. We compare the lowest item-criterion correlation in an index to the item-criterion correlations for the other items. If they are low as well, then we keep the item in the index. If the other items have item-criterion correlations that are higher, then we examine the Cronbach alpha for the index with the item deleted. If the Cronbach alpha for an index with the item removed is lower than the Cronbach alpha for the index with the item, then we keep the item in the index. If an item has a higher correlation with an index other than the one that contains it, we examine the content of the item and the two indexes to see whether it makes more sense to delete the item or to move it to the other index. On rare occasions, we have kept the item in the original index.

Missing Data: When a case has values missing for variables in an index, the value of the index is the mean of the values observed for the case for variables in the index. This rule permits the calculation of each index for most subjects. In our regression and factor analyses, we replaced missing information on any index or single variable used in an analysis with the mean of the respective index or variable.

NOTE

1. Terri McNulty, one of Finch's graduate students at Stony Brook, studied the application of these strategies on mathematical models similar to ones that we believe held in the LESFU data as part of her research project for her master's degree. Her results confirmed the effectiveness of factor analysis strategies like the one described here.

References

BOOKS AND ARTICLES

Alcabes, Abraham, and James A. Jones. 1985. Structural Determinants of "Clienthood." *Social Work* 30, no. 1:49–53.

Beck, Bertram M. 1979. *The Lower East Side Family Union: A Social Invention*. New York: Foundation for Child Development.

Bostwick, Gerald J. Jr., and Nancy S. Kyte. 1988. Validity and Reliability. In Richard M. Grinnell, Jr. (Editor), *Social Work Research and Evaluation* pp. 111–136. Itasca, Ill.: F. E. Peacock.

Briar, Scott. 1966. Family Services. In Henry S. Maas, *Five Fields of Social Services: Reviews of Research* pp. 9–50. New York: National Association of Social Workers.

Citizen's Committee for Children of New York. 1971. *A Dream Deferred*. New York: Citizen's Committee for Children.

Cochran, William G. 1983. *Planning and Analysis of Observational Studies*. New York: John Wiley and Sons.

DeMaio, Theresa J. 1984. Social Desirability and Survey Measurement: A Review. In Charles F. Turner and Elizabeth Martin (Editors), *Surveying Subjective Phenomena*, vol. 2 pp. 257–282. New York: Russell Sage Foundation.

Draper, Norman R., and Harry Smith. 1981. *Applied Regression Analysis*. 2nd ed. New York: John Wiley and Sons.

Durkheim, Emile. 1951. *Suicide*. Glencoe, Ill.: Free Press.

Eyesenck, Hans J. 1952. The Effects of Psychotherapy: An Evaluation. *Journal of Consulting Psychology* 16:319–324.

Fanshel, David, Stephen J. Finch, and John F. Grundy. 1990. Foster Children in a Life Course Perspective New York: Columbia University Press.

Fanshel, David, and Eugene B. Shinn. 1978. *Children in Foster Care: A Longitudinal Investigation*. New York: Columbia University Press.

Fleiss, Joseph L. 1981. *Statistical Methods for Rates and Proportions*. 2nd ed. New York: John Wiley and Sons.

Hollis, Florence. 1964. *Casework: A Psychosocial Therapy*. New York: Random House.

Hunt, J. McVicker. 1948. Measuring Movement in Casework. *Social Casework* 29, no. 9. pp. 343–348.

Jones, Mary Ann, Renee Neuman, and Ann W. Shyne. 1976. *A Second Chance for Families*. New York: Child Welfare League of America.

Kinney, Jill, David Haapala, and Charlotte Booth. 1991. *Keeping Families Together— The Homebuilders Model*. New York: Adine De Gruyter.

Lagey, Joseph C., and Beverly Ayers. 1963. Community Treatment Programs for Multi-Problem Families. In Benjamin Schlesinger (Editor), *The Multi-Problem Family*, pp. 55–71. Toronto: University of Toronto Press.

Lenski, Gerhard E., and John C. Leggett. 1960. Caste, Class, and Deference in the Research Interview. *American Journal of Sociology* 65, no. 5:463–467.

Magura, Stephen and Beth Silverman Moses. 1986. Outcome Measures for Child Welfare Services, Theory, and Applications. Washington D.C.: Child Welfare League of America.

Maluccio, Anthony N. 1979. *Learning from Clients—Interpersonal Helping as Viewed by Clients and Social Workers*. New York: Free Press.

Maluccio, Anthony N., Edith Fein, and Kathleen A. Olmstead. 1986. *Permanency Planning for Children*. New York: Tavistock Publications.

Maluccio, Anthony N. and Wilma D. Marlow. 1974. The Case for the Contract. Social Work. 19, no. 5, pp. 28–37.

Mayer, Jerome E., and Noel Timms. 1970. *The Client Speaks—Working Class Impressions of Casework*. Boston, Mass.: Routledge & Kegan Paul.

Meyer, Carol H. 1984. Working with New Immigrants (Editorial). *Social Work* 29, no. 2:99.

National Commission for Children in Need of Parents. 1979. *Who Knows? Who Cares? Forgotten Children in Foster Care*. New York: National Commission for Children.

Perlman, Helen Harris. 1968. *Persona: Social Role and Personality*. Chicago: University of Chicago Press.

Rapoport, Robert N. 1987. *New Interventions for Children and Youth: Action-Research Approaches*. New York: Cambridge University Press.

Reid, William J., and Ann W. Shyne. 1969. *Brief and Extended Casework*. New York: Columbia University Press.

Ripple, Lillian, 1957. Factors Associated with Continuance in Casework Service. *Social Work* 2, No. 1, pp. 87–94.

———. 1964. *Motivation, Capacity, and Opportunity: Studies in Casework Theory and Practice*. Chicago: School of Social Service Administration, University of Chicago.

Rubin, Allen, and Earl Babbie. 1989. *Research Methods for Social Work*. Belmont, Calif.: Wadsworth Publishing.

Tukey, John W. 1977. *Exploratory Data Analysis*. Reading, Mass.: Addison-Wesley.

Weissman, Harold H. 1978. *Integrating Services for Troubled Families*. San Francisco: Jossey-Bass.

Wells, Kathleen, and David E. Biegel. 1990. *Intensive Family Preservation Services: A Research Agenda for the 1990s*. Cleveland, Ohio: Bellefaire/Jewish Childrens

Bureau and Mandel School of Applied Social Sciences, Case Western Reserve University.

Young, Dennis R. 1985. *Casebook of Management for Nonprofit Organizations*. New York: Haworth Press.

DOCTORAL DISSERTATIONS BASED ON RESEARCH PROJECT

Alvelo, Jaime. 1986. Foster care, Preventive Services, Puerto Rican Mothers, and Informal Supports. New York: Columbia University School of Social Work.

Chu, Fungsim Amelia. 1991. Problem Improvement in a Foster Care Prevention Program. New York: Columbia University School of Social Work.

Li, Peter. 1988. The Cultural Perspectives of Help-Seeking of the Lower East Side Family Union's Chinese Clients. New York: Columbia University School of Social Work.

DOCTORAL DISSERTATIONS CURRENTLY BEING CARRIED OUT

Perez-Koenig, Rosa. An Exploratory Study of the Social Work Associate's Investment in Cases at the Lower East Side Family Union and Its Relationship to Outcome Variables and Ethnicity. New York: School of Social Work, New York University.

Index

About the Authors

DAVID FANSHEL is Professor in the Columbia University School of Social Work.

STEPHEN J. FINCH is Associate Professor in the Department of Applied Mathematics ar.d Statistics at the State University of New York at Stonybrook.

JOHN F. GRUNDY served as a senior research associate at Columbia University of Social Work at the time of this study.